Palgrave Studies in Financial Services Technology

Series Editor
Bernardo Nicoletti
Rome
Italy

The Palgrave Studies in Financial Services Technology series features original research from leading and emerging scholars on contemporary issues and developments in financial services technology. Falling into 4 broad categories: channels, payments, credit, and governance; topics covered include payments, mobile payments, trading and foreign transactions, big data, risk, compliance, and business intelligence to support consumer and commercial financial services. Covering all topics within the life cycle of financial services, from channels to risk management, from security to advanced applications, from information systems to automation, the series also covers the full range of sectors: retail banking, private banking, corporate banking, custody and brokerage, wholesale banking, and insurance companies. Titles within the series will be of value to both academics and those working in the management of financial services.

More information about this series at
http://www.springer.com/gp/series/14627

Michael Naylor

Insurance Transformed

Technological Disruption

palgrave
macmillan

Michael Naylor
School of Economics and Finance
Massey University
Palmerston North, New Zealand

Palgrave Studies in Financial Services Technology
ISBN 978-3-319-63834-8 ISBN 978-3-319-63835-5 (eBook)
DOI 10.1007/978-3-319-63835-5

Library of Congress Control Number: 2017948716

Printed on acid-free paper

This Palgrave Macmillan imprint is published by Springer Nature
The registered company is Springer International Publishing AG
The registered company address is: Gewerbestrasse 11, 6330 Cham, Switzerland

Contents

List of Figures

1
Exponential Change

Introduction

Insurance has traditionally been a very conservative industry, and this includes conservatism in the way it has used information technology. This conservatism applies to both companies' interactions with clients and to interactions within the company. This conservatism is about to change as the insurance industry is currently on the crest of a combination of technological advances in technology which, when combined, will utterly disrupt the current insurance industry and its interactions with clients, and disrupt up to 80% of current insurance job activities. Coping with this challenge will be the key insurance management issue for the next few decades, and success at adapting to technological disruption will be the defining characteristic of industry survivors.

Some of the elements of the disruptive technologies have been around for a while; others are new, whilst some are not yet useable. Each of these technologies has individually, as yet, not had much impact on insurance, and this has lolled the insurance industry into complacency. This complacency is starting to crack with the insurance consultants from 2015 waking up to the possibilities, so that by 2017 discussion

M. Naylor, *Insurance Transformed*, Palgrave Studies in Financial Services Technology,
DOI 10.1007/978-3-319-63835-5_1

of technological disruption was the fashion. No commentators, however, have realized that it is the combination of these technologies which is the disruptor, not the impact of each individually. No commentator has realized that when added together, the small impacts of each technology will combine to create utter disruption in the insurance industry, so that insurance will emerge as an industry transformed.

While these technologies will disrupt all industrial and service sectors, PWC (2015) and the World Economic Forum (2015) argue that in the next decade insurance will be the most disrupted of all the major service sectors. This disruption is not a once-off; it will be continuous and geometrically increasing challenge, that is, the rate of change will increase, so disruption will increasingly increase. Insurance companies who do not respond dynamically will not survive as the ability to respond innovatively to disruption will become as vital in insurance as it has in mobile phones. The key management skill in the future will be the ability to fundamentally transform companies so that they are able to cope with continuous change. Most current insurers will struggle with this, resulting in a sector ripe for disruptive external entrants.

Disruption is also occurring because customers' experiences with technological leaders in other sectors are transforming their expectations of insurance customer service. Consumers do not now judge their customer experience of an insurance company against that of other insurance companies, but instead judge it against their superior experiences with digital leaders such as Amazon. Yet insurers still tend to benchmark themselves against other insurers instead of benchmarking against possible external disruptors. Who would have guessed that the PC manufacturers would create a product which would destroy incumbents in diverse industries such as telephones, diaries, maps, and photography? Insurers need to understand the scale of the transformation needed or risk being left behind.

This meta-study outlines the key disruptors, outlines how these will impact on the insurance sector, including advisers, and what insurers will have to do to survive. It is vital to understand that these changes will not occur as a stand-alone Uber moment, but will consist of a series of increasingly high waves of disruption. There is no end point - the future is one of increasingly fast change. Insurers need to reimagine their product and their industry.

The end result and the timing are uncertain, so the research can only provide informed speculation. While society as a whole will undoubtedly be better off because of the coming changes, some insurance companies, and their workers, will not be. The question is: 'what is the likely impact of the looming technological disruption on the insurance industry, on insurance advisers, and on jobs?'

The Third Wave

Historians generally recognize two waves[1] of technological change in the modern era: (i) the late eighteenth-century steam/mechanical industrial revolution, and (ii) the late nineteenth-century electric power/motor car revolution. Both of these transformed society and led to far higher average income and better lives for society. Both were, however, quite disruptive to existing social structures and employment. The first industrial revolution, for example, involved a change from a society which was 90% agricultural and rural, to one which was 90% industrial and urban. A lot of the benefits, which we now enjoy and see as essential, were not appreciated by common people at the time, with major protests against both the water wheel and the motorcar. However, in every case, society as a whole gained. The current IT revolution, which started about 1970, should be recognized as constituting a third wave, one which will transform our society as thoroughly as the two earlier industrial revolutions did.

It is useful to understanding to note that each of the first two waves took 80–100 years or more to work its way through its impact on society, with most of the social impacts occurring only towards the end of the wave. This is because technological revolutions involve a combination of inter-linked technologies, each embodying a small change which builds on the others, ensuring that the depth and spread of change

[1]Some Historians include a third or fourth wave, but these do not change my point.

speeds up only over time. The initial stages of the first industrial revolution, for example, had little impact outside the cotton industry for about 50 years, and then it transformed society. The social impact of the IT revolution as it nears its 50-year mark, while it has changed society in a number of ways, should thus be seen as only at an initial stage, with the biggest social changes due to occur over the next 50 years. The scope and scale of those substantial changes are only now starting to become evident. Many of these future changes will be unexpected and unforeseeable.

Exponential Change

Exponential change is change which follows an ever-rising upward curve, so that changes occur at an ever-increasing rate. For example, it took 38 years for radio to reach 50 million people, 20 years for phone, 13 years for the television, 3.6 years for Facebook, 88 days for Google Plus, and 35 days for Angry Birds. Most people find this type of change hard to deal with, as even though we think we are now used to change, humans typically have an inherent tendency to be unable to visualize exponential change. For example, the Internet was originally invented in the mid-1970s, but it only become useful outside a narrow niche after the invention of a graphical browser by Netscape in 1994. At that stage, nearly all forecasters failed to see its potential. Cliff Stoll, a respected network expert, argued in a 1995 Newsweek article[2] that 'online shopping and entertainment were an unrealistic fantasy' and 'the truth is that no online database will replace your newspaper' and then he poured scorn on predictions that we would soon be downloading books via the Internet. Commercial use was seen as impossible. Thus, looking back, while the Internet revolution which has occurred now seems obvious, in 1995 it was nearly unimaginable. Also, nobody predicted in 1980 that in 30 years' time each of us would be carrying the power of a 1980s mainframe computer

[2]Stoll, C (1995) 'Why the Web won't be Nirvana,' Newsweek, Feb 27 (original title 'The Internet? Bah!').

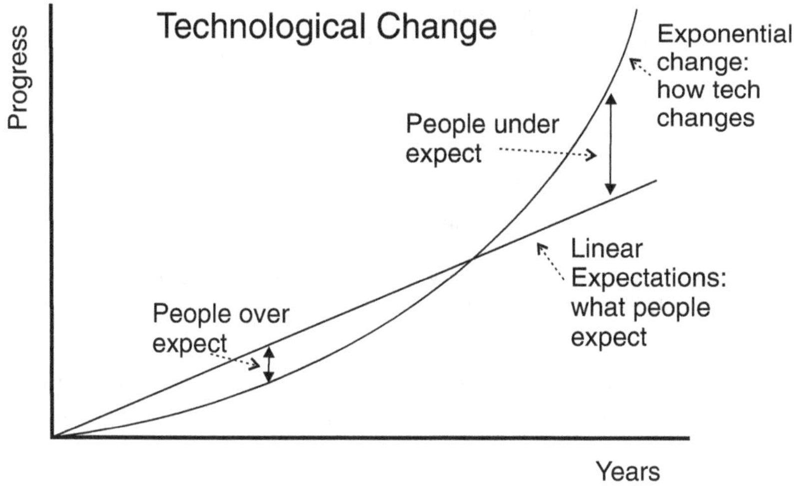

Fig. 1.1 Linear vs. Exponential change. *Source* Author

in our pockets. We currently find it nearly impossible to forecast the potential of a mobile device with 1000x today's capability.

The reason for this inability to predict the future is because we are hard-wired to expect change to be linear. This means that when they forecast a transformative event, people will assume that future changes continue at about the same rate as past changes, with an equal rate of change and equal social impact over each time period. However, technological change is predominately nonlinear, normally exponential. This means that initial predictions of transformative change tend to be wrong. An inherent issue with complex exponential change is that 80% of the social change tends to happen in the last quarter of the period. This is because for most technologies to be useful, a number of structural transformations have to occur first, and these have to work together to be transformative. Most technologies also require changes in businesses/social structures before they can have a major impact. As most social change does not occur until a number of technologies interact, and this takes a while, social changes tend to accumulate during the last stage of the technological revolution period. These assumptions are contrasted in Fig. 1.1.

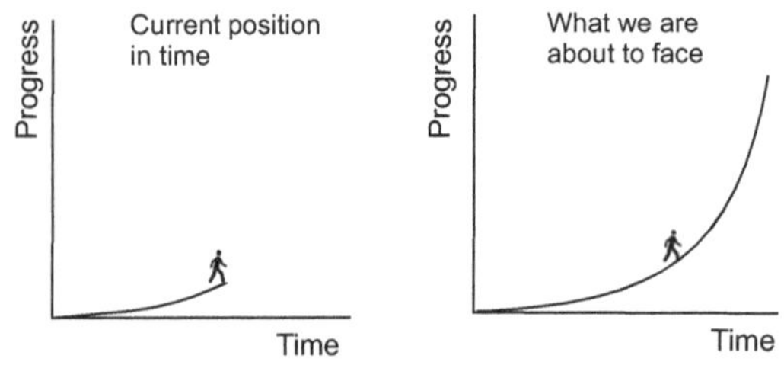

Fig. 1.2 What we expect based on where we are at the moment vs. what the future is actually like. *Source* Author

The result of this faulty expectation is that people tend to be underimpressed by the rate of change during the first 2/3rds of a disruptive revolution, just before they are shocked by the rate of change during the last 1/3rd,[3] as shown in Fig. 1.2. This has occurred with the impact of IT, which so far in occupational terms, typists apart, has not had as much disruptive impact as people predicted in the 1990s. Even experts get this wrong. In the mid-1980s, AT&T hired McKinsey to forecast mobile phone adoption by the year 2000. They predicted 900,000 subscribers. The actual number was 109M, off by 120 times!

It is important to remember, however, that the underlying technological change has been unprecedented. Brynjolfsson and McAffe (2011) state that the effectiveness of computers increased 43m-fold between 1988 and 2003, and Nordhaus (2007) notes that during the 1980s and 1990s the computing costs fell by an average of 64% per year. The paradox is that up until about 2006, the impact of IT on overall rates of productivity was minor. Even since then, change has occurred at a rate we can cope with. Over the next 50 years, however, this will reverse, with society currently very ill-prepared for the drastic changes which can be expected. The rate of change will particularly accelerate over the last 3rd of the IT revolution, creating society-wide disruption.

Society is often initially skeptical about transformative technologies and tends to focus on the transformative technology's potential for destruction, rather than creation; in Plato's *Phaedrus,* Socrates worried

---

[3]For a commentary on rate of change of technology see: http://waitbutwhy.com/2015/01/artificial-intelligence-revolution-1.html.

that the recent invention of writing would have a deleterious effect on youth, as it would harm their memories; when books started to roll off Gutenberg's press, many argued that the books would be confusing and harmful by overwhelming young people with excess information; when Marconi invented the radio, many worried that children's minds would be damaged by dangerous ideas and family life would be ruined; many experts warned against the cancer risk from mobile phones. Possibly, some early homo sapiens warned of the dangers of fire?

Yet once transformations have taken place, society tends to regard them as obvious. For example, experts struggled for decades to achieve even basic language recognition. Many experts regarded IBM's Jeopardy goal as impossible. Yet people now regard the ability of Siri to talk and respond naturally as a trivial achievement. Larry Tesler quipped that 'Intelligence is whatever machines haven't done yet.'

The Ah-Ha Moment

Within every technological revolution, there comes moments, 'ah-ha' events, when humanity realizes with the shock the potential and scale of the looming revolution.

One of the core elements of the current revolution is the ability of software to handle complex tasks. One of the key 'ah-ha' moments came at the 2007 3rd Darpa[4] autonomous vehicle challenge. When the challenge started in 2004, creating software able to handle driving was widely regarded as far too complex to be automated; driving was a 'complex task,' which is defined as a situation involving ill-defined rules, a fluid, dynamic, environment, and the need for instantaneous adjustment based on real-time feedback.

Up to that point, analysts had assumed that software could only be used where there were well-defined and repetitive tasks amenable to yes/no rules, within a restricted environment. Sure enough, vehicles in the 2004 Darpa challenge failed to handle open desert, mostly crashing shortly after starting. Two of the top experts in the field, Levy and

[4]Defence Advanced Research Projects Agency.

Murnane, in their 2004 book, explained why handling 'complex tasks' like driving was just about impossible for a computer and would take many decades to solve. They stated that the idea of software being able to handle the complexity of ensuring a computer-driven car made a safe turn across a flow of irregular oncoming traffic was just laughable, as detecting and predicting the movement of other vehicles was extremely complex, and was too unpredictable to be reduced to set rules.

The software community was thus stunned when in the Darpa 2007 challenge, autonomous vehicles successfully handled a complex urban mock-up, happily obeying road rules, and safely interacting with other vehicles. The speed of improvement in the ability of software to handle complex feedback was stunning and unprecedented. You can now watch Google cars do even more complex tasks on YouTube. Autonomous cars have now driven themselves across the USA (99% of the time).

The idea that software could handle complex tasks changed everything - programmers worldwide have since then been busy re-examining complex areas previously thought too hard. By 2016, the sense of wonder at autonomous driving is starting to fade and we now find it hard to understand why we were stunned that cars could drive themselves. Our expectations of what software can handle have been transformed.

This ah-ha moment had huge implications for the disruptive impact of technology, as programmers eagerly attacked many tasks previously regarded as impossible. For example, speech recognition was for decades seen as impossible, yet 5-year olds now expect Siri to understand them. These complex tasks often involve a type of programming called 'artificial intelligence,' which involves creating a generalized program which is 'teachable' by importing large data sets and running these through the program so it weights responses based on past events. In 2011, these AI techniques were used to create software which could win at the TV game show 'Jeopardy,' which was previously regarded as impossible for software because of its subtle and complex word-play questions, and then, even more impressively, in 2016, to beat the reigning world champion at the game of Go, also previously regarded as impossible. As most insurance tasks involve easier algorithms than these tasks, there are few areas of insurance inherently immune to computerization. Compared to playing Go, most underwriting tasks are child's play.

There is no question that the insurance industry is far behind technologically. Millennials find that frustrating. We live in a world where if you want something you go on your phone and get it instantly. The insurance industry currently just is not like that.

Hype and the Technological Innovation Cycle

Gartner Corporation[5] argues that the inability of humans to cope with exponential events leads to new technologies going through a 'hype-cycle,' whereby expectations about technologies tend to be initially over-hyped, and then because they cannot deliver fast, there is disillusionment, followed later by actual solid products. Gartner Hype Cycles contrast product maturity versus hype/expectations and provide a graphic representation of the maturity and adoption of technologies and applications. The Hype Cycle is shown in Fig. 1.3. Each Hype Cycle drills down into the five key phases of a technology's life cycle:

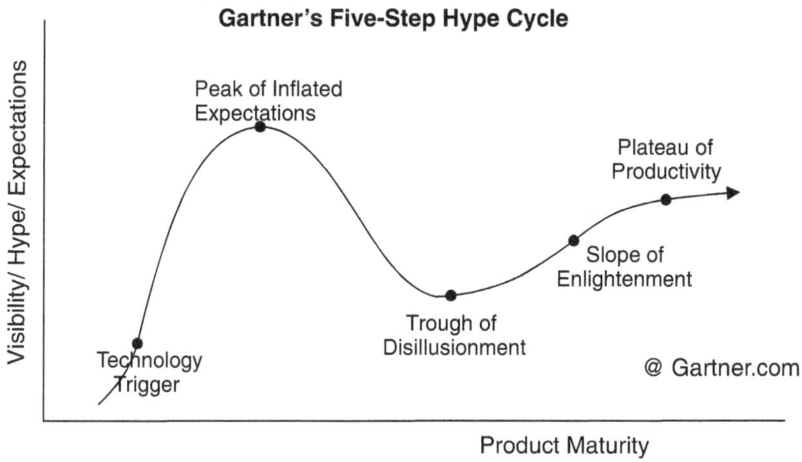

Fig. 1.3 Hype vs. Product maturity. © Gartner, used with permission

[5]Gartner.com; http://www.gartner.com/technology/research/methodologies/.

Technology Trigger: A potential technology breakthrough kicks things off. Early proof-of-concept stories and media interest trigger significant publicity. Often, no usable products exist and commercial viability is unproven.

Peak of Inflated Expectations: Expectations reach a fever pitch. Early publicity produces a number of success stories - the scores of failures are ignored.

Trough of Disillusionment: Interest wanes as experiments and beta products fail to match expectations. Producers of the technology shake out or fail. Investments continue only if the surviving providers improve their products to the satisfaction of early adopters.

Slope of Enlightenment: Product users start to understand how to use the technology productively. More instances of how the technology can benefit the enterprise start to crystallize and become more widely understood. Second-generation products with far fewer faults appear from technology providers. More enterprises fund pilots; conservative companies remain cautious and start to fall behind (Fig. 1.4).

Plateau of Productivity: Polished third-generation products arrive. Mainstream adoption starts to take off. Criteria for assessing provider viability are more clearly defined. The technology's broad market applicability and relevance are clearly paying off.

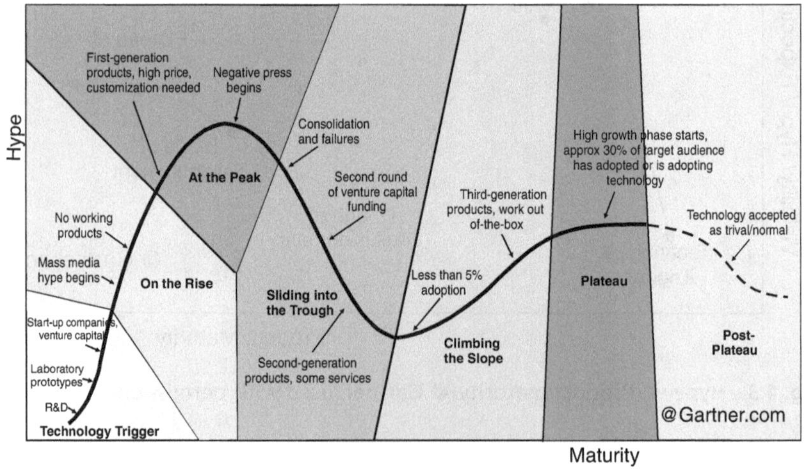

Fig. 1.4 Gartner Hype Cycle phases. © Gartner, used with permission

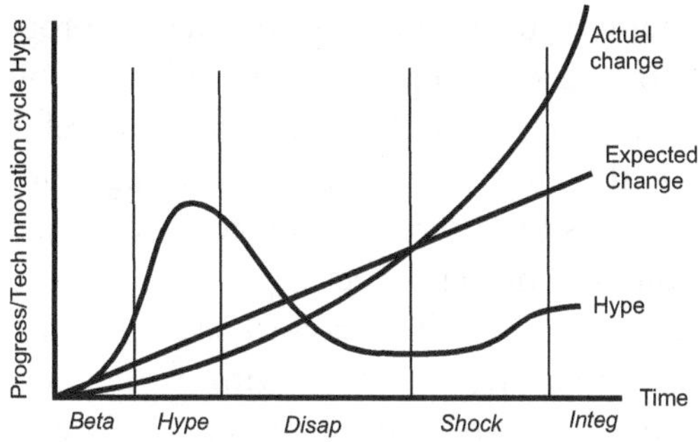

Fig. 1.5 Exponential change and the Hype-cycle. *Source* Author

Maturity: Mature products drop off the chart, as do failed products. The hype is over and the products are seen as 'normal.'

When the faulty reaction to exponential change shown in Fig. 1.1 is combined with the Gartner Hype Cycle this creates, a *technological innovation cycle*. This is shown in Fig. 1.5.

Beta—New technologies are normally only understood by and available to a small number of high-tech users. The technology is normally immature, in beta format, and both users and producers are unsure of how the technology can be best used. Products are difficult to use. The only users are those prepared to spend time and effort working with imperfect technology, either because they are fascinated by it or because they like the prestige of having tech which no one else does. The technology tends to undergo substantial change during this stage as it tends to just be a vague collection of exciting ideas. Many of the initial firms do not survive.

Hype—Technologies which survive the beta stage get hyped up initially in the technology media, and then in the general media. Excitement spreads as new possibilities are discussed. These tend to assume that the technology will have a major social impact in the near future. The difficulties and imperfections of the technology are ignored. As stock valuations soar, heavy investment takes place. This is the best time for market leaders to issue a stock market IPO.

Disappointment—Generally, the new technology takes a while to spread, and little actual impact on social structures or life style is observed. Expectations of change exceed actual progress, so impatience with the slow pace of impact grows. This is despite the technology maturing from a vague collection of ideas into useful products. The media move onto the 'next big thing.' Non-using companies reassure themselves that there is little threat. Producers are thinned out to those with useable products or deep pockets.

Shock—Products become useful, easy-to-use, and increasingly widely available. As actual progress catches up with expectations, the technology spreads and market share soars. Consumers discuss usefulness and whether or not to buy the product rather than fantasizing about possibilities. When progress soars past existing incumbent technology, producers of now-non-viable existing products find themselves scrambling to keep their products viable and rush to produce some version of the superior technology. A substantial proportion of old-product firms goes bankrupt or are taken over. Profits of new-tech firms soar, though cash flow can be under pressure due to rapid expansion.

Integration—The product becomes the new 'normal,' and consumer focus turns to the comparative merits of features. If the market is competitive, profits margins drop as firm struggle to provide the most features at the lowest cost. As technology is standardized, low-cost producers expand market share. Old-tech producers become a fading memory.

For incumbents, the lesson is that the beta versions of disruptive technologies will initially seem to be a minor threat and then will seem to 'come-from-nowhere' to take over a market. In a world of exponential change, where everything is changing, the biggest risk is standing still.

It is useful to distinguish between normal 'incremental technologies,' those which lead to little societal change, and 'disruptive technologies,' those which change the way society or business runs. Nearly all the technological changes which insurance companies have encountered so far have been incremental and could be dealt with by iterative change to existing business systems. What the insurance sector is facing now is a collection of technologies, which when combined, creates a perfect storm of technological disruption. This cannot be handled by incremental adjustments, but needs a transformative change.

References

Brynjolfsson, E. R., Hitt, L., & Kim, H. (2011). Strength in numbers: How does data-driven decision-making affect firm performance? *Social Science Review Network*, April.

Economist (2014). *The Third Great Wave*, special report, October 4th.

Levy, F., & Murnane, R. J. (2004). *The new division of labor: How computers are creating the new job market.* USA: Princeton University Press.

Nordhaus, W. D. (2007). Two centuries of productivity growth in computing. *The Journal of Economic History, 67*(1), 128.

PWC. (2015). *Insurance 2020 & Beyond: Necessity is the mother of reinvention.*

World Economic Forum. (2015). *The future of financial services: How disruptive innovations are reshaping the way financial services are structured, provisioned and consumed.*

2

Key Technological Disruptors

The coming disruptive revolution will involve not just AI programming, but also a range of disruption drivers of the IT revolution, which are evolving at about the same time. The drivers are:

Internet of Things

One of the key elements of a connected world is sensor chips, called 'telematics', which give constant real-time feedback to data centers on their current state. An unheralded breakthrough for telematics came in July 2015, when it was announced that scientists had discovered how to power these devices by Wi-fi.[1] They can also be powered by radio waves. This is revolutionary as it means that no internal power will be needed, no need for wires or changing batteries, thus enabling the insertion of these devices into everything. In 2015, five quintillion (10 to the power of 18) chips were added to things which were not computers.

[1]For a discussion, see Talla et al. (2015). In general, these devices need no internal power to transmit as they use the energy provided by radio and other waves used to connect with them.

M. Naylor, *Insurance Transformed*, Palgrave Studies in Financial Services Technology,
DOI 10.1007/978-3-319-63835-5_2

The recent drastic reduction in the price of these sensor chips means that they are now being embedded in everyday items like cars, fridges, groceries, street lights, and drains.

Morgan-Stanley/BCG (2013) forecast that wearable telematics will rise from 6M in 2013 to 248M in 2017. McKinsey (2015) estimates that the number of self-supporting interconnected devices, in general, will grow from 5M now to 50B by 2025, which is probably an underestimate as they assumed that these devices would need a power source. The total number of networked items is far higher than that once you include all the unintelligent items which will be tagged so that telematics can notice them and thus control them. General estimates are that there were 10 million sensors of all types connected to the Internet in 2007, and in excess of 3.5 billion by 2013. The total number of telematic devices, including non-networked and non-self-supporting, could exceed 10 trillion by 2025 and is expected to surpass 100 trillion by 2030. These sensors will provide a flow of real-time data whose size exceeds most analysts' imaginations. A new Internet protocol has just been agreed to enable these huge numbers of telematics to be individually labeled. Generation 6 Internet is being built to deal with the mind-boggling data flows.

The widespread use of telematics has huge implications. The obvious implication is examples like: if every grocery item is tagged/linked, your fridge can record what is used and help the cupboard create a shopping list; your car can tell your insurer's computer how you drive; street lights can tell the data center when they fail, or turn on only when your car tells them you are approaching; swarms of nanobots can examine pipes; your doctor can embed a small chip which can analyze your blood, warn you of dangerous trends, make changes to and adjust your automatic injector, alert emergency services if you suffer a medical emergency, give them medical details, with your location. It could even arrange an autodrive ambulance so no human needs to be involved.

The less obvious implication is that up until about 2012, it was assumed that Internet traffic would mainly involve human-created activities, with Internet growth projections based on the estimates of human activities and the percentage of the world population which was connected. Now, it is realized that in the future, Internet traffic demand will soar primarily predominantly due to a link between things, rather than between people. McKinsey (2015) estimates that the number of Web-linked telematic devices by 2040 will run into hundreds of billions, implying that human-sourced Web traffic will be less than 5% of all Web traffic. Forbes (2014) found that 50–70% of home owners will consider buying smart home devices in the next five years.

The interconnection of telematic devices, the exponential increase in data inflow, and active analysis of the data received will be transformative in nearly all industries, and thus has huge implications for businesses. The most powerful use of telematic data will involve using two-way feedback to predict failures before they occur, and to fine-tune performance. There will have to be a large investment in capturing, sorting, and analyzing the immense data flow, as well as acting on the resultant information. The amount of work required to effectively use the ever-increasing inflow of data will be a major issue for businesses, and the survivors will be those who solve this problem. Businesses will have to learn how to use the data to gain competitive advantage.

The implication for insurance is that all insured objects will give constant real-time feedback to the insurer's data center. Examples would be the minute-by-minute driving history of every driver or the minute-by-minute blood pressure, blood chemistry and heartbeat of every patient. Chips linked to patient can report back to the doctor's computer, which can call an ambulance if the metrics indicate a need before a problem actually occurs. The data from multiple clients can then be compared, for example, the driver behavior and car reaction of nearly every driver on the road, in every traffic environment, or changes in body chemistry which leads to illness, can be compared and trends found. Seriously, ill patients could carry an intelligent medicine injector, which can get feedback from a specialist. Drivers can be alerted before their cars break down while drivers who are driving erratically can have their cars turned off or controlled remotely. A house can identify if a stove is overheating, or can tell police where all stolen items are now located.

In insurance terms, we are currently in the third wave of telematics. The first wave was beta experiments by Norwich Union and Progressive in using black boxes for collecting automobile insurance data. This saw battles over regulations and intellectual data. With these settled, the second wave trial programs were expanded to a number of other insurers, and real-time networked data explored. The current wave of innovation will involve telematic use in Auto insurance becoming routine, especially in commercial fleets, and an expansion of trials of telematic use into other insurance types, with a focus on health.

It is important to note that the limited data flow we currently receive from the limited number of telematics installed is poorly used. This is because up until recently companies have struggled to store the flood of data. They are thus typically analyzing only a fraction of it. McKinsey (2015), for example, estimates that we are currently using less than 1% of all currently available telematic data. An example they cite is that a typical offshore oil rig now has about 30,000 sensors, but less than 1% of the information received is ever used, with only about 300 sensors actually monitored. Modern cars can have 1000 sensors, data from which is mostly ignored, and none gathered centrally in real time. Very few insurers have setup systems to access data from these sensors. We are also only using telematic data for anomaly detection and control systems, instead of taking advantage of its use in areas like optimization and prediction. The major reason for this limited use of telematic data has been the substantial costs and difficulties of storing and analyzing it. As will be explored below, these limitations have now been removed.

Data Storage and Cloud Computing

The arrival of mobile devices meant that IT users had to stop being tied to the memory of a single device, otherwise they could not move seamlessly between devices; accessing email on the move is difficult if emails are stored on a PC hard drive. The introduction of 'every-where Wi-Fi' has allowed IT to escape physical confines. A necessary part of mobility has thus been the creation of huge external 'cloud-based' data storage facilities.

This centralizing and scaling up of data storage has had the side effect of allowing drastic continuing drops in prices, and this has reinforced the trend toward cloud storage. For example, Amazon's costs of storing cloud data has been falling by about 50% every three years since

2006, and costs are forecasted to drop even faster as the scale increases exponentially. PWC (2015) states that the cost of storing a gigabyte of data in the cloud dropped from 25 cents in 2010 to 0.024 cents in 2014.

Cloud computing has also meant that internationalization of services can occur without the customer being aware of it, as nobody is aware of where their data is stored, who is managing the service, or who is analyzing that data. This has allowed the use of cheaper data storage locations, e.g., those with lower cost electricity or cold external air. It also allows secure multiple backups.

This near-zero marginal cost of data storage is essential as insurance companies who use telematics will find their need for data storage skyrocketing. Cloud computing is thus vital as it means that insurers (i) will have no need to run their own data servers, (ii) will find that the cost of storing the huge data quantities created by the other trends manageable, and (iii) data storage is now scalable, with insurers only renting storage as they need it. Cloud computing also allows its interlinking with mobile devices and the internationalization of data banks.

The cost of local data storage has also plummeted. In the year 2000, one gigabyte of hard drive space costs $44, by 2012 it had dropped to 7 cents, and by 2016 to less than 1 cent. In 2000, it costs $193 per gigabyte to stream video, by 2010 it had dropped to 3 cents, and by 2016 to fractions of a cent. The amount of data able to be transmitted on an optical network has also been doubling every nine months for the last decade. The marginal cost of most data storage and transmission is thus dropping close to zero.

Big Data

Traditionally, mathematics has assumed that data on 'everything' is not available, so we need to make do with a limited sample of data. Statistical theory, surveys, and nearly everything actuaries learn is thus based on assessing how closely this limited sample matches the entire population. This theory will, however, soon be archaic as the internet of things and cloud computing means that now we can very cheaply collect *all* the data. The world's production of data grew 2000-fold between 2000 and 2012 and is expected to double at least every 10–18 months for the foreseeable future. Approximately, half of all the data the world has created in its history has been created in just the last 10 months. In 2015, data was growing by 2.5 quintillion bytes a day (18 zeros) or 8 zettabytes per year (21 zeros). The use of real-time telematic data could soon make these forecasts of data increase underestimates, with data probably doubling every six months. Notice that this is an exponential curve.

The issue for traditional data analysis method is that the size of the data flow is so large that no person can usefully access it directly. A new mathematics of big data is consequentially evolving which uses algorithms and software to automatically analyze the database for trends, and then either summarizes it, or alerts an operator to preset changes, or uses it to predict adverse patterns. Examples would be management alerted if a truck driver started driving erratically, or if the failure rate of a particular type of part increased, or if those who buy alcohol at 1 a.m. have more heart attacks. Patterns of data which predict house fires or link types of food purchase to types of sickness, can be discovered. The extent of these huge data sets has had the side effect of providing large enough training sets for software algorithms to learn to handle non-routine cognitive tasks, hence starting the process of creating the Artificial Intelligence (AI) software required for complex tasks.

The efficiency gains possible from effective analysis of big data, combined with telematics and AI software, are huge, with McKinsey (2015) estimating a gain of 1% additional growth in GDP per year for the next decade. They argue that the potential profit from use of business to business telematics is three or four times the size of consumer telematics. An example would be a global oil giant, which could link sensors at petrol stations, which give real-time information on types of fuel sold, to refineries - to adjust the mix produced, to trucks - to adjust deliveries, to oil rig - to adjust volume pumped. Sensors would alert staff when things are about to fail, so they can be replaced. All this can be done with no human making a decision, only supervising. It has been estimated that this style of change could improve the efficiency of most sectors by 100–200%.

Big data is analyzed using three different methods:

Machine learning: The process of training computers how to 'learn' interesting patterns in data and how to adapt automatically when data changes over time. With machine learning, algorithms are trained for a time in order to build models, which are then used to direct automated marketing and operational decisions, adapting as more data is gathered once the AI is 'live.' This learning can be supervised or unsupervised.

Supervised learning: Supervised learning algorithms take independent variable inputs, such as user clickstream data and dependent variable outputs like purchase data, and create a model for how they relate to each other. Once it fits, it can be used as a predictive tool.

Unsupervised learning: This is also called 'data mining.' It is unsupervised learning which looks for patterns and relationships within the data itself, without concern for outputs. The focus is on its useful for segmentation and customer insights.

The biggest current barrier to use of big data analysis is that universities are only now starting to create postgraduate courses in big data, so skilled staff will be in short supply for at least the next decade or so. Since most of the IT revolution depends on these data analysts, this is the major limiting factor to the speed of transformation. The relative unattractiveness of insurance companies to these graduates could be a major barrier, which the insurer able to attract the best staff likely to gain an unbeatable competitive advantage.

Digital Natives and the No-Wait Generation

There is a generational shift in consumer attitudes taking place. GenRe (2014) argues that the millennial population cohort group (now aged 18–34) will represent over 50% of the global workforce by 2017, and over 75% of the global workforce by 2025, and their spending power will soon surpass baby boomers (now aged 52–70). Millennials were raised with the idea that the first place to learn something, share something, or buy something is the Internet.

The generation born after the millennials have used laptops from young, so are 'born digital', and use their tablet as their primary contact with the world. They have played with film-quality digital games from an early age. They will increasingly grow up in a house where a talkbox controls house functions, so that they expect to talk to software. Their expectations about interaction with companies are substantially different to that of baby boomers and exceed the already high expectations of the millennials.

Zaptitude (2016) found that 70% of millennials surveyed feel disconnected from financial service providers because those providers do not package products or services in a manner they feel comfortable with. Zaptitude argues that millennials feel that financial service providers 'speak in an alien language, which makes the millennial feel invisible.' Readers can imagine how digital natives will respond - Facebook and Web sites are old techs and scanning documents is dinosaur age. They will expect to interact verbally with an insurer's AI system, getting instant answers. An insurer who thinks 'being digital' is adding a Web page will suffer the fate of the dinosaurs.

Bain (2015) found that even among the non-digital natives, the proportion that plan to use a Web channel for buying insurance will rise from 35 to 79% over the next two years. They also plan to interact with insurers in quite different ways. For business, a key aspect is that these consumers will increasingly interact with Web sites via social networks and will increasingly review the goods and services provided. Nearly all purchases are first researched online, including service quality.

McKinsey (2012) found that 80% of users interact with social networks at least 5 times a week. They also find that the speed and scale of adoption of social technology by consumers have exceeded that of previous technologies, yet estimate that only about 5% of possible uses of social networks have yet been discovered.

Shirky (2010) argued that social networks are a unique invention for business as they encourage consumers to cooperate together to create rich new forms of interaction. This collective effort feeds back in a way which ensures that individuals work together in a way that they could not achieve alone. This ensures that the joint output exceeds individual efforts by a multiple. Businesses cannot control this, only encourage it.

People now rely on their social networks for everything from advice on movies, on relationships, on product reviews to decide what is interesting. The use of social networks is thus transformational and has changed how people think about customer relationships. The implications of this generational change in favor of social networks for businesses are huge. Company Web sites will have to do more than act as one-way portals for corporate communications, product promotions, customer services, and e-commerce, and instead become interactive two-way communication channels and lock into social activities.

While these new generations value face-to-face contact with providers, their base expectation is an extremely high level of Internet and personal service, and a seamless integrated experience. Their primary contact with business will be Web-based, and their expectations about the Website will be extreme. They will expect your network to interact with their devices automatically and your Web page to integrate with your customer service. Every possible device must be supported. Your company will have to integrate into online social networks and from within the ecosystem, provide useful and active feedback to enhance lifestyles. Quotes, service, and feedback must occur within minutes.

In particular, companies have to respond to feedback in a two-way conversation, rather than treating the Web as a push mechanism for the company's views only. Complaints must be responded to within an hour and responded to publicly. This can be very positive if handled in a way which the crowd approves off; mistakes are accepted, and it is the response to mistakes which increases or decreases reputations. The ability to enhance ratings via customer feedback then becomes a sales tool vital for the new generations. The ability to respond to public feedback from customers in a manner which enhances reputation is a skill most insurers have yet to master.

If your business doesn't meet these expectations, you may as well not exist. For example, these generations won't phone; they expect to Skype via your Web page. Expectations around the visual presentation of your Web service are extreme, similar to an advanced-level digital game platform. Film-quality video tutorials or news blogs are expected. Very few current insurers even come close to these expectations.

Digital natives are correctly labeled as the 'no-wait generation'. The essence of this is that consumer expectations around level of customer service are raising rapidly, with declining patience for any delays in response or administrative errors. Phone centers or text messaging which takes 30 seconds to answer are regarded as archaic. Satisfactory customer feedback and respond to complaints/issues is expected in terms of hours rather than days. A question must be asked only once, and then be available to all other staff, regardless of platform. These extreme response attitudes are rapidly migrating to other generations. Only a keyword software-based AI response system can respond with this degree of rapidity and scale to wide fluctuations in demand. Call centers will always struggle.

Millennials also eagerly swap consumer experiences online, with over 70% discussing possible purchases with friends online and 75% browsing online customer feedback. Unmet expectations will be immediately discussed online. The main forums are social networks especially video outlets, as fewer than 25% watch more than 10 hours of TV a week, and very few read print newspapers. Insurer reputations can be irretrievable damaged within a week, meaning that insurers will not have time to fully discuss response strategy, and instead must have protocols prearranged. It is surprising that in 2017 insurers still regard setting up a Facebook site as leading edge.

It is also a mistake to assume that the older baby boomer clients aren't also technologically literate, don't desire digital contact opportunities, and don't have changing expectations. CEB (2013) found that the wealthier segment of the 55+ age population has high technological expectations, and that wealth management company customer relationship management (CRM) systems are persistently lagging behind the dynamics of older customer preferences. Baby boomers do, however, have lower response expectations.

In a fast-paced world where bad experiences are immediately uploaded, insurers will either evolve excellent customer service or die. These extreme expectations and tendency to communally review experiences online mean that social capital is now the key currency for companies. Mistakes in customer response are accepted, but the company response to issues must be excellent. Because of changing generations, firms which do not engage the way digital natives expect will be out of business by 2025.

Software, not Hardware

Some experts have predicted future disruption being based on robots. This is unlikely to be true. The initial drivers of the IT revolution were indeed physical; e.g., reduction in transistor size, worldwide optical fibers, and mobile devices. While these advances will continue, their impact will lessen hereafter, as advances in physical technology have opened up the space for software innovation.

A reason is that in a number of key areas, like automated cars or general-purpose robots, we have reached the stage where the key factor inhibiting most progress is now software limitations rather than hardware. A second reason is that current redesign of computer chips to incorporate RAM will substantially enhance speed. A third reason is that computer speed will not be an issue, with a predication that the first useable quantum computer will be available by 2020 and in general use by 2030 and will hundreds of times faster than today's best supercomputer. The result of this is that past limitations due to physical processing capacity will disappear. Analyzing huge data sets will not be a problem.

The implication of this is that solving the software issues will lead to exploding uses for physical technology. From that point in time software innovation will be the key driver and will start to dominate. It has been speculated by experts that so far, we have only discovered 1% of all the possible uses of the Internet. Uses for software will explode as fast we can code them. The more processing intensive uses like AI will particularly explode. Insurers need to pay close attention to leading edge software innovations in all sectors.

Artificial Intelligence and Complexity Science

Predicted improvement in the areas of artificial intelligence and complex adaptive systems mean that software could, within 5 years, handle problems regarded today as 'impossible'. Traditionally, software has been created using a large set of simple 'yes/no' rules. This required the problem to be solved to be broken down into a long series of simple steps. The data set was assumed to be stable and the relationships to be unchanging. Forecasting systems were thus created by using 'predictive analytical systems' which assumes fixed relationships between variables based on prior data. This then postulates a single future by forecasting this relationship forward. This meant that the range of problems which could be solved was limited by (i) those areas where the data meet the stability requirements, (ii) those areas which the programmer thoroughly understood prior to starting, and (iii) those areas which can be solved by iteration within a reasonable time.

These restrictions are about to be largely removed by an alternative approach, 'complexity science', which, in contrast, structures the problem by using a number of elements which interact with each other in a dynamic network of 'nodes' whereby the weightings on links between nodes change as the system learns. Outcomes are not just yes/no but a complex array. The programmer does not have to understand how to solve the issue or impose solution frameworks. Complex adaptive systems do not pre-specify logical sequences but create a system of rules, which software 'agents' work within but are not constrained by. These agents then examine data sets and look for patterns and learn as they go. Therefore, there is a multiple of future paths dependent on exactly how the elements evolve. There is no assumption that relationships between elements are stable or that what happened in the past will reoccur. Nor is there an assumption that all elements will react in the same way to another variable. Diversity in response is allowed. A typical node network is shown in Fig. 2.1.

Complex software programs can thus find patterns not apparent to humans and the systems get better as the data sets increase in size and as the number of runs increases. The software is thus 'learning' rather than having answers preset. The key element is discovering how the elements interact and how the relationships evolve over time. Important here is finding paths which lead to stability rather than to chaos.

In 2007, Fei-Fei Li, the head of Stanford's Artificial Intelligence Lab, gave up trying to program computers to recognize objects and began labeling the millions of raw images that a child might encounter by age three and feeding them to computers. By being shown thousands and

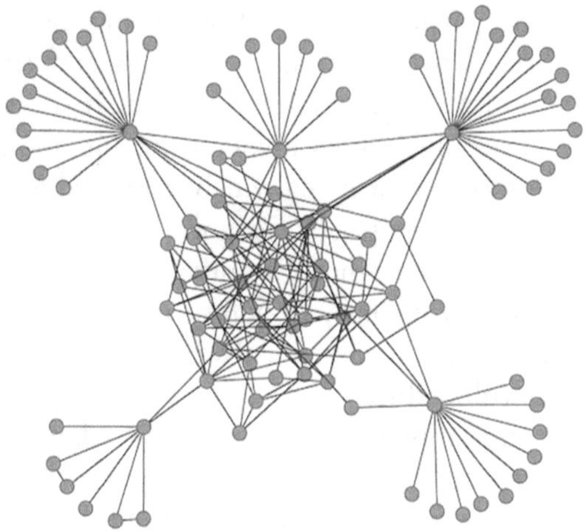

Fig. 2.1 A dynamic node network. *Source* Author

thousands of labeled data sets with instances of, say, a cat, the machine could shape its own rules for deciding whether a particular set of digital pixels was, in fact, a cat. In 2015, Dr. Li's team unveiled a program that identifies the visual elements of any picture with a high degree of accuracy. An image recognition challenge called 'ImageNet' achieved their breakthrough in 2012, when software successfully recognized 85% of images by using AI methods. In the 2015 imaging challenge, the winning team achieved 96%, surpassing human achievement. IBM's Watson machine relied on a similar self-generated scoring system among hundreds of potential answers in its *Jeopardy* victory. During its Go victory, the AlphaGo AI, created a strategic move never seen before, which involved substantial short-term sacrifice, for long-term strategic domination.[2] One of the reasons for this move was that AlphaGo assessed that it would surprise its human opponent so much that they would respond poorly. That move was true innovation by an AI program.

Predictions of complex adaptive systems are thus dynamic and can solve problems in areas where the relationship cannot be carefully

[2]https://www.technologyreview.com/s/602094/ais-language-problem/?mc_cid=c6c808bdae&mc_eid=e1c76a51f6.

predefined. They are particularly useful in (i) finding patterns in data which are too obscure to be visible to humans and (ii) finding patterns in overwhelmingly large amounts of data. In particular, an area of AI called 'deep learning', which involves systems finding patterns by crunching big data sets, is now being widely exploited to power Internet search engines, translate Web pages, recognize voices, and detect fraud.

When combined with the other disruptive technologies like big data, telematics, cloud computing, etc., AI will be the key disruptive technology for any industry which relies on data. Insurance, being based on data, is particularly vulnerable.

Research into and application of complex adaptive systems was restricted and limited up to 2005 by limited computer power and small data sets. Progress was slow. It was overhyped and went into the disappointment phrase.

Since 2012, however, the arrival of big data and corresponding computing power able to run a huge number of scenarios has transformed the field. Modern computers can run billions of scenarios to find the few scenarios which offer optimal results in a way humans cannot match.

An important AI technique is called 'artificial neutral networks', which has an input layer, an output layer, and a number of hidden processing layers (see Fig. 2.2). Data is fed into the input layer and the problem is

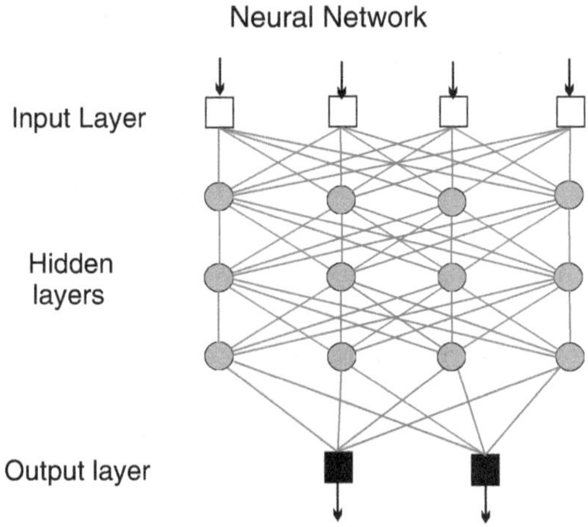

Fig. 2.2 Neutral Network. *Source* Author

then separated into aspects and each hidden layer pathway attacks an aspect of the problem. Each 'node' or 'neuron' tries to learn from past mistakes by adjusting the weight it puts on a particular facet of the problem. By running a large data sample through enough layers, multiple times, the system adjusts the weights until a sufficient level of accuracy is obtained. This is called 'training' the system. Advanced systems can have over 30 layers, which is only possible with very powerful computers.

Learning can be 'supervised', which involves labeled data and instructions of what to look for, or 'unsupervised', which involves unlabeled data and allowing the program to find its own correlations. The latter is particularly useful for insurers who want to discover new links between claim rates and customer attributes, or to find undetected types of claim fraud.

The more complex AI applications are still limited by current processing power, but new chip advances will soon limit these areas to only the largest problems. These deep searches can find relationships which are complex in ways which could only be discovered once big data sets are used. The bigger the data set, the more can be found, so the capacity of these systems will improve on the exponential scale, as telematic data becomes available.

The importance of very large data sets for training means that Internet search companies have a nearly unsurpassable advantage in creating very accurate AI systems. The only way insurers will be able to compete is by joining an ecosystem with a firm which has access to huge data sets, as well as expertise in the most advanced AI systems. The newness of the field means that advanced level expertise is a major constraining issue, with insurers forced to compete for scarce Ph.Ds with far more exciting employers. Charan (2015) argues that any organization that is not already math and AI-based, or is unable to become one soon, is already a legacy company. Insurers need to set up AI research centers and retrain actuaries in AI and big data methodologies.

It needs to be noted that AI is really a portfolio of technologies, and for this type of software to become autonomous a number of related technologies need to be sufficiently advanced at the same time. Progress, however, has not been even across all fields; with AI researchers making much greater progress in some fields such as natural language processing and data analysis, and far less progress in other fields of AI such as decision-making and deductive reasoning. This is due to scientists in the mid-to-late 2000s achieving a breakthrough in the way they thought about neural networks, or the systems that allow AI to interpret data. Along with the explosion of raw data made possible by the Internet, this discovery allowed machine learning in related fields to take off at a near exponential rate. Other fields of AI research, in contrast, are plodding along merely at a linear pace.

This doesn't mean scientists won't make breakthroughs in lagging AI fields, but it does mean that, for now, there are limits on fully autonomous software. This is vital, because in the meantime, the uneven advances made are pushing programmers toward creating very specific kinds of artificial intelligence. For instance, consumers are already seeing our machine-learning research reflected in the sudden explosion of digital personal assistants like Siri, Alexa, and Google-Now—technologies that are very good at interpreting voice-based requests but aren't capable of much more than that. These 'narrow AI' have been designed with a specific purpose in mind: to help people do the things regular people do, whether it's looking up the weather or sending a text message.

Narrow, specialized AI is also what companies like IBM have been pursuing. It includes, for example, algorithms to help radiologists pick out tumors much more accurately by 'learning' all the cancer research we've ever done and by 'seeing' millions of sample X-rays and MRIs. These AI systems act much more like glorified calculators: They can ingest way more data than a single person could hope to do with his or her own brain, but they still operate within the confines of a specific task like cancer diagnosis.

The limitations of this unbalanced AI progress are however minor, as current IT capacity vastly exceeds what insurers currently use IT for, so it will take a decade for insurers to reach any processing limitations and by then AI advances will offer insurers virtually unlimited opportunities. Within a 5- to 10-year time frame, more even progress in AI will result in products which will transform our lives. The expected pace of change is such that insurers who are not currently racing to understand and implement current advances will soon be too far behind to ever catch up.

This differential progress also has major implications as to what kinds of tasks can be automated, and thus what job activities will be at risk of being replaced by software. This means that loss of specific job activities to software will not occur all at once, but will occur one by one. However, as this process will probably be exponential the impact on jobs will seem like an increasing wave, giving workers and employers little time to react to one change before the next change occurs.

Hyperscaling

BCG (2015) argues that within the digital revolution there have been two prior secondary waves of disruption. The first wave was the dot-com era, which was characterized by falling transaction costs altering the trade-off between information richness and reach, so that suddenly rich information could be broadcast widely and cheaply altering how products were sold. Company value chains were open to attack by outsiders. An example of this was Microsoft giving away Encarta to promote PC sales and incidentally destroying Encyclopedia Britannica.

The second wave was the explosion of Web businesses, which was characterized by the disappearance of scales of economy for many products. This allowed long production tails and collaborate production, called 'economics of community'. An example was Encarta being replaced by Wikipedia. Successful companies actively adapted these waves. Unsuccessful companies tried to restrict the trend and disappeared.

BCG argues that we are now entering a third wave, which is characterized by what they call 'hyperscaling'. This involves creating huge networks based on a common AI system because of the importance of obtaining as wide a range of data as possible to train complex systems. This means that competitive scale will be beyond any individual business and gives an unbeatable competitive advantage to businesses who can cooperate with other related businesses to standardize and share data and systems. Data has to be regarded as infrastructure, and the collection and use of huge data sets across a business ecosystem will be a defining characteristic of insurance survivors.

Note that it is the combination of Wi-fi-linked devices, big data, cloud computing, and advanced software, which is now enabling progress at a far faster rate than the previously the previous stand-alone systems could achieve. This third wave will allow us to harvest the fruit of computerized administration systems in a way which has so far not been possible. Insurers have to make strategy decisions increasingly based on data access.

Voice and Visual Recognition

Hard things for humans - like calculus, financial market strategy, and language translation—are easy for a computer, while easy things for humans - like vision, motion, movement, and perception - are hard for a computer.

Voice recognition, for example, is hard for computers, and accurate recognition took far longer than analysts predicted. A key problem was that 95% or even 98% accuracy was not considered good enough by consumers. The largest initial hindrance was lack of large data sets in multiple dialects and of everyday speech. A key breakthrough was the release of the Justice Department's store of millions of Enron emails which gave analysts examples of real-world communication. This data set enabled the creation of respectable voice recognition and translation systems and the linking of these to central data stores is now generating huge data sets for algorithms to work on.

The ah-ha moment, however, came in 2011 when IBM's computer beat the two top all-time champions on the game show Jeopardy. This is impressive as Jeopardy is a complex verbal game requiring a deep understanding of verbal word plays and complex spoken language with hidden meanings, as well as learning from past mistakes. Involvement in Jeopardy was thus long considered a complex task impossible for a computer. These achievements mean that voice recognition has passed the breakthrough stage, the point in the graph where exponential technological progress breaks through linear expectations.

The implications of accurate voice recognition are large. Already most large corporations have either replaced telephone receptionists with software or are considering it. While Siri was initially crude, it has recently become workable. As frustrating as some of these current systems are, improvements at an exponential scale indicate that your next receptionist will probably be software. Call center operators will follow. In the future, most interactions with software can be expected to be voice-focused.

Similarly, visual recognition is at the breakthrough stage, so that face recognition systems will soon be routine to handle Skype calls and visitor reception. Nearly, all the physical engineering issues which hindered visual recognition are solved, meaning that progress from this point is software-related. Autonomous cars can now meet 99% of the visual demands on them to recognize obstacles, and within 5 years will match or exceed the capacity of human vision, especially in situations where spectrums like infrared are more useful, for example, at night or during storms. Recently, an app was released which allows a person to take a photograph of a stranger on their mobile and then instantly search the Web for information on that person, with about an 80% success rate at establishing their identity.

Advances in animation are linked to this and are also disruptive. Initial work on animated characters revealed that while humans were happy to accept a 90% accurate human animation as a cute copy, they strongly rejected any animation which was more than 90% but less than 100%, as it became ‘creepy’. This is called the ‘valley of death’ or ‘uncanny valley’, in the industry, as revealed by the adverse reaction to the movie Polar Express. Work by movie companies like Weta have, however, since advanced animation to the level where animated heads are now accepted by consumers.

Soul Machines is working on producing talking heads for chatbots which are eerily realistic. These have expressive faces which convey emotion in line with the spoken content - so it can express surprise or frown when asking customers about uninsured areas. They can also read customer emotions via the Webcam or smart phone app. Current versions seem stilted, but it would be an unwise insurer who assumed that, given exponential rates of improvement, these systems will not dominate future CRM systems.

For companies, the key issue is not the ability of animated heads to perform in a movie setting where thousands of hours of programmer time can be invested on a limited preset sequence of moves, but the ability of an animated head to respond in an ad hoc manner to a diverse range of customer queries. While this area is less advanced than voice recognition, within 5–10 years animated heads will be available to answer simple Skype queries and redirect more complex ones. Within 10–20 years, nearly all customer queries and advice, whether physical or online, will probably be handled by animations.

Insurers need to be aware that once combined with image recognition and voice recognition, AI systems are currently being designed which will be able to answer 90% of all text, phone, or skype queries without the customer being aware that they are not talking to a human. These systems are able to recognize which questions or situations require them to refer to a human supervisor.

There is a strong tendency for humans to respond to chatbots as if they were humans and therefore expect an appropriate human response. A difficult area which is currently being focused on is the ability to handle jargon, irony, sarcasm, and exaggeration. For example, if a customer says 'I've been waiting on the claim payment forever', AI systems can work out that they just mean a very long time. AI systems can be programmed to make jokes and to simulate 'social intelligence', especially tact, wit, and charm. Apple has put a lot of effort into making Siri likable, recognizing that occasionally this requires imperfections or kookiness.

Importantly, these systems will soon be able to recognize emotions and provide appropriate emotional responses. The increasing ability of software to pick up human facial clues on Skype calls will make these systems seem emphatic, with customers finding it very hard to tell if a human is speaking to them.

Research with psychology chatbots has shown that if the right style of questions or responses is programmed in, humans trust these digital agents and provide intimate financial or personal information. There is some evidence that humans prefer admitting failing to a digital agent in preference to a human. Given that these systems will collect data on customer reactions, insurers will than be able to trial different emotional or facial reactions to customers and see which generate the highest probability of a desired customer response. Differing facial types can also be trialled.

An important aspect of this is that software can be scaled to large or small demand, at very low marginal costs, and can be fine-tuned to accurately follow company policy. The software will never get bored or irritated or take leave and can be scaled infinitely if demand soars due to an emergency.

Digital Agents

One of the basic problems for users of the Internet is how to cope with the overwhelming size of choices. Every year, 8 million new songs are produced, so how does a consumer decide which few to listen to? If a keyword search reveals 3 million possible Web pages, how to rank the top 10? Platforms like Google use algorithms based on your own past Web searches and match these to what people with similar search histories clicked on next. Because this 'people-like-you' recommendation so closely matches your preferences, these have proved to have very high click-through and sales conversion rates. Relying on platform algorithms, however, places power in the hands of the platform. They control what you see next and what you buy. They also control the balance between repeating past patterns and experiencing new ideas/products outside your immediate comfort zone. This is 'people-like-you-generally-dislike-these-but-learned-to-like-this-one'.

The leading edge of Web users is therefore increasingly interacting with the digital world via the use of AI 'digital agents'. These are programs which contain useful personal information and carry out Internet tasks on behalf of its owner, and search the Web widely based on your preferences, rather than what a platform allows you to see. They can be customized to look past the answers which platform algorithms provide. They are increasingly being used to search for bargains, arrange activities, and autonomously make simple payments. They will liase with other household systems and create shopping lists, and keep track of appointments. For example, they will be aware of upcoming dinner parties, check the fridge contents, and arrange buying, book services, and ensure other attendee's digital agents are aware of the event. They can thus be visualized like a digital butler.

The agents are frequently voice-activated and likely to be the heart of future human contact with computers. Increasingly, they will use animated talking heads to communicate with their owners. Within insurance, these agents will offer financial/insurance planning, search for the best price/condition deals, and arrange cover via communication with insurer Web sites. Customers will set the buying parameters and then let the agent explore the Web for the correct product. Because they will have no time restrictions they will explore the Internet more thoroughly than customers would. Over time, the agent will increasingly learn their owner's preferences and may suggest interesting new products or services. An as yet undefined area is what weighting these digital agents will place on brand or reputation when making buying decisions. Customers can give their agent feedback about the product, which the agent will then upload to product review Web sites. Therefore, product review may become increasingly agent rather than human based.

Insurers will have to interact with these agents, computer to agents, to ensure their product ranks high within the agent's selection algorithm. This will be essential for dynamics insurance which involves a series of micropayments. Minor insurance claims will, in general, be handled by these agents. Insurers who do not have a system which interacts with these agents, will not be in the market.

Block-Chain Payment Systems

Payment over the Internet has always been an issue as the identity of the next party in the chain has to be verified. This has meant a need for third-party vendors who can guarantee each payment. This imposes cost and has hindered the development of micropayment systems.

Block-chain systems involve the use of a sequence of encrypted ordered records, each with a timestamp and link to the previous step. These are highly resistant to modification and thus the sequence can record transactions between two parties in a verified, permanent, and low-cost manner. This substantially removes the need for third-party payment systems and will be a vital part of real-time insurance as it will allow near-zero-cost transactions. This is a vital part of smart admin systems. Outside of that role, however, block-chain technology will be less important as a disruptor for insurance than it will be for finance.

Robotics

While current factories are becoming highly mechanized, this does not generally involve 'robotics' or mobile machines. The key issue is that current autonomous machinery is highly specialized and only able to adapt to a restricted range of uses, and because they have limited awareness of humans, for safety reasons they have been kept within set areas. Future use will involve unspecialized machines equipped with artificial intelligence (AI), which will be capable of learning multiple jobs, improving from experiences and mistakes, and because of multiple sensors will be safe enough to move among the general public. Progress toward this has been slow, however, with the Darpa Robotic Challenge not showing the same rate of change as autonomous car challenge exhibited.

This lack of momentum is about to change, however, especially once issues around unstructured environments, sequence planning, and tactile response are solved. Substantial progress can thus be expected in the future, especially independently mobile machines. Most of the key technology issues have been solved, from vision to manual dexterity to balance. One of the key reasons for the current slow progress is that the integration of the various robotic components depended on software developments, and these are only just being developed. This makes current humanoids jerky and not very useful. The creation of realistic robot faces is well behind that achieved in animation.

In the immediate future, the high cost of initial models will restrict their use to dangerous or extreme situations. Within a 10-to 20-year framework, however, autonomous machines which are truly adaptable and can be safely used beside humans will be developed and will fall rapidly in price. They will become common in areas where staff is hard to find, like elderly health care or food preparation. The best estimates of the employment impact of moveable robotics are the loss of around 15% of all jobs, mostly in factories. For insurance administration, the impact will be minimal; software and AI are likely to be a lot more important.

Insuring the value of these robots is conversely likely to be a growing area in the medium term. MGI (2013) found that the market for household cleaning robots is currently growing at more than 20% per annum, though from a very small base. Most middle-income households will eventually use a robot for nearly all household jobs which require mobility, though this is more likely in a 20-year time frame. The market for general purpose robots is potentially larger than the car market and is drawing in a lot of serious investment. However, because these robots will be equipped with location sensors and control over the Internet, their theft will be unviable, and as they get more reliable, claims for damage will become rare, so insurance revenue will be low. Issues relating to data security and hacking are sources of revenue.

3D Printing

3D printing has since 2000 evolved from an idea to a hobby to a reality, with printing now using a range of materials, including metals and biomaterial. Commentators have disagreed on the ultimate cost viability of printing industrial components routinely, but development on an exponential scale has substantial implications, for example, a drastic decrease in the need to trade internationally. While this technology will have limited application to the insurance industry, it will impact via the ability of suppliers to produce whatever parts are needed, rather than maintain large parts stores. For example, once repair shops or customers have access to high-quality 3D printers, then car insurance firms only need to supply repair shops with the software for a part, rather than the part.

SwissRe (2016) points out that 3D printing is starting to create a range of insurance issues, e.g., are replacement parts being made to a good quality, do printed medical implants create more or less risk, are there differences in user instructions, and are there potential malicious hacking issues?

Energy and Material De-intensification

People have a limited capacity to consume most types of goods, that is, most physical goods have a 'low-income elasticity'. The main reason for the severe shrinking of agriculture from 90% of production before the industrial revolution to 2% today was that people did not buy much more food as they got wealthier, so rapid increases in agricultural productivity caused rapid decreases in agricultural employment. The same has occurred with industrial goods, where the share of industrial employment peaked in most Western countries by 1980. The physical products we do buy contain less content, for example, beer cans weigh 80% less in 2016 than they did in 1973. In the future, cars will be computers on wheels. Services, in contrast, tend to have high income elasticity, so that people buy more services as their incomes rise, so that service employment has expanded.

We are thus entering a 'post-material' world, where any increase in income will result in more spending on software and entertainment, rather than physical goods. This, together with the increasing efficiency of modern manufacturing, will mean that consumption of energy and materials have just about peaked in the developed world with a decline probable. Emerging markets will follow. Demand for insurance for physical products, contents insurance, will thus rise slower than GDP. If they want to retain their cash flow, insurers have to increase their revenue from non-risk insurance-related services.

References

Bain & Company. (2015). *Global Digital Insurance Benchmarking Report 2015: Pathways to success in a digital world.*

Boston Consulting Group. (2015, July 24). Navigating a world of digital disruption. *BCG Perspectives.*

CEB. (2013). *TowerGroup wealth management client experience survey.*

Charan, R. (2015). *The attacker's advantage: Turning uncertainty into breakthrough opportunities.* Public Affairs, February.

Forbes. (2014). Internet of things by the numbers: Market estimates and forecasts.

GenRe. (2014). *Marketing to the millennial mindset.* GenRe USA.
McKinsey. (2012). *The social economy: Unlocking value and productivity through social technologies: consumer financial services.* McKinsey Global Institute.
McKinsey. (2015). *The internet of things: Mapping the value beyond the hype.* McKinsey Global Institute.
MGI. (2013). *Disruptive technologies: Advances that will transform life, business and the global economy,* Technical Report. McKinsey Global Institute.
Morgan-Stanley/BCG. (2013). *Wearable devices: The internet of things becomes personal.* Boston, MA: Boston Consulting Group.
PWC. (2015). *Insurance 2020 & beyond: Necessity is the mother of reinvention.*
Shirky, C. (2010). *Cognitive surplus: Creativity and generosity in a connected age.* New York: Penguin Press.
SwissRe. (2016). *How 3D printing will reshape the insurance landscape,* Centre for Global Dialogue, New York.
Talla, V., Kellogg, B., Ransford, B., Naderiparizi, S., Gollakota, S., & Smith, J. (2015). *Powering the next billion devices with Wi-Fi.* ArXiv:1505.06815.
Zaptitude. (2016). Investing in millennials. *Research Report.* www.zaptitude.com.

3
Types of Insurance

House & Contents Insurance

Property insurance insures your home against the risk of fire or other damage. Most home insurance provides cover only up to the 'sum insured'—a capped amount, that is, the limit of what can be claimed. Home owners with mortgages are normally legally required to insure their property against loss or injury to others. It also provides some 'third party' cover if we damage someone else's belongings in the house we are living in.

Contents Insurance protects personal belongings, both in and out of the house. Tenant's/Renter's insurance applies only to those who rent their home.

Automobile Insurance

Automobile insurance will pay to repair or replace your automobile. 'Comprehensive' motor vehicle insurance is the most common and it covers loss, theft, or damage to a vehicle. It also covers accidental

M. Naylor, *Insurance Transformed*, Palgrave Studies in Financial Services Technology,
DOI 10.1007/978-3-319-63835-5_3

damage to the other car or property you damage, or liability risk. Cheaper options are 'third party' and 'third party, fire and theft' cover. Third party insurance covers for damage to another person's vehicle or property, but not yours. Extending third party insurance to fire and theft covers the risk of your car being destroyed by fire or stolen, too.

The cost of insurance will vary depending on your age, claims history, the level of excess you are prepared to take, and the make and type of vehicle. Most countries make some type of auto-insurance compulsory.

Personal Insurance

Life insurance provides a lump sum of money on death. In some cases, a portion or the entire 'sum insured' is paid out before death if you are diagnosed with a terminal illness. There are different types of life insurance cover. The most common one today is term life insurance, which covers you for a fixed number of years such as the length of our mortgage. Investment 'whole of life insurance' has no maturity and is popular as an investment in countries where it is tax advantaged.

Trauma insurance (also called critical illness) provides a lump sum if you suffer from certain illnesses or injuries such as cancer, heart disease, or paralysis.

Income protection insurance pays a percentage of your income on an ongoing basis if you suffer from named illnesses.

Disability insurance pays out a lump sum for permanent disablement through sickness or accident.

Medical insurance covers private hospital and other medical bills in case of sickness.

Travel Insurance

Travel insurance policies cover belongings against loss or theft, extra costs if your flights are canceled, and medical treatment for accident or illness while traveling. Travel insurance policies usually have exclusions for preexisting conditions and unattended baggage. There are often many conditions and exclusions in travel insurance policies.

Business Insurance

Commercial property insurance policies provide for property having a business use. In addition to providing coverage for loss, damage, and liability issues, on both the premises and contents, business owners buy protection for the indirect loss of business costs associated with having to suspend operations while recovering from an incident.

Business interruption/loss of earning insurance covers expenses incurred if the business is unable to operate.

Business owner's policy (BOP) packages all required coverage a business owner would need. Often, BOP's will include business interruption insurance, property insurance, vehicle coverage, liability insurance, and crime insurance. This can be customized to a company's specific needs. Typically, a business owner will save money by choosing a BOP because the bundle of services often costs less than the total cost of all the individual coverages.

Commercial Auto-Insurance protects a company's vehicles. If a business does not have company vehicles, but employees drive their own cars on company business this provides 'non-owned auto liability' to protect the company in case the employee does not have insurance or has inadequate coverage.

Worker's Compensation provides insurance to employees who are injured on the job, providing wage replacement and medical benefits.

In exchange for these benefits, the employee gives up his/her rights to sue the employer for the incident. This protects the company from legal complications. Some countries require companies to have this insurance.

Liability Insurance

Business Liability Insurance provides protection when the policy holder is financially responsible for injury or damage they cause to others. The policy provides both legal defense costs and damages if employees or products or services cause bodily injury or property damage to a third party. This includes area like accidental pollution.

Professional Liability Insurance (Errors and Omissions Insurance) provides defense costs and damages for failure to or improperly rendering professional services. Professional liability insurance is applicable for any professional firm.

Directors and Officers Insurance protects the directors and officers of a company against their actions that affect the profitability or operations of the company. If a director or officer of the company, as a direct result of their actions on the job, finds himself or herself in a legal situation, this type of insurance can cover costs or damages lost as a result of a lawsuit.

Data Breach Insurance provides cover for accidental or unauthorized breaches of data. If the business stores sensitive or nonpublic information about employees or clients on their computers, servers, or in paper files they are responsible for protecting that information.

Medical Malpractice Insurance provides covers for medical institutions and personal.

Marine/Shipping Insurance

Marine insurance covers the loss or damage of ships, cargo, terminals, and any transport or cargo by which property is transferred, acquired, or held between the points of origin and final destination. Cargo insurance is a sub-branch of marine insurance, though Marine also includes onshore and offshore exposed property, hull, marine casualty, and liability. Marine open cover is generally open-ended with no expiry date and can be canceled without prior notice.

Shipping insurance covers goods transported by mail or courier. Depending on transportation method, it can be divided into marine cargo transportation insurance, continental cargo transportation insurance, aviation cargo transportation insurance, and parcel transportation insurance.

There are three internationally-used transport insurance categories: (i) *Free of particular average* (FPA) is the narrowest form of cover as the insurance company does not cover you for partial loss or damage to the cargo. You are only covered if the entire consignment is lost or damaged, for example, when a ship sinks, or by fire. (ii) *With average* (WA) cover extends the FPA clause to include partial loss arising from heavy weather and sea water damage. Both FPA and WA can usually be extended to include protection from theft and pilferage. (iii) *All risks* (AR) cover is the most comprehensive cargo insurance, providing protection against loss or damage from external causes. It does not cover loss or damage arising from delay, inherent vice (deterioration or damage without outside help), losses as a result of inadequate packaging, weight loss from drying out, or market changes. Risks from war, strikes, riots, and civil unrest are also not covered, but can be covered at extra cost.

Transport and marine insurance is often brokered and terms can be extensively modified.

4
The Impact of Disruptive Technology

Not Business As Usual

For the reasons explained in earlier chapters, the insurance industry worldwide, which in general has been a laggard in the use of advances in IT, is on the brink of a major technological-induced disruptive revolution. Because the essence of insurance is data analysis, insurance as a sector is likely to face far greater disruption than most other sectors as the combination of disruptive innovations will uniquely impact more on data analytics than other sectors. Fundamentally, insurance is about the pricing and selection of risk. The Internet of things, Wi-fi mobility, and big data will fundamentally change the type of risk data insurers use, how they assess risk, how they price risk, and how they deal with customers. This change will be complex. For example, while self-drive cars and other innovations could reduce claim rates drastically (self-drive cars can even be programmed to deliver unauthorized drivers to the nearest police station), they will also reduce premiums and cash flow drastically, and lead to the virtual elimination of car insurance as a viable stand-alone industry within 20 years.

M. Naylor, *Insurance Transformed*, Palgrave Studies in Financial Services Technology,
DOI 10.1007/978-3-319-63835-5_4

While insurance has often been responsive to technology, unfortunately, during the last decade, while the IT world has transformed, the insurance industry has been focused on business-as-usual in an effort to survive the troubled times of the GFC and associated regulation changes. IBM (2006) explores reasons for this tendency of insurers to lag technologically, concluding that insurers tend to focus on the optimization of products and processes, and accept this incremental change as though it were innovation. During the coming disruption, however, insurers which display continued passivity to technology will no longer be able to survive, as the cost advantages of technological leaders or external disruptors will destroy the cost base of laggards. Christensen (1997) argued that new resources plugged into old processes and values does not constitute a change-capable organization.

Brynjolfsson et al. (2011) found that companies which were in the top third of their industries in terms of making data-driven decisions were, on average, 5–6% more productive, and the gap was increasing. McKinsey (2016) found that the top 25% of digital adapters in insurance had revenue growth twice the rate of the other 75%, while achieving a 26% expense ratio vs. 32% for the rest. McKinsey argues that digitizing the top 20 insurance processes would reduce human service costs by between 30 and 50%. These kinds of cost reductions are achievable within five years and would reduce non-adopter profit margins to near zero. Past five years cost will drop even faster. External disruptors are starting to enter the insurance sector with US$2.6B invested in insurance-related start-ups in 2015, up from $135M in 2010. At the end of 2016, there were in excess of 1300 InsurTech start-ups aiming to transform the market, and this is rising fast as the sector is viewed by potential disruptors as ripe for the plucking. The key issue for this book is how insurance companies and their employees will respond to these changes.

Middle-level insurance management is often aware of and informed about these issues. Yet surveys of what issues senior insurance company management are worrying about, rarely mention technological change or external disruptors as the top issue. Insurance management is thus, in general, unprepared for what is coming. Those insurers who are aware,

are only starting to explore the implications. Most have yet to react. Very few understand that they have to reimagine their industry.

This is in contrast to financial markets and banking which have undergone significant change. For example, financial markets no longer have floor traders, with complex trading decisions being handled by the millions by software with IT-trained staff overseeing rather than being involved. McKinsey (2015) notes that more than a dozen European banks have replaced older statistical-modeling approaches with machine-learning techniques. Some have experienced 10% increases in sales of new products, 20% savings in capital expenditures, 20% increases in cash collections, and 20% declines in churn. The banks have achieved these gains by devising new recommendation engines for clients in retailing and in small- and medium-sized companies. They have also built micro-targeted models that more accurately forecast who will cancel service or default on their loans, and how best to intervene.

Costs of Production

The costs of producing a product are a balance between fixed, 'one-off,' costs and marginal, 'per unit,' costs. Most industrial products have substantial marginal costs so there is always a limit to how low prices can drop. By contrast, software has substantial fixed costs of creation but very low marginal costs of reproduction.

Figure 4.1 illustrates the difference between the traditional insurance cost model and the new. Normally, we assume that: (i) as fixed costs are

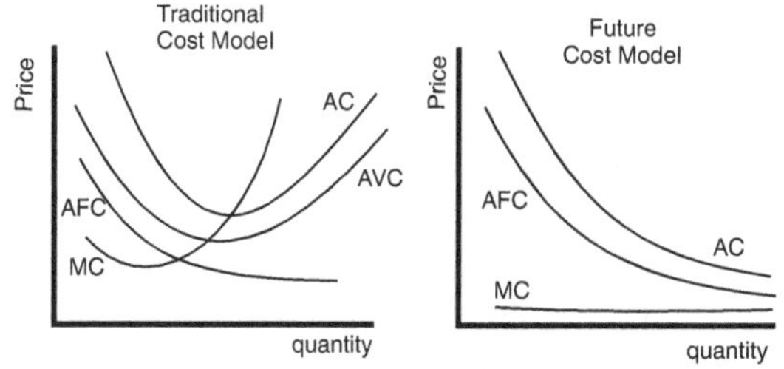

Fig. 4.1 Fixed vs. marginal cost diagram. *Source* Author

spread over more outputs then the 'average fixed cost' (AFC) continually falls, (ii) marginal costs (MC), the extra cost per output, tend to rise as we try to squeeze more and more output from our fixed system thus MC tends to rise as output expands, (iii) thus average total cost (AC) per output tends to fall and then rise. The high level of marginal cost occurs because each output requires materials, workers, shipping, etc.

For software products, there are typically very little costs to reproduce or distribute a product once it has been produced. Conversely, the costs to initially produce a product may be high. Thus, the long-run average cost, or the cost per product, tends to continually fall as total sales rise. The marginal profit per product is high. For example, if it costs an IT firm $10M to produce an App, and $1 to reproduce and distribute each copy, and it charges $100 per copy, then once it has sold one hundred thousand copies and has covered its costs, then it makes $99 profit per extra copy. Alternatively, it could drop its price to $10 a copy, to shut out new entrants, who cannot cover their fixed costs at that price. This means once a minimum market size is reached, so that the fixed costs of production are paid, prices can be set at a very low level.

There is thus an advantage to large international insurers who can create an expensive but efficient and world-leading IT system and then spread the cost over its worldwide network. It is very hard for smaller firms to react. The implication of this for employees would seem to be that if your occupation type is large enough worldwide to justify the initial investment in creating the software, then, if you can be replaced by a program, you will eventually be replaced. However, things are not that simple. The price of many service activities will certainly be drastically lowered, as automation drops the costs of individualization and customization to pennies and makes them become routine. The key thing to be understood is that if these services have a reasonable 'price elasticity of demand,' then this drastic drop in per-service cost can easily increase overall demand so much that more workers are required, even if each service embodies only a fraction of the traditional amount of human labor. For example, during the industrial revolution while hand loom operators lost their jobs, as each mechanical loom worker could produce 1000× the output, because the price of cloth dropped to a fraction of what it had been, demand for cloth increased so much that overall employment in the cloth sector increased substantially. Another useful concept here is 'income elasticity of demand,' mentioned earlier—does the overall increase in income mean that people want to buy more of that good? In sectors like entertainment, overall demand will rise as IT transformation increases incomes.

Servicization

Traditionally, companies have visualized consumer demands as being best met by producing a product; people have a need for transport so a car is produced, people have a need for travel accommodation so a hotel is built, people have a need of music at home so a record is produced. This product was priced at cost plus a reasonable profit margin. Digitization disrupts this model because it allows the creation of perfect copies at a very low marginal cost.

Rifkin (2014) argues that this creates revenue issues for companies who produce very low marginal cost products. This is because competition frequently drives price down to marginal cost. Customers naturally demand that their needs are met at a price near to this low marginal cost, rather at a price which allows the full costs of production to be recovered. Summers and DeLong (2001) argue that when marginal cost is near zero, this can mean that firms are unable to cover fixed costs, and therefore are unable to sustain their position in the market. This is illustrated by many software apps being distributed for free, with provider income arising from add-on services. The implications of this possible future for insurers are profound. The main implication is that surviving insurers will need to create a wider range of income streams.

This pricing quandary was first felt by the music and media industries from the late 1990s when music download and news Web Sites started to destroy demand for the physical product, yet did not provide an adequate replacement revenue stream. Many producers tried to resist the technological innovations, by imposing access fees or via legal actions. These rearguard actions have had little impact on the waves of technological innovation. When products can be provided at near zero cost and copied indefinitely, transformation is inevitable.

The only viable producer solution has been to reimagine consumer demand in a way which is financially viable. This basically involves providing the basic product at low cost and then making profit from a range of add-on services which the consumer values. This transforms products to services, which is called 'Servicization.' Rather than being a product which is produced at a set time and place, there is a flow of real-time value-added services. There is not a onetime purchase but an ongoing relationship. There is not a sales price but a subscription. Once reimagined this process opens up a range of previously unimagined service-based sales opportunities.

Kelly (2016) argues that when copies are near-free, companies need to sell flow attributes which can't be copied. Some of these are: (i) *Trust* is valuable, as it can't be copied or stored. In a world of unlimited supply, brand reputation becomes increasingly the main factor for buyers. (ii) *Immediacy* is valuable; customers want instant availability. (iii) *Personalization* is valuable; customers want a service modified to their exact needs. As these needs change, this requires an ongoing two-way conversation. (iv) *Service support* is valuable; a near unlimited supply of data or information means that advice, interpretation, or guides on how-to-use are vital. (v) *Authenticness* and *data security* are valuable. (vi) *Accessibility* without ownership is valuable; this removes the need for maintenance.

Consumers do not want LP records, they want music. Trying to sell an LP record with a fixed selection of songs, chosen and sound-edited by an expert, is outdated. What consumers value is being able to select their own mix of songs, being able to edit, or modify those songs to suit their taste. They want and will pay for; an expert they trust, or a group of friends, providing recommended selections from the overwhelming mass of songs; software which allows them to stretch or reduce song length without the sound essence being affected; being able to access sound tracks for each instrument, so they can produce their own modified copies; being able to share, discuss, review, or rank songs, with people like themselves; live performances; and live streaming. Similar disruption is occurring in travel, automobiles, media, publishing, banking, and other industries. The revenue available from all these services was not visible to record executives when the digital revolution happened. Insurance needs to focus on the imagining how they can invent a wide array of similarly innovative value-added services.

Administration

One of the main impacts of the looming disruption will be substantial pressure to create completely automated, software-based internal administrative systems backed by AI, often called 'intelligence process automation' (IPA). This means that every activity, which can be done by software, telematics, or drone, is done without direct human involvement.

IPA comprises five aspects: (i) *robotic process automation* - this handles routine administrative tasks in software, (ii) *smart workflow* - this is process management software, which integrates activities done by humans and software, (iii) *machine learning* - algorithms which identify patterns in data, providing superior analysis, (iv) *natural language generation* - software that allows interactions between humans and software, based on translation rules, (v) *cognitive agents* - technology which combines machine learning and natural language generation to create a digital workforce. It is vital to understand that the future is not a question of software vs. humans, but rather how these two can work together to create services which customers value.

Insurance is a very administrative process - its chief output is a promise and is thus more vulnerable than other sectors to external disruptors with superior IPA skills. An insurer with a fully automated, digital, adminstrative system would have the ability to carry out most activities at a substantially lower marginal cost, and therefore undercut its competitors. While insurance has always been interested in the use of computers, incumbents have recently been struggling to upgrade disparate legacy systems. Therefore, recent advances in the technology sectors have left most incumbents well behind the leading edge of IPA best practice. As will be explained later, despite increased spending in IT systems, it may be difficult for incumbents to catch up in time.

The IT Productivity Paradox

Spending on IT systems has become a major headache for most service sector companies since 1980. Spending has become increasingly heavy with Carr (2003), showing how IT went from 5% of capital expenditures in 1965 to 15% in the early 1980s, to 30% in the early

1990s, to 50% by 2000. The problem is that despite these increases and the fact that IT is now the backbone of the business, productivity improvements which can be related to this IT expenditure seems minimal. This is called the 'IT productivity paradox.'[1]

One explanation for this is that because IT capital expenditure alone does not confer a competitive advantage, but merely keeps a firm in the game, spending on IT merely reduces prices so no extra revenue is gained. IT in a physical sense also has to be combined with the ability to use that IT capacity via related changes in management systems and across the full range of administrative activities, so that IT becomes integrated. IT is just a resource; it has to be used wisely.[2] IT investment has so far been used to cut cost rather than allowing most firms to differentiate themselves or expand revenue. It is thus likely that most insurers will be forced to substantially increase IT expenditure and revolutionize their business processes just as the cost of staying in the industry, with minimal extra profit gained as no sustainable competitive advantage is achieved.

An additional complication, which will be explored further below, is that the future success will require insurers to form business networks with related companies. A key part of these relationships will be the integration of data systems, including data formation protocols. Thus, insurers not only have issues with integration of their disparate legacy internal IT systems, they will have to integrate across previously disparate industries. Insurers have little experience with this and are unlikely to be technological leaders, and so are vulnerable to external entrants who have these skills.

Legacy Systems

Many commentators argue that most current insurers could struggle to cope with the changes because of issues associated with lagging legacy IT systems, poor reputations, negligent social capital with customers,

[1]For a background see Schryen (2013).

[2]This is discussed in Wernerfelt (1984) and Breznik (2012).

and an inability to become flexible fast enough to cope with new 'born digital' competitors. Large insurers, especially those born from multiple mergers, are already struggling to cope with current demands for efficient IT systems due to poorly integrated multiple legacy systems. They are likely to be unable to cope with the future demands for the complete recreation of their IT and management systems, in an environment where the IT systems of external competitors are moving forward at a rapid pace. The ability to stay up with IT system technological change will become a vital characteristic of survival, as the future changes in IT are not only increasing but the rate of increase is increasing, so the need for change is increasing - exponential change.

One of the problems insurers have is that, perversely, because their business is data based, insurance companies have always seen the advantages of computers and were early adaptors, investing heavily in the 1970s and 1980s. At that stage, packaged software was in its infancy so insurers developed most of their systems in-house to cover specific functions. They are thus frequently stuck with inflexible, outdated, legacy IT systems.

This has led to a number of IT issues for current insurers: (a) many systems were written in older code, which is less flexible than modern code, (b) there is a mix of in-house and packaged systems, which are often incompatible, (c) the code in many systems was not well documented, esp. later modifications, and staff involved have retired, so it is nearly impossible to effectively optimize the code, (d) types and specification of data were created as isolated silos, so have to be extensively modified to be compatible, (e) as new technologies have emerged, insurers have tended to layer these on top of existing systems, rather than rebuild and integrate, (f) most data analysis takes place in batches, not real time, and (g) existing IT processes were not created with any ability to accept real-time data. While most industries have these issues, the early adaption of IT by insurers perversely makes their issues more acute. Most insurers also struggle with multiple incompatible legacy systems from mergers as well as myriad sources of input data which are non-standardized and incompatible with their IT systems.

Thus, systems and IT transformation will require insurers to invest substantially in replacing existing IT systems, in standardizing, absorbing, and utilizing the huge new data flows, in partnering with telematic embedders, in new Web-based customer interaction platforms, in automated policy/claims/billing software, in changing work patterns and mind-sets, and in retraining/restructuring staff. Product line silos need to disappear to enable a company-wide, integrated seamless process to occur.

The need for large investments to reinvent systems means that overall IT costs may increase substantially in the short term, even as marginal cost per-client falls in the medium term. Since IT systems and management systems were also created together with differing products set up as separate streams, re-engineering an insurer into an integrated company can be very difficult, as management processes and business models will have to be transformed as the IT system is transformed, as is discussed in later sections.

Given that the computerized administrative systems will be the heart of the insurer survivors and its structure will determine the way in which an insurer can react to challenges, outsourcing of IT is problematic as decisions made by the IT consultant will impact directly on the structure of business processes. As noted earlier, the need for change is more about the business procedures than about the physical software. Thus, the recreation of IT systems has to be seen as a key strategic management issue to be decided at the highest level. Note also that for insurers their core IT systems are the essence of their business, 'mission-critical,' and cannot be turned off or allowed to fail as they are transformed. Thus, IT transformation has to occur in a moving system.

Note that before insurers can exploit the exploding streams of new data, they will need to transmit it, to store it, to create software to analyze it, and then decide which trends can be responded to by the software versus which trends need to be brought to human attention. They will require agreed protocols about data standardization and security, both within the firm and across their ecosystem. All of these are complex tasks requiring expertise in areas which incumbent staff may not be strong in.

The large size, the unstructured nature, and the diverse formats of big data mean that extracting useable insights is not easy. For example, many call centers now provide contact staff with all correspondence with a customer on screen. In an era of big data, this is not possible as information on a client will be multi-channel and overwhelming in size. All contact employees need just the information they need, all they need, but no more, and they need it in a way which is easy to comprehend at a glance.

A particular issue with big data is that its size, and complexity and the requirement that many sources of data be combined before trends can be found, means there is no simple way to examine data - it cannot be 'eyeballed.' Instead, big data requires the creation of data visualization systems whereby a mass of data can be distilled to key variables. The way data is presented to humans will be critical to what kind of insights can be achieved.

Deciding exactly what trends or detail each employee needs is a complex problem, when it is still unclear exactly what insights big data will reveal. The information will need to be presented to contact employees in a dynamic framework, with a dashboard so more is available if required. Data visualization will thus be a key skill, a field which is only starting to establish itself. This will require substantial investment as initially the required data visualization software will have to be customized in-house.

These complexities led Morgan Stanley/BCG (2014) to argue that most existing insurers are too complex and siloed to be able to change and adapt with adequate speed and flexibility to survive against 'born digital' disruptors. They argue that it is easier for external firms with already integrated systems to add insurance as a product than it is for insurers to transform. Zoeller Consulting Principal Kent Hopper argued, in an Actuaries Summit in May 2015, that today's insurers are outdated dinosaurs who will not survive. Hopper argued that this is because the future requires 'companies to be data based, agile, consumer orientated, mobile, smart and predictive,' whereas current insurers are 'HQ-based, process-centric, analogue, one-size-fits-all, and too risk-orientated.' The result is that 'insurers are facing increasing costs, with declining sales and customer loyalty'. Modern companies 'respond to customers in seconds, not weeks.'

In the past, established insurers have been protected from new entrants by the high fixed costs of developing systems and distribution capacities. In the new digital era, however, these barriers have disappeared, as many IT-based companies have better existing systems than insurers do, making it easier for new entrants to develop the required systems than it is for existing insurers to transform their systems. The obvious advantages to customers of the future IT-based insurance will also remove most regulatory barriers.

Firms have to get past the idea that they can survive by adding to existing legacy systems with a few Web site or apps. They need, instead, to reinvent entirely how they operate. The core skills of successful future insurers will be an ability to create and utilize extremely client friendly software, an ability to create data networks, and an ability to build social capital.

The refocus on IT systems also changes the scale of dynamics in insurance, as the ability to rent IT capacity via the cloud means that large insurers will no longer have a size advantage in term of IT capacity. Effective software, not ownership of mainframes, will be the key insurer asset.

A key element in the survival rate of existing insurers is the speed of entry by firms from outside the current insurance sector who already have these skills, as well as social capital. These external entrants will find it easy to enter and destroy the market of those insurers too slow to respond. An illustration of the ability of out-of-sector firms to disrupt is the destruction of Kodak by firms from the electronic sector.

Customers

A key impact of the impact of Web-product-comparison has been the growing strength of customers versus companies. As explored earlier, a key to company success in the future will be the level of their social capital. This has not traditionally been an area which insurance companies have focused on or been successful at. Insurers have instead focused on internal issues like pricing risk and controlling internal costs.

They rarely interact with customers directly. One of the key impacts of digitization is that it will transform insurance from a seller's market to a buyer's market.

The disconnect between life insurers' value proposition and today's customers[3]

Imagine Susan, a 34-year-old high-school teacher who is expecting her first child and hence decides to buy a life insurance policy. First, it is very unlikely that a provider will proactively reach out to her, or know she is about to undergo a life-event. If she tries to shop for a policy online, she may be intimidated by complex products and technical terminology that is confusing and makes her feel incompetent.

If she looks for an agent and is lucky enough to find one that she feels she can trust, she is likely to have concerns about how much the policy will really cost, the meaning of all the fine print, and whether the agent is more interested in her needs or in a quick commission.

If Susan overcomes these doubts and decides to buy a policy, she will begin what may be an arduous application process: lengthy forms with sensitive medical questions, weeks of waiting, and little transparency on where things stand. She may wonder why the process is so complicated and time-consuming when many companies in other industries offer convenient, fast (and mostly digital) services.

If she has questions on her coverage after buying the product or wants to change her policy, she will likely struggle with the limited self-service options offered by the insurers and may find that her agent has moved on.

Such 'pain points' may make Susan abandon the process or take her business elsewhere.

McKinsey (2016) argues that the traditional insurance product creates six 'insurance disconnect points' along the customer's purchase path, each with reasons why prospective customers fail to be converted into loyal customers. These pain points are:

[3]Example is from McKinsey (2016) *Transforming life insurance with design thinking.*

1. *Awareness of Product:*
    (a) Limited product engagement.
    (b) Doubts about product value.
    (c) Incomplete product understanding.
    (d) Tendency to put off purchase (seen as a disagreeable chore).

⬇

2. *Consideration of Purchase:*
    (a) Low trust in delivery.
    (b) Limited rapport with broker.

⬇

3. *Purchase Decision:*
    (a) Confusion about product features.
    (b) Doubt if product is right fit.
    (c) Feeling of 'being sold to'.

⬇

4. *Application Process:*
    (a) Frustration about delay and lack of transparency.
    (b) Feeling rejected when application turned down or terms imposed.

⬇

5. *Customer Care:*
    (a) Limited, or no access, to quick, easy, self-service tools.
    (b) Limited product flexibility.

6. *Claims:*
    (a) Feeling vulnerable and overwhelmed.
    (b) Need for emergency bridge help.
    (c) Feeling taken advantage off when under emotion and financial pressure.

These business-leakage drivers create some of the main problems with personal risk insurance: (i) low customer engagement, (ii) limited ability to meet the expectations of Generation Y or millennials, (iii) large, inflexible, stock of legacy polices, and (iv) slow product change cycles.

The movement of customer acquisition from intermediation via agents toward direct sales will also reduce customer stickiness and increase retention issues. IBM (2015) found that only 37% of US customers trusted their own insurer to a reasonable degree. While customers of agents trusted their own agents, non-customers did not, in general, trust agents. IBM also found that 40% of customers who did switch providers did so because their old insurer could not meet their changing expectations. They also found that 58% of respondents think that insurance companies are more difficult to deal with than tech-based firms. Given that acquiring new customers tends to cost about four times the cost of retaining existing customers, changes in customers' stickiness can have substantial cost implications.

The insurance industry generally rates low in terms of client trust, with Equinix (2014) stating that insurers rate below banks in terms of trust, which is bad given the public hatred of banks after the GFC. PWC (2014) argues that companies which do not refocus from a product orientation to a total customer-centric orientation will not survive past 2025. They found that the top three customer needs were: (i) accessibility, (ii) tailored to customer, and (iii) content explanation.

They argue that most companies who try to respond to the challenges of the digital era put digital innovation at the forefront of their strategy. This is a mistake as it should be the customer who is the focus; IT developments are the means to that end, rather than the end. Many existing insurance companies, however, may find that their legacy of poor service in customers' minds and the resultant low social capital is a hurdle impossible to reverse. Companies with existing expertise in building social capital in other fields, and high social capital, can thus be expected to enter the insurance market as they will be viewed positively by customers.

McKinsey & Company (2016) argue that for generations, insurers have delivered their promise of financial security with the help of strong actuarial functions, intermediated distribution channels, complex products, limited service, rigid processes, and cumbersome customer interactions. In the future, customers will reward transparency, speed, and flexibility.

Another IT-based change has been the evolution of groups of customers with similar risk profiles bought together by Web-based software. Current products are aimed at an amorphous average, yet many customers differ from that, resulting in them not being offered cover or feeling disconnected from the product and difficult to market to. Traditionally, groups with similar differing needs have had to find each other and mutually identify themselves, an information problem which was difficult and expensive. Now, use of deep-social-data-and-web-search-algorithms enables specialist companies to identify these differing customers and offer them to as a group to insurers who are seeking that risk profile. Groups of customers can also create their own groupings via software and bulk-buy from insurers. The insurer can then create a customized communication strategy and additional sales opportunities. An example of this would be cancer patients who are seeking travel insurance for short restorative trips.

A key question is how accepting customers will be of the new technology. The answer at this stage is that customers are happily accepting elements like adaptive-cruise-control, use of Siri, software telephone receptionists, online shopping, at a fast pace. The willingness of customers to accept new approaches seems to be increasing over time, e.g.; customers accepted smartphones far faster than they accepted the initial mobile phones.

An example of this is the Japanese Web-marketplace, Rakuten, which purchased an underwriter and now offers insurance to its wide network of existing customers. In New Zealand, the main online shopping Web site, TradeMe, is already offering the most popular insurance premium comparison engine and has taken the first small step to selling policies on behalf of insurers. It is only another small step away from selling its own policies, underwritten by reinsurers. The fact that these disruptors have not yet entered a particular market is not a good reason for the delay.

Legislators in some countries may be unable to keep up, but the possibility of online insurers or advisers operating from a foreign jurisdiction which has state-of-the-art legislation will give some impulse to politicians to reform. The lagging elements at this stage are insurance companies and advisers. They will either update or lose business.

Digitization will transform insurance from a seller's market to a buyer's market - the customer will be a king. Insurers do not currently treat them as such. While traditionally insurance customers have been static, accepting poor service and finding switching difficult, the new breed of customers are becoming restless and looking for alternatives, as switching difficulties have been slashed. Capgemini/Efma (2016) details comprehensively how Generations Y and younger have drastically different and more demanding customer expectations than baby boomers and argues that insurers will have to adopt. They found that, in general, customer expectations are evolving faster than insurers' ability to innovatively address these expectations. Customers' disappointing insurance experiences led them to be open to external disruptors. Customer stickiness is falling.

It is vital to note that modern consumers do not judge their customer experience of an insurance company against that of other insurance companies, but instead judge it against their experiences with digital leaders such as Amazon. Yet insurers still tend to benchmark themselves against other insurers instead of benchmarking against possible external disruptors. In terms of a quality real-time omni-channel interface and a quality customer experience, insurers, in general, perform so poorly that they are seen as 'in a different world' from the digital leaders, and therefore vulnerable. This means that being the 'best insurer' in an area is meaningless as a metric for long-term survival.

Morgan Stanley/BCG (2014) argues that, so far, insurance customers have found their insurance online satisfaction in the bottom 10% of their overall online experiences, perceiving their needs as significantly unmet and the products as expensive and inflexible. Customer expectations have changed faster than insurers have realized, with expectations that they should be able to engage with insurers via multiple channels,[4] especially mobile devices, without being bogged down in lengthy and annoying phone conversations.

Morgan Stanley/BCG (2015), in a worldwide survey, found that 50% of insurance customers indicated they would switch to any insurer offering superior mixed-channel service, with 80% of all customers willing to consider new digital insurance products, and this peaked at over 85% in the 25–35 age group, and at over 90% in the highest income group. About 85% were willing to divulge personal information, if significant premium reductions were offered. It is interesting that insurers were seen as the 3rd most trust-worthy industry in terms of handling personal information, which gives a basis to work from.

The most important change that social media has created for insurers is that they can no longer create their reputation in isolation from customers - the value of a company's reputation is now co-created with customers. It is no longer a one-way process, from the PR department to the customer, it is now inherently two-way. Most insurers have not yet recognized this, nor understood what this means for reputation value creation.

Castriotta et al. (2014) argue that insurers need to use the DART model (Dialogue, Access, Risk assessment, Transparency), and that the

[4]For omni-channels customer expectations, see Target Group (2015).

relative absence of insurers from social media platforms has meant that they are not visible to digital natives and when they are present they tend to *talk to* customers, rather than *talk with* them, which is worse than being absent. This played a major part in the declining sales to this generation. Instead, insurers need to build high-quality digital spaces where customers can interact and feel deeply involved in activities which are not strictly related to the world of insurance. The key future insurer social media skill will be able to create dialogue to jointly solve problems. Digital laggards are rapidly disappearing from customer awareness.

Digital natives, in particular, will switch to more in-tune newer entrants, who will meet their expectations of substantially lower costs and superior online service. Surveys show that digital natives exhibit little insurer brand loyalty, but have robust service expectations. Experience with CRM systems is cumulative so first movers in this area will enjoy significant competitive advantages. GEICO is an example of a new entrant to auto-insurance which has used heavy investment in IT to cut admin and claim costs while pleasing customers. This has meant that it has grown its market share significantly faster than older competitors, who are now struggling to catch up.

Note that there cannot be one-answer solutions. Most insurers use CRM systems which are reactive, and not proactively in-tune with customer needs. Yet research shows that customers, in general, prefer low-touch self-service options when browsing or researching, but when something goes wrong or they are confused, they want high-touch, personalized service. The younger generations will not put up with the current low level of insurer service and will actively switch. Consumer technology firms which already offer this style of customer service, and have established social capital with the digital generation, are prime candidates for disruptive entry into the insurance sector.

Another key element is that customers are becoming more diverse, demanding that companies engage via multiple channels. This is due partly to growing ethnic diversity, but is also due to differing capacities of customers to react to the accelerating technological changes. Thus, a key skill for survivors will be the ability to retain and simplify existing channels to retain low-tech clients while expanding new channels to attract high-tech clients. Any indication from insurers that they regard users who are reluctant to move to new channels as illogical would be harmful to their reputation.

A better way to define customers than by birth is in terms of those who embrace technology, 'Digitals,' versus those who do not. BCG (2016) found that 5% of over 55s embrace leading edge technology vs. 25% of those aged 31–54 and 33% of millennials. This makes digitals about 20% of the current US auto-insurance market and growing. When compared to non-digitals, digitals switch more frequently, (14% switching within the first 9 months vs. 7%), do more product research (70% vs. 47%), use multiple channels (30%), are more likely to use price comparison sites (35% vs. 25%), are more likely to take an agent or broker recommendation (21% vs. 6%) or employer recommendation (10% vs. 3%), are less motivated solely by price (69% vs. 84%), are more motivated by loyalty programs (34% vs. 18%), are more likely to use banks (42% vs. 24%) or Internet providers (38% vs. 17%) or household service firms (18% vs. 8%), and are less likely to purchase direct from an insurer (52% vs. 77%). The implication of this cultural change is that Internet-based firms are more likely to survive in a world of digital insurance than current insurers are.

Yoder and Rao (2015) found that 71% of insurance CEO's surveyed regarded the increasing diversity of customers as a major disruptive trend. Product suppliers and distributors will have to create a more diversified range of products, which are simultaneously simpler yet broader, and offer an ability to be customized to customer needs at minimal additional cost. This may require multiple brands with different images or customization. The younger generations, in particular, will not be satisfied with a few standardized choices. Customers will demand seamless and efficient feedback and a positive response to their request for customization within a consumer-centric culture. They have become used to this from online retailers and will not comprehend why insurance companies can't tailor products. In a world where McDonalds offers the choice of 'build-your-own burger' via a software interface, insurers need to offer customized products. Mass-customization is the future.

An essential reason for product simplification is that, as Equinix (2014) argues, with technological complexity increasing and customers' available time decreasing, it is no longer reasonable for companies to take a 'buyer-beware' stance. Society will increasingly expect the burden of protection to fall on those creating the product or service. Providers who do not fulfill this expectation will face a devastating backlash from society. Producers whose products or services are seen to be 'unfair' via confusion will lose client trust. Insurers will have to reduce the perceived complexity of their products while being completely transparent and compliant with regulation.

Disintermediatization

Two big themes in other areas of financial services have been the automation of administration and the separation of distribution from production. The growth of software in administration, the ease of international transfer of information, and the vital nature of social capital mean that insurance companies no longer need to do be involved in all areas of the insurance business. Theory argues that integrated companies only exist because internal operations are cheaper than external contractors. The Web and explosion of data is changing these cost structures. An example is banks and the finance sector, which disintermediatized in the 1990s, e.g.; mortgage originators developed who originated and then on-sold loans to merchant banks who then spiced and diced and then on-sold to investors.

There is amble proof from other sectors that category killers often can offer one area far cheaper than an integrated provider can. McKinsey (2016) points out that every part of the insurance value chain is currently under attack by an external disruptor who can potentially do that part of the chain better than the incumbents. Why should one company find insurance clients, as well as underwrite clients, manage big data, process claims, and hold capital to fund claims? Business functions like creating a brand name, dealing with customers, underwriting, holding risk, handling claims could all be handled by different companies in a way which is seamless for the customer. Insurers can outsource areas which can be handled by a specialist suppliers of each of these services at a lower cost. Insurers have resisted disintermediatization so far, but may in the future be forced to go down this route. This may occur because current new entrants are focusing on part of the insurance chain.

Most administrative aspects of insurance can be replaced by software, so external firms with a high level of customer skills can easily enter by creating or buying the appropriate software,'an insurance company in a box,' adding this to their existing products, and outsourcing areas like claims. An IT-focused firm could provide a Web-interface, backed by data analytics, with non-programmable areas outsourced, or by selling to existing customers as a franchise, or by distributing via an outside chain. KMPG (2016) argues that technology has evolved to the point where new insurance organizations can be virtually 'stood up' in a matter of weeks by renting everything from servers through to customer interfaces. World Economic Forum (2015) argues that all links in the insurance value chain are at risk from a new entrant aggressively moving into one link, using contractors to supply other links and utilizing new sources of capital, like cat bonds. It is now relatively easy for an external disruptor to enter.

These developments could lead to product development, distribution, underwriting, claims, and risk capital supply, being the area of niche players. As telematics allows a finer pricing of risk, insurance may be sold as a loss-leader by customer product providers in other industries. Insurers thus need to assess which aspects of their operations are vital and need to be in-house and which aren't. Insurers may, for example, decide to withdraw from customer contact and focus on risk analytics. Insurers need, however, to retain core business units as history is full of examples of companys which sliced off what seemed less important areas only to find that they ended up losing a key future business skill. The value of these core units is not just the profit but the business cultural learning. This type of disaggregation is very likely a strong future trend for insurers

Big Data and Analytics

Traditionally insurers have had very infrequent contact with the customer, only at policy inception, renewal and claim time and therefore know little about their clients. KPMG (2014) states that current insurer client data is historical, shallow, and based on very few interactions. The new sources of data will give insurers substantially larger amounts of far higher quality data about their clients and they will thus be able to use software to assess each client individually. Combining this with automated administrative, customer contact, and underwriting, systems will allow insurers to offer customized policies at low additional cost, as well as substantially reduce client churn and increase satisfaction. KPMG (2015) thus argues that effective use of big data will be one of the most important sources of future insurer competitive advantage. It is not just a temporary trend but a massive and permanent change in the data used by insurers. It will change the way insurers interact with their clients, the way they underwrite, and the way they structure their administration. It will be as much about software and systems as data. Big data as a competitive tool involves mainly the way data is used and analyzed rather than the actual data. CII (2015) argues that big data analytics is a game-changer and insurers who do not fully integrate the new methods into their structures will not survive.[5]

On the up-side, insurers will gain a greater depth of understanding of personality profiles, buying trends and behavior, vastly exceeding what could be previously imagined. Yoder and Rao (2015) argue that the combination of big data, telematics, and complexity analytics, will allow insurers to move away from simply descriptive (what happened) and diagnostic (why it happened) analysis toward predictive (what is likely to happen next) and prescriptive (determining how to ensure the right outcome) analysis. Multiple scenarios can be run and likely outcomes role-played. This will create more robust supply chains and stronger conversion rates. Insurers will gain an in-depth understanding of why customers insure or don't insure, and be able to individualize customer

[5]Boobier (2016) provides a good summary of data analytic issues in insurance.

approaches so as to maximize sales. The key here to the use of increased data is automated administration, as this will ensure there is a very low marginal cost to what would have previously been an expensive chore if done by workers. Underwriting will also be more accurate as it will be based on a rich depth and breath of detailed data on causal variables.

Current analytical underwriting and claims systems have been shown to have the ability to increase the speed and cut cost of underwriting and claims processing by up to 100x, often reducing claims processing times from months to minutes. Similar techniques can be applied to customer relations, or sales data, pinpointing what issues or styles are important for each segment of the market. Probably, more importantly, successful insurers will use detailed underwriting analytics to allow them to offer personalized products, with products broken down into blocks, and customers choosing the mix of products that suit their needs and their budget, with the insurer able to provide detailed and personalized advice at each step. This will allow them to construct tailored and personalized products, rather than the traditional one-fits-all model. How, for example, do higher risk members of the white, female, suburban, SUV-driving group differ from higher risk members of the white, female, city-center, non-car-owning group? Does gym attendance 2x a week differ in health outcomes from 4x a week? Customers will feel the insurer has been listening to their needs and differences. Special risk or small group customers, now deemed uninsurable, will be easier to handle. Groups of customers with desirable characteristics will be able to interact and seek group discounts.

Michal Kosinski showed in 2012 that on the basis of 70 Facebook 'likes' they could know a persons' social and purchase preferences better than the person's friends could, by 150 'likes' they could out-perform what the person's parents knew, and by 300 'likes' predict better than their life partner. Adding in additional social media and mobile phone data allowed them to predict a person's preferences better than the person themselves could. Firms have built on this style of analysis[6] to develop very detailed psychological profiles of nearly every person in

[6]Facebook has tried to prevent use of its data for this, but multiple other sources of data are available.

selected countries, showing how to target the emotionally appropriate appeal. This involves variation in multiple areas like message, graphics, style, color, font. Rather than one TV ad, an insurer could send out 100,000 differing targeted digital ads. Feedback from response to this can then be used to target the next round of ads.

Analytics will also allow customized client contracts, for example it may reveal if a customer belongs to a group likely to lapse, or to change providers, and at what point in time or in what circumstances this lapse is most likely to occur, and will then give the insurer the capacity to provide a personalized insurance experience or policy contact structured in a way most likely to retain that customer.

Big data is also starting to revolutionize risk assessment, which because of the growing size of data sets and their very intensive nature, means that patterns can be found which are not visible when assessing a sample data set. For example, in health care, the digitalization of millions of client medical records has allowed software to compare each client's individual symptoms with their genetics, their family background, their gut bacteria, their environmental factors, and other factors to create optimal and personalized treatment plans, and individualized medicines, all with minimal human oversight. New patterns have emerged which have drastically changed some traditional ideas about optimal treatment. Patients no longer have to be put into categories and treated as groups.

Complexity arises because data needs to be combined from as wide a range of sources as possible, many of which can be quite different; for example, minute-by-minute purchase data, location data, text, online comments, blogs, and call center communications. Combining these diverse sources can yield unsuspected insights. A useful source of data for insurers is retail data from loyalty cards. KPMG (2014) points out that current insurer client data is historical, shallow, and based on very few interactions, whereas loyalty card data is deep, rich, and real time. An example of the possible gains is the discovery by Woolworths Australia that customers who drank lots of milk and ate lots of red meat had a significantly lower auto-insurance risk than customers who drank spirits, ate lots of pasta, and filled their petrol tanks at night.

Gathering the data to create these types of insights will require proactive collaboration with other companies in the industry and in unrelated industries. This will require sector-wide data standardization agreements as well as a transformation in insurer attitudes to data. Insurers currently tend to treat data as private property and handle it in siloed, furtive, and undisclosed ways. Yet the larger the database, the more the insights, so that in the future, insurers who refuse to collaborate with a wide ecosystem will suffer a competitive disadvantage large enough to bankrupt them.

The major issue facing insurers, who have always been fundamentally in the data business, is that the overwhelming size of the future stream of data means that they will struggle to cope unless they fundamentally change the way they analyze data. Software, not people, has to scrutinize the data for meaning and then present limited aspects of it to humans. Data analysts will not visually purview data but will build AI systems to mine it for useful insights. Skills in leading edge data visualization are rare, yet unless managers get access to data in a form which can be used for strategic decisions, they may as well not have the data.

Commentators thus argue that if you're a huge, data-driven, business, you will either have cutting-edge AI driving your company products, or you're out of business. Key skills will be big data analytic skills and data presentation skills, as well as deep knowledge of customer behavior. Workers with outstanding skill sets in all these three areas are limited and will be in high demand. Workers with only IT skills will need to work within multi-skill teams.

Existing data software suppliers may not survive the transition if they do not have skills in AI mining of large and disparate data volumes. Instead, social media firms or consumer Internet players, who do have experience in AI mining, will probably take over supply of data software. Many new players in this area already exist, e.g., Captora uses data science to personalize and evolve customer-specific marketing material. UK payday loan firm Wonga used social data to cut its default rate from 50% to less than 10%. Insurers thus need to be proactive in using a range of software suppliers, and even ceding control of this area.

CII (2015) argues that the two key customer issues with big data are: (i) the value which customers experience or perceive from its use and

(ii) the extent to which insurers' handling of big data builds or undermines trust. Insurers need to have an intensive and ongoing conversation with customers about data collection and use, so that customers experience a shared realization that the changes will be mutually beneficial. These two issues are linked as insurers currently have very little contact with customers and engage in no trust building exercises. Within this scenario, the use of increasingly inquisitive data thus has myriad issues. This means that data decisions cannot just be taken according to the law, but must be carried according to what the public considers is right, so the insurer can be actively and publicly proud of their changes.

The Chartered Insurance Institute, CII (2015), argues big data is the most important issue for insurers for the current century and that successfully handling big data will be the defining characteristic of successful survivors. They argue that two issues in particular require professional judgment: (i) social sorting and the issue of how to handle those customers who will be worse off, and (ii) the right balance between personalization and pooling of risk. There will be a number of issues which will involve complex managerial or ethics decisions and these will need to be proactively dealt with. An example here is how to deal with elderly drivers whose telematics indicates they are a risk to other road users, or how to deal with families who have an inherited cancer risk gene?

Other issues CII (2015) identify include: (i) given real-time risk data, how much can the rate/premium fluctuate before the customer starts to regard insurers as unstable institutions, (ii) how will customers deal with knowing that the insurer knows a lot about them which the customer did not actively tell insurers, especially if sourced from informal social media, (like photos of the claimant attending a big party before driving, or trying to sell a customer a change in their life cover because the client searched online for baby products), (iii) can individual clients set differentiated rules on what data can be collected on them, (iv) will data trading across firms lead to customer unease, especially if the same piece of data can mean different things in different contexts (like increased purchases of plus-sized clothes), (v) will the public trust of insurers drop if software dominates in decision making, (vi) can premiums decisions based on correlations between not-obviously related data be justified to clients, in terms of causation, (vii) will personalized underwriting and the related increase in pricing complexity lead to confused and disgruntled customers, (viii) what happens when automated pricing or claim software fails to know an important fact which makes the decision unethical from a human viewpoint, and (ix) how to embed ethics and professional principles into automated decisions.

It is vital that automation does not decrease the ability of insurers to think critically about the issues, and the ability to reflect upon the implications which flow from that decision. Human oversight of automated administrative systems will be required as software can make decisions which seem incredibly stupid to humans. This requires insurers to run as wide a range of scenario tests on software as possible and to carefully set limits whereby the software brings an issue to humans for checking or decision. Software, especially AI programs, needs to be structured so humans can oversee it and actively intervene if the 'right decision' is not being taken.

All these challenges mean that existing insurers will have to create entirely new IT, data flow, and decision systems based on new management processes. KPMG (2015) argues that the issue for current insurers is that in large organizations data is normally trapped into silos and locked behind access controls so it is virtually impossible to gain an integrated overview of reality. Data governance and ownership is also normally spread across an organization so that there is no centralized view of what data they have and how it is used, so that it is impossible for any creative new uses of the data to be envisioned. Some of the most useful insights will come from comparing diverse data sets which seem to have no connection. KPMG argues that the management culture shock of moving from legacy systems to what will be required is profound. This implies that external companies who already use big data effectively will find it easier to move into insurance than insurers will find it to transform their legacy systems. To survive, insurers will need to see the changes as a big opportunity for self-transformation rather than as a big challenge they have to overcome. Management needs a proactive enthusiastic response.

McKinsey (2015) argues that companies embarking on machine learning should: (i) Firstly, investigate all feasible alternatives; (ii) secondly, pursue the strategy wholeheartedly at the top executive level; and (iii) thirdly, use existing executive expertise and knowledge to guide the application of that strategy. The people charged with creating the strategic vision may well be (or have been) data scientists, who will need guidance from top executives overseeing other crucial strategic initiatives. More broadly, McKinsey argues that companies must have two types of people to unleash the potential of machine learning; 'Quants' who are schooled in its language and methods, and 'Translators' who can bridge the disciplines of data, machine learning, and decision making by reframing the quants' complex results as actionable insights that generalist managers can execute.

McKinsey argues that behavioral change will be critical, and one of top management's key roles will be to influence and encourage it. Traditional managers, for example, will have to get comfortable with their own software variations. Frontline managers, armed with insights from increasingly powerful computers, must learn to make more decisions on their own, with top management setting the overall direction and zeroing in only when exceptions surface. The front line will have to be provided with the necessary skills and setting appropriate incentives to encourage data sharing.

Executives should think about applied machine learning in three stages: description, prediction, and prescription.

- The *description stage* is about collecting, developing, and analyzing databases. This online analytical processing is now a routine activity.
- The *prediction stage* is more difficult as current technology already allows businesses not only to look at their historical data but also to predict behavior or outcomes in the future. While data quality can be an issue, McKinsey argues that past IT investments have equipped most companies with sufficient information to obtain new insights even from incomplete, messy data sets, provided of course that those companies choose the right algorithm. Adding exotic new data sources can in fact be of only marginal benefit compared with what can be mined from existing data warehouses.
- The *prescription stage* is the opportunity for the future and therefore must be where top executive attention is focused. The aim is to predict *what* customers are going to do; only by understanding *why* they are going to do it, can companies encourage or deter that behavior in the future.

While some current executives may see a software driven future as threatening, over time, AI software will become culturally invisible in the same way technological inventions of the twentieth century disappeared into the background. The role of humans will be to direct and guide the algorithms as they attempt to achieve the objectives that they are given.

Telematics and Dynamic Insurance

The linking of built-smart connected products with Wi-fi networks has profound implications. Porter and Hepplemann (2015) point out that this is more than the linking of products by the Internet, but is a transformation in the nature of products and the way we use them. The data processing innovations of the 1970s on, and the Internet innovations of the 1990s on, left products largely unchanged. Now products, which are everywhere, will be transformed. The resultant cultural change will be profound.

This telematic connectivity can be: (i) *one-to-one* - one product joining to one central unit, (ii) *one-to-many* - one central unit joined to many sensors, or (iii) *many-to-many* - each sensor joined in a network to many others. It is the last which is the most transformative, as a smart connected product has qualitatively different implications than just a smart product.

Insurers are, in general, not up-with-the-play in the area of the Internet of things. They are currently either ignoring the Internet of things or viewing it negatively. What insurers need to realize is that telematics offers them a qualitatively different way to handle claims and relate to clients.

The impact on insurance claims could be immense. Claims will be a lot easier - as insurers will get real-time feedback from their telematics. For example, the networked chips in the car will inform the insurer's computer instantly of the crash, call emergency services, and software can instantly assess who was to blame by comparing the two cars' records, inform the tow truck and book the car repair, and make all payments, all without human intervention. Smoke alarms can already phone both you and the fire brigade, notify the repair service, and then talk to the oven or fridge or TV to ascertain the cause. A biochip can sense the results of changes in diet, exercise patterns, or health indicators, before the customer or their health professional is aware of any health issue.

Once real-time data feedback from telematics is added, the consequences for rate-making are revolutionary. The feedback from embedded devices will enable premiums to be set on an individual basis by software, and adjusted in real-time as insured behavior changes - what is called 'dynamic insurance.' Clients will be underwritten individually, with premiums dynamically set based on feedback from the telematic devices. For example, the analytics may reveal that a particular activity is risky for that kind of customer, and rather than excluding it, the insurer could offer cover at a different rate during that time, as long as the customer uses appropriate telematics to indicate to the software when to charge a differentiated premium. Clients who engage in an unauthorized temporary pattern of risky behavior can have their insurance immediately canceled.

The use of networking will allow the creation of real-time dynamic risk-rating, which will transform the insurer relationship with clients. Thus, for a networked linked car, a client who changes from a pattern of limited driving to intensive commuting for a short while may find their premiums jump for that period, whereas a client who drives more safely will find their premiums drop. Thus, premiums may be set weekly or even shorter, based on usage. Since insurers will get real-time feedback on when cars are used, it will be possible to offer innovative products. For example, several insurers have started using telematics to trial asking car owners to pay a 'driving premium' when they actually drive, with a 'residual premium' if the car is parked in the garage. Given that cars are parked for an average of 95% of their lives, it would have a huge impact on the distribution of premiums, with heavy users of cars paying multiples of the premiums which light users pay. Higher rates could be set for evening or holiday driving.

Retailers are already putting tiny Wi-fi-linked spots on goods, so if they are stolen they can be tracked by a mobile phone. In trials, this has led to rapid multiple arrests and decimated the shoplifting community. The flow-on effect of theft becoming non-viable is that premium income for contents insurers will drop sharply.

It is a common mistake in insurance circles to think of telematics as impacting solely in the area of general insurance. Morgan-Stanley/BCG (2013) argues, however, that personal risk areas like medicine are rapidly developing a range of Wi-fi devices to monitor those with medical conditions, including wrist devices which can monitor blood components, in real time. Ralph Lauren's Polo-Tech shirts stream various athletic health data to the wearer's mobile phone. Health providers could issue acute patients with this kind of clothing so software can track key indicators and alert staff if preset levels occur. Stick-on patches (bio-stamps) are being developed which read blood contents. The patient can then be warned to seek help or their mobile phone can confirm location and contact an emergency health service. Linked to a mobile phone these can send a continuous stream of updates to a hospital computer so that unusual trends can be spotted before the patient may be aware of them. Treatment plans and drugs can be modified based on real-time feedback, especially if an auto-drug-dispenser is integrated into the overall system. This will lead to preventative treatments likely to cut health costs. With the computerization of hospital administration, all tests, all services, all patient health metrics can be linked to the insurer so immediate payment can be offered and trends in the effectiveness of drugs or procedures analyzed.

Taken a step further, these devices could be installed in the healthy clients, to record exercises, heart pressure, calorie or alcohol consumption, etc., with large premium discounts given to clients who follow agreed risk reducing behavior. Changes in blood chemistry would reveal to the software what the client is eating and could send the client feedback, offering discounts or increases. Life insurance can then be underwritten based on these indicators.

The sharing of personal information is part of everyday life for millennials and any privacy concerns will be quickly outweighed by the substantially lower premiums. Algorithms will quickly work out what combinations of behavior led to less claims and offer discounts to selected clients if they improve their habits. Health researchers will have an unprecedented database of information to establish definite cause and effect relationships which will allow illnesses to be identified at an early stage. The focus will shift from sickness to health. This is only possible cost-wise if customers and their telematic devices interact via software, so the marginal cost of altering premiums is near to zero.

Individualization

Digital natives will not accept a standardized product from a firm which does not seem to be paying them much attention. Expectations are that the firm should work hard to gain their business, that the firm must listen to the needs of the digital natives, and that the firm must personalize both advice and products to fit. This response and personalization should be universal and rapid. This kind of customer service cannot happen at a reasonable cost and within the expected time frame without the majority of the administrative process being automated and analysis provided by AI software. Increasingly all insurance customers will be underwritten, and dynamically, rather than just at policy inception, or renewal. The integration of that pricing software with big data will allow insurers to very accurately price policies.

Insurance staff will oversee the creation of products via testing and improving the software, rather be directly involved in product creation. This will demand staff who have a deep understanding of the interaction between software and customers, as well a heavy investment in IT systems.

Client discrimination will no longer have to be on the basis of gross characteristics like gender or age, but on actual causal factors. The obvious issue that individualization creates is how to deal with customers who have genetic or other unchangeable issues which put them into high-risk groups. Legislators will have to come to arrangements with insurers on how to provide these groups with required insurance cover. On the up-side, individuals from groups who currently face underwriting issues, like young drivers, will be able to prove that they do not individually possess the behavior patterns which make that group high risk. Note also that for the EU, use of personalized rates based on dynamic data derived via telematics will enable the impact of gender neutrality to be limited.

A likely future trend is the creation of *personal data agents*. This is an App which holds your personal Internet information, all data about you, including your real-time Web surfing history. Some firms now pay to obtain surfing history, and this can be handled and paid for by the App. It is likely that clients will provide permission for insurers to use their data via an agent and will be able to set data access boundaries.

Data-Focused

The current focus of insurance management is on strict cost control, so that premiums can be kept competitive. These costs, however, are difficult to control and estimate, as underwriting estimates are created prior to a policy issue, and are only updated at renewal time. Even then, if clients are found to be higher risk than estimated, there can be legal or regulation issues around substantial premium increases or policy refusal. Client data is currently sparse and fuzzy, with contact only at renewal or claim time, and clients are grouped into broad categories. In general, despite being data focused, insurers currently know very little about their clients.

The new era of real-time big data via telematics means that insurers will have a qualitatively different quality of data on clients. They will be able to price far more accurately, and dynamically change prices, if initially-set risk parameters are exceeded. The big data sets will enable insurers to more accurately understand causal factors and create predictive models of risk. They will be able to offer clients attractive premiums if they meet certain behavioral conditions.

The impact of telematic big data on pricing is a revolution. Currently, insurers use actuarial-based statistical algorithms based on compiling past data and event occurrences to forecast annual event probabilities. The new approach will be based on the structural drivers behind events as well as any conceivably related data. By being able to examine real-time structural data on casual factors, insurers will be able to price risk very finely, as well as customize risk to individual clients and adjust premiums on a real-time basis. Insurers will have to create systems to track risk in real time and adjusting premiums or reserves - for example, tracking the spread of infectious diseases, tracking spending on health or unhealthy food products by customers, tracking weather risk, or tracking trends in burglary by street and house type. The sheer size of this data means that the job of tracking and responses to clients need to be primarily software based, with human staff overseeing. SAS (2013) argues that insurers need to move to a predictive claims process rather than a reactive, thus enabling smaller liquid reserves and higher profits.

This requires insurers to reimagine themselves, to change their vision of their business from being one of providing insurance products to being one where they are data companies with real-time links to customers, specializing in personal products and services. This will enable insurers to expand their product range to provide real-time data-based services to clients. Because big data will provide highly accurate predictive indicators, insurers will move from compensation after an event to advice and warnings on how to prevent an event. Examples would be data on traffic congestion, parking availability, weather, relevant retail discounts, health events, lifestyle tips, and using that to communicate alerts and helpful tips to clients. The aim of these may seem initially to be to reduce client risk, but the real aim would be to integrate the company into customer lives. An insurer could then brand itself as handling a customer's lifecycle management, with the aim to minimize the events which lead to claims.

Another area is reducing client churn. Currently, insurers have little idea what occurs inside client's heads when they decide to renew or not renew. Does sending a client an incentive to renew reduce churn because the client is attracted to the incentive or increase churn because the client is reminded that they can switch? What parts of the brochure does the client who renews read? What behavioral characteristics distinguish those who renew from those who don't? What types of interactions with friends or what online reviews decrease policy churn? What style of channel contact most appeals to that type of client? Which style of contact repeals a type of client? What type of non-clients could be influenced by an e-newsletter? Which members of a particular social network are most influential in the buying decisions of other members? These persuasive modelings have proven success in diverse fields, but are little used in insurance due to inadequate data.

It needs to be remembered that by itself big data is useless and overwhelming - the key is the ability to extract useful customer insights. Often this can mean creating new methods of sourcing data, of standardizing data, of understanding what outcomes are required, of analyzing the data, of integrating data from multiple sources, and of using the results to guide decision making. There are two main reasons for negative outcomes when using big data: (i) unreliable or unsuitable data, often provided by external sources and not properly incorporated into the organization's own environment and (ii) the analytics team missing an important component of data because they didn't fully understand the business situation. Thus, managers are needed who both understand the new data analytical methodologies and who understand the insurance business.

This will require heavy investment in physical IT capacity, in big data analytical staff, and in creating new management decision-making procedures to make best use of the new insights. There will need to be a willingness to source expertise and software from outside the company. The overwhelming mass of data also means that high-level data presentation skills, via the use of dashboards, are a vital new area.

Improving the quality and usefulness of data is vital. BCG (2016) argues that the most important steps are;

1. *Be clear about the question*: Insurers need to be clear about the potential new uses for data, assess the benefits or costs of the new use, and then determine exactly what issues arise. For example, how can existing high-value-customer retention rates be increased? What determines client stickiness? Then assess what issues arise, like regulatory, and consider the uses for the data in terms of technical, organizational, and data stewardship feasibility.
2. *Determine the necessary types and quality of data*: Seizing an opportunity may require multiple sources of data, both internal and external, which may be in differing formats and quality. This has to be assessed along multiple dimensions: (a) *Validity* - the degree to which the data confirms to logical criteria, (b) *Completeness* - the degree to which the required data is available, (c) *Consistency* - the degree to which the data is the same in definition, rules, format, and time, (d) *Accuracy* - the degree to which the data reflects reality, (e) *Timeliness* - the degree to which the data reflects the most recent information.
3. *Define clear targets for improvement*: Normally, some aspect of the data types will be missing or suffer quality issues. A gap analysis needs to be undertaken to determine the baseline and the target for each type of data. The benefit vs. cost of improvements needs to be analyzed. Real-time dashboards can determine quality gaps.

4. *Determine the causes of bad data*: Poor quality data can arise from many causes, whether gathering, processes, staff management, or technology. Management incentives may have to be changed as collection or processing staff may have more incentive to input speedily rather than checking quality. The cost of correcting these needs to be weighed against the lost opportunities elsewhere in the business due to faulty data.
5. *Assign an internal business owner to data sources*: Data must be 'owned' to become high quality. Someone needs to be assigned who can oversee all stages of the data flow and creating end-to-end information models. These models will include the master data, the transaction data standards, and the metadata. The data owner is not the same role as a data quality officer, as they focus on business deliverables and benefits rather than technology.
6. *Scale what works*: It is important to start small and quality check new systems. However, too many data projects cherry-pick high quality data and the best staff for trials, leading to projects floundering when they are applied systems-wide on normal data by normal staff. The checking will be as much about changing management processes and incentives as about technology. Flexibility and innovativeness need to be built in so the company can quickly move onto the next transformation.

CII (2012) points out that two potentially large problems exist with the use of large complex data analytical systems. One is that unseen instabilities can occur within large interconnected systems and led to instability and sudden crashes. The second is that the systems only predict based on existing data, they cannot predict scenarios which have not yet occurred within the data period - the Black Swan problem. The latter has the prime cause of Lloyds near bankruptcy in the 1980s and the recent Global Financial Crisis. To combat this, managers of complex systems need to build in stability control break points, run extensive scenario analyses, and understand client psychology. It is well known, for example, that insured people behalf differently than non-insured, and therefore loss rates for new products may well be higher than expected. Data managers will need to be twinned with managers who have extensive client experience and a grounding in insurance behavioral theory.

Insurance Rates

The use of big data to set individualized rates and premiums with the associated improvement in customer's risk behavior will have the effect of reducing and spreading insurance risk. This is shown in Fig. 4.2.

For the majority of customers, the change will be beneficial as their insurance premiums will drop and they receive useful feedback on risk reducing activities. There will, however, be an increased group whose premiums will rise. This may be because they: (i) engage in risk increasing activities, or because (ii) they have genetics or lifestyles disadvantages which are outside their control. Insurers or insurance regulators will need to ensure this latter group have arrangements made to guarantee that they receive appropriate insurance cover. This is discussed in a later chapter.

Safer Lifestyles

The combination of many of these changes, together with advances in medicine in areas like genetics and organ printing, means that lifestyles will be a lot safer. Car accidents will largely disappear, houses will not

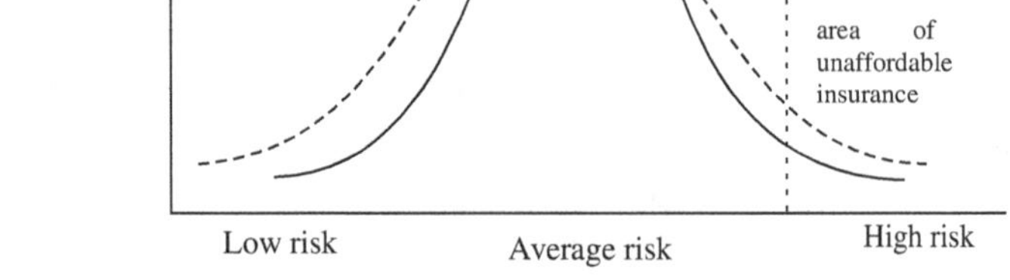

Fig. 4.2 Changes in the spread of insurance rates. *Source* Author

burn or be burglarable, people will not die prematurely as often, etc. As a result, many of key pillars of the current insurance industry will either disappear or face sharply reduced premium flows. This is complex, however, as reduction in premiums and increased flexibility will potentially expand markets, bringing in currently un- or underinsured clients, as will be explored later.

Robo-Advice

A new but growing trend is using software to provide financial and insurance advice based on a limited financial questionnaire. This advice is nicknamed 'robo-advice', is already provided by firms like Future Adviser, and is being introduced by the major index fund providers. Using the example of the rate of increase in the sophistication of accounting software, indicates that within 5 years it will be increasingly hard to tell the difference between humans and software in terms of advice for routine clients. While current financial robo-advice is crude it is improving fast and the sophistication of robo-advice will rapidly improve once artificial intelligence programs are applied. One of the key aspects is thus how fast robo-advice software can include details like Federal and state taxation, and region-specific investment advice as well as up-to-the minute news.

This type of personalized financial and insurance advice will suit situations where the clients have no unusual or complex features so that standardized solutions can be offered, which suits the least wealthy 60% of clients. The advantage of robo-advice is that because of its very low per unit cost, it can be offered to run-of-the-mill-clients for a very low fee. Asset managers like Charles Schwab are already introducing these systems to deal very cheaply with clients with as little as $5000 in funds.

Currently, the combined assets under management in the USA via robo-advisers are less than US$20B, against US$17T for traditional managers, and no individual robo-adviser has yet to reach the size required for sustained profitability. Given the capacity of robo-advice to continually improve, however, while continually and substantially cutting cost to clients, there is no reason, however, to use the current size of the market as an indicator of the future size. US fund managers who use robo-adviser are currently doubling their funds under management every few months. Even if this slowed to an annual doubling of demand this would see robo-funds-under-management exceed human-advised funds within a decade. In 2014, US$290M was invested by venture capitalists into robo-advice start-ups, which has also been more than doubling every year. Robo-advice is not a fad; it is the future of the majority of financial advice.

Most firms offering robo-advice include it within a Web site which also offers educational videos, trade-execution, portfolio management, investment news, as well as tax advice and statement filing. Once avatars are added, which can offer video advice and respond to standardized questions, it is easy to envisage that average income retail clients will see little reason to seek out a human adviser for value-added advice. Financial advisers are unlikely to be concerned about the migration of the average income client to robo-advice as they offer too little potential fee income to make it profitable to spend much time advising. Banks and other large financial institutions may offer robo-advice to these clients as a loss-leader, to attract clients to take out mortgages or transfer investment funds.

The structural issue is that while financial advisers may retain a high share of baby boomers who are used to the personal touch, the market share of robo-advise fund managers is particularly strong amongst the under 30s and the millennials. While these younger, computer savvy clients are currently unlikely to be wealthy enough to interest an adviser, the danger is that when they do acquire wealth in a decade or so, advances of robo-advice technology, combined with their decade of using robo-advisers, will mean that it will be difficult for human advisers to attract them.

Another likely market which advisers may be worried about losing are affluent individuals who are highly computer literate and feel uncomfortable discussing financial affairs with a person. Given that these may include high-net-worth individuals, it will be difficult for the average adviser to attract them unless they set up a very advanced Web site, with the added capacity for personal advice for those with complex needs.

Given that the key skills involved would be customer service, brand trustworthiness, and quality software, it is also likely that software or Web-firms like Google could easily add these robo-advice sites to their existing services and have a competitive advantage over those existing financial service providers who suffer from low brand trust.

Another key skill to success in robo-advice will be analysis of the data collected from clients. Over time data analysts will be able to spot trends which distinguish the financially successful from the less successful and help all clients achieve their goals. The ability to analyze big data then becomes vital, especially when trying to ascertain which behavioral finance characteristics determine financial success, or which types of advice best promotes the right customer response. There will be an advantage to financial firms like banks which have a more complete set of client financial data, including income and spending patterns. Small firms which create smart software, however, can also be successful if they can obtain enough base data to fine-tune their models. Cloud computing means that there is no longer an inherent advantage to large firms simply because they can afford mainframe computers.

It is the careful analysis of this big data set which will allow robo-advice to be tailored to more detailed client profiles so that advice is not generalized but specific to each client. Clients can be offered advice relating to what the software identifies as that client's behavioral weaknesses. This can then be tied into insurance advice and individualized underwriting. This can be complimented by mining of social media so that current concerns can be identified and advice offered. Algorithms can then be used to create predictive models of financial needs, product preferences, and customer interactions.

Carefully constructed robo-adviser financial Web sites will thus be able to offer education and news which is specific to a narrow set of clients and make clients feel as if the robo-adviser understands their needs, without the cost factor of human involvement. There is psychological evidence that investors are more willing to share personal data with an anonymous data warehouse, as the software will make no value judgments about life choices.

While robo-advice will not be able to match human advisers in the next decade in terms of understanding the myriad financial and emotional reasons why individuals either succeed or fail in achieving their financial goals, agent-based learning software is currently being built which will, within five years, start to approach human adviser capacities at an exponential rate. Asset managers or dealer groups who do not respond adequately will be left behind. Note that retaining client trust in the privacy and the integrity of the process is vital and any providers who exhibit abuse of this trust, or suffer data security breaches, will lose irretrievable market share.

Rao (2015) argues that there will be three generations of robo-advice software:

1. *First generation*: These are currently available and are stand-alone programs targeted at the self-directed end users. They allow users to aggregate their financial data, create a unified portfolio, obtain generic advice, determine portfolio optimization based on life-stage and execute trades. These programs use simple segmentation and portfolio optimization assumptions.
2. *Second generation:* These currently being trialed and will be aimed at both end users and advisers. These allow integration between investors, advisers, and clients and are based on wrap programs. The increased information available allows more customization of advice and allows advisers and institutional traders to interact dynamically with clients, offering real-time news and trading advice.
3. *Third generation*: These are being planned and will be available within a five to ten-year period. These will build off advances in Artificial Intelligence learning software, and will have the ability to improve advice based on feedback from client behavior. These will offer life-long personal financial planning advice by combining the mining of big data and social media to inferring investment behavior, spending and saving patterns, behavioral mistakes, and risk preferences, using learning agent modeling to create a model of 'someone-like-you' persona for the end user.

This third generation will watch how the clients react to advice and modify advice based on this. It will monitor economic and market data and offer investment and insurance advice based on current conditions.

By adding a Web-avatar, this advice can be delivered in a personal way using techniques designed to be most persuasive. The software will run scenarios and illustrate how differing portfolios will react to possible futures. This can then easily be combined with banking and tax advice.

A key element of the third generation will be client feedback on how they feel about the advice. The collection and use of increasingly large databases on client reaction will enable algorithms to be created which will improve the sophistication of the advice, making it pleasing and relevant to clients at an exponential rate. Advances in computer voice modulation will fine-tune how to sound the most persuasive, as will advances in avatar face movements. The integration of the lessons from psychology and behavioral finance will be vital to this feedback process and is the aspect which robo-advisers will probably struggle with the most.

It is going to be difficult for small advice firms to match the IT investment and data warehouses of large mutual fund or banks. The key to their survival will be the availability of high-quality software from 3rd-party vendors.

Conclusion

The insurance industry has been built on its ability to detect, analyze, and manage risk. Capgemini/Efma (2016) argues that the insurance sector is changing in four fundamentals ways: (i) most key risk variables, the determinates of risk, are changing and becoming more individualized, less random, (ii) in general, risk is decreasing and becoming more avoidable, (iii) the nature of risk ownership is changing and becoming more communal, and (iv) new techniques are causing shifts in basic insurance business principles and models as connected technology and risk mitigation reduce loss.

The insurance industry is in general a laggard in terms of both its adoption of technology and in the extent to which it has been impacted by disruptive innovators. These, of course, go together, as insurers have not been pushed to innovate. Insurance, however, has now reached a tipping point, where a perfect storm of technological innovations will coincide to generate in the immediate future a step-up in both the impact of disruptive innovators and the requirement for insurers to adopt technological solutions.

The insurance industry needs to urgently start making strategic decisions on how to survive. It needs to reimagine its product into an array of currently unoffered value-added services. In most cases, this transformation will involve extensive use of external change consultants.

Dynamic Insurance

Insurance has traditionally been a static product: sold once, with a risk-rating set largely for the life of the client or product. Clients did not think much about insurance and insurers did not know much about their customers. Neither the insurer nor the client engaged much with the other.

The future of insurance has to be as a dynamic product: sold in modules, with real-time risk-pricing dependent on the client activities, with the ability of either side to add or subtract aspects of the product and respond to temporary specials. The insurer and the client will engage on a continuous basis, with the insurer having a rich and deep knowledge of the client, and the client choosing an insurer on the basis of the warmth of the engagement, the worthwhileness of their value-added services, and the attractiveness of their pricing. This involves combining both pay-as-you-use and pay-how-you-use data with real-time feedback.

References

Boobier, T. (2016). Analytics for Insurance: The real business of big data, Wiley, UK.

Boston Consulting Group. (2016). *How to avoid the Big Bad Data Trap*, BCG Perspectives, October 2.

Breznik, L. (2012). Can information technology be a source of competitive advantage? *Economic and Business Review, 14*(3), 251–269.

Brynjolfsson, E. R., Hitt, L. & Kim, H. (2011). *Strength in numbers: How does data-driven decision-making affect firm performance?* Social Science Review Network, April.

Capgemini/Efma. (2016). *World Insurance report.*

Carr, N. (2003, May). IT doesn't matter. *Harvard Business Review*, 5–12.

Castriotta, M., Floreddu, P. B., Di Guardo, M. C., & Cabiddu, F. (2014). Disentangling the Strategic Use of Social Media in the Insurance Industry: A value co-creation perspective, chpt 4 in *Social Media in Strategic Management: Advanced Series in Management*, 63–86.

Christensen, C. M. (1997 & 2011). *The innovator's dilemma* (4th Ed.). NY, USA: Harper Business/Harvard Business School.

CII. (2012). *Future risk: How technology could make or break our world.* London, UK: Chartered Insurance Institute.

CII. (2015). *Big data and insurance: A conversation.* London, UK: Chartered Insurance Institute.

Equinix. (2014). *Challenge to change: three-part series*, Acord/Global Futures & Foresight.

IBM. (2006). *Insurance 2020: Innovating beyond old models.* New York, USA: IBM Institute for Business Value.

IBM. (2015). *Capturing hearts, minds and market share: How connected insurers are improving customer retention.* New York, USA: IBM Institute for Business Value.

Kelly, K. (2016). *The inevitable: Understanding the 12 technological forces that will shape our future.* New York, USA: Viking.

KPMG. (2014). *An industry transforming: insurers and intermediaries in a fast changing, digital world*, white paper.

KPMG. (2015). *Big Data: The big factor driving competitive advantage.* Frontiers in Finance.

KPMG. (2016). *Empowered for the future: Insurance reinvented*, KPMG International.

McKinsey. (2015). *An executive's guide to machine learning.* McKinsey Quarterly, June.

McKinsey. (2016). *Transforming life insurance with design thinking*, May.

Morgan-Stanley/B.C.G. (2013). *Wearable devices: The internet of things becomes personal.* Boston, USA: Boston Consulting Group.

Morgan-Stanley/B.C.G. (2014). *Insurance and technology: Evolution and revolution in a digital world.* Boston, USA: Boston Consulting Group.

Morgan-Stanley/B.C.G. (2015). *Insurance and technology: The emerging role of ecosystems in insurance.* Boston, USA: Boston Consulting Group.

Porter, M. & Heppelmann, J. (2015, November). How smart connected products are transforming competition. *Harvard Business Review.*

PWC. (2014). *Insurance 2020: The digital prize—taking customer connection to a new level.*

Rao, A. (2015). *The rise of robo-advisers*, Insurance Thought Leadership, PWC, June.

Rifkin, J. (2014). *The zero marginal cost society: The internet of things, the collaborative commons, and the eclipse of capitalism*. London, UK: Palgrave-MacMillian.

SAS. (2013). *Predictive Claims Processing: Transforming the insurance claims life-cycle using analytics*, SAS White Paper.

Schryen, G. (2013). Revisiting IS business value research: What we already know, what we still need to know, and how we can get there. *European Journal of Information Systems, 22*, 139–169.

Summers, L., & DeLong, J. B. (2001). The 'new economy': Background, historical perspective, questions, and speculations. *Economic Review of Federal Reserve Bank of Kansas*, USA.

Target Group (2015) 'Distribution Channels in Insurance: Understanding the Customer Viewpoint'.

Wernerfelt, B. (1984). A resource-based view of the firm. *Strategic Management Journal, 5*(2), 171–180.

World Economic Forum. (2015). *The future of financial services: How disruptive innovations are reshaping the way financial services are structured, provisioned and consumed.*

Yoder, J., & Rao, A. (2015). *Insurance at a Tipping Point*, Insurance Thought Leadership, PWC, June 20.

5

What Insurance Companies Need to Do

Management during Disruptive Waves

Christensen (1997) in his classic book points out that technological disruption can blindside even successful companies. Commentators often argue that only weak or badly run firms fail when faced with a market challenge. In fact, Christensen argues that even well-managed companies, those who scan for looming market challenges, listen astutely to customers, and invest aggressively in new technologies, can fail to foresee and meet disruptive innovations.

Christensen distinguishes between 'incremental innovations' and 'disruption innovations,' with the differentiating factor being that incremental innovation can be accommodated within existing business models and disruptive innovations cannot. In that sense, 'disruptive innovation' is wider than technology, as non-technological areas can also involve disruptive innovations.

Markides (2006) divides disruptive innovation into three types: (a) disruptive technological innovations, (b) disruptive business model innovations, and (c) disruptive product innovations. These will have differing disruption pathways. This book is has so far focused on the first type,

M. Naylor, *Insurance Transformed*, Palgrave Studies in Financial Services Technology,
DOI 10.1007/978-3-319-63835-5_5

but disruption in the other two areas will arise as a consequence. For example, the use of real-time data is technologically based but will redefine the insurance business model from a product to a service. This will expand the insurance market to new customers and into new products. This implies that there will be waves of disruption of differing types.

Christensen (1997) points out that an aspect of disruptive innovation is that it occurs in waves, with each wave having distinct characteristics. The management style which suits each wave can be quite distinct, so that companies which were successful in one wave fail to handle the next. For example, IBM dominated the mainframe market, but stumbled after the emergence of minicomputers. In fact, no mainframe manufacturer managed to handle that disruptive wave. An emergent firm, Digital Equipment Corp, dominated the minicomputer market, alongside Data General, Prime, Wang, Hewlett-Packard, and Nixdorf. These emergent firms, in turn, failed to handle the change to desktop personal computers, whose market was dominated by the new emerging firms: Apple, Commodore, Tandy, and a revived IBM. Of these new firms, only Apple managed to survive the shift to portable laptops and recently to tablets and phones. Firms whose expertise was in very different sectors, like Samsung, have entered the mobile market.

This disruption outcome is similar whatever the pattern of the disruptive waves, whether the change arrives in a rush or is slow, whether the changes were complex or simple, or whether the innovation is an extension of existing technologies or new.

Christensen notes that the blindsided firms were, in the main, well managed, with Digital Equipment in particular praised in the Peters and Waterman (1982) classic 'In Search of Excellence,' just two years before it ran into trouble. Christensen argues that the basic problem is that well-managed firms follow patterns of behavior which are best practice only in terms of the current environment, not in terms of the new environment; each innovative stage has differing best-practice management requirements, and it is often the best managed firms, those who are sure of their excellence, which have trouble recognizing the need for transformation. It is precisely their excellence at adapting to the old environment which causes issues handling disruptive waves.

Christensen thus argues that when facing an uncertain future, with multiple possible waves, most of which will end up insignificant but several transformational, a different style of management is required. Given that customers will have even more limited knowledge of the future, management may be justified in following counterintuitive methods like not listening to customers, in investing in lower performance products with lower margins, and in aggressively pursuing small rather than large markets.

Christensen argues that these aspects occur because disruptive technologies are typically cheaper, simpler, smaller, and easier to use than existing technology. They are initially aimed to lower-end or more forgiving customers. Any survey of existing customers tends to lead to the new product being scorned and rejected. Imagine asking mainframe users in the early 1960s about their impressions of the new-fangled minicomputers!

This dichotomy occurs because the disruptive innovation is typically evaluated by its new users by a different metric than customers of the existing technology use. For example, existing market customers may prize speed, while new market customers prize flexibility. To both customer sets, switching to the other product reduces usability. This means that customer surveys of new innovation product attributes will have to involve customers who not currently are in the market or have not yet considered what they want.

In terms of existing metrics, disruptive technologies, therefore, tend to underperform compared to existing technologies, so are ignored by market leaders who are focused on fine-tuning their market-leading products. However, because the disruptive technologies provide more customers with an experience closer to what they actually want, even if they are unaware of it, disruptive technologies progress at a faster rate and rapidly end up more performance competitive. Indeed, the new product often creates new markets, which could not have been imagined prior to its introduction. It needs to be noted that the initial customers are commonly technophiles who may value different attributes to latter users; they are less price sensitive, more fault tolerant, and more demanding of advanced features.

Adner (2002) shows how differing structures of demand along two or three preference attributes create three possible outcomes: (i) The two technologies exist in isolation in different markets, (ii) the two technologies converge in the same market and compete, and (iii) the newer technology disrupts the old. All three of these outcomes are likely in different parts of the insurance sector.

Christensen (1997) distills his ideas about the problems of waves of disruption into five principles. These apply to each wave of disruption, so that yesterday's emergent innovator becomes today's struggling incumbent.

1. *Customers and investors control resources*: Within successful companies, managers are often under the illusion that they control company resources. They normally have well-developed, rapidly working, systems for killing ideas which customers don't want. They thus find it difficult to allocate resources to new technologies which customers currently don't seem to want, and then find it hard to reallocate resources when customers suddenly decide they do want the technology, especially if these are customers from outside the existing profile, and the market is seemingly small and low margin.
2. *Large companies find small markets difficult*: Emerging technologies start small and offer few enticements to existing large market leaders. Thus, incumbents typically decide to 'wait-and-see.' Given, however, that there are typically significant first-mover advantages, lack of initial engagement can condemn incumbents to playing eternal catch up; especially, if the disruption involves a new type of customer who the incumbent does not understand.
3. *Markets that don't exist can't be analyzed*: Sound market research and good planning are embedded parts of market leaders. These techniques fail when faced with disruptive innovations as the ultimate use and extent of products are not established and customers cannot know if they appeal. Who would have guessed, pre-mobile phones, that people would prefer to play games or take photos with their phones?
4. *Company processes are more inflexible than people*: Good companies often assume that staff who are capable within current structures

will deal with a new task. Yet, the disruptive innovation often can't be dealt with until company processes drastically change, and then, the staff may not be as capable within the new environment. A new business model is required, which may cannibalize the existing profit stream.

5. *Disruptive innovations typically exceed customer capacity*: Within disruptive waves, typically technologies will include multiple features which will be ignored, until the market can absorb previous changes. These new features are often so innovative that the market fails to understand that a product can be used within an entirely different setting. Therefore, products can seem to initially under-perform, followed by an extremely rapid change, as customers' mind-set changes. Companies often inadvertently 'over-satisfy,' and end up too up-market, opening up a space at the lower end.

Christensen argues that what these principles result in is the 'innovators' dilemma'—good companies begin their descent into failure by listening to their best customers and then aggressively investing in the products and services which their most profitable customers want. The innovation maximizes a different metric, one which does not appeal to existing customers, but does to ill-serviced or non-serviced customers, customers who do not suit the incumbent's existing business model. Managing the right way ends up being wrong.

It is common for individual teams within incumbents to be aware of the disruptive innovation and to have developed their own version before the disruptor brought their product to market. Yet, it is uncommon for the senior managers of incumbents to approve the transition in time.

For innovative unproven technologies, an issue is that disruptive technologies will at the start typically seem unprofitable, have no demand from existing customers, be technologically crude, and generally not make sense as a rational place to invest resources. Financial and marketing analyses will thus show the innovation as a near certain failure. Given that 90% of possible innovations will come to nothing, it is near impossible for a manager to successfully argue that an incumbent should transform itself because of a possible disruptive innovation before that innovation has established itself in the market. Research shows that predicting which 10% of innovations will succeed is near impossible.

Christensen argues that incumbent delay also occurs for innovations which are the obvious next step, innovations where incumbents may have a performance advantage. This is mainly due to the fact that the innovation is inferior at the start, so the most profitable existing customers do not typically want the new innovation. The current product may be quite profitable and have a strong growth path. Feedback from suppliers and customers within the wider network will thus confirm the existing business model. It is therefore hard to visualize a new product possessing a superior growth path.

Disruptive innovations thus enter by servicing a market the incumbent handles badly, who value a different metric to the core customers. The disruptor then improves its performance on all metrics and starts to nibble at the lower-end incumbent customers, those over-serviced by the main metric. The incumbent finds this hard to respond to, as altering their product to service lower-end customers would alienate core customers. Eventually, the disruptor ends up servicing the mainstream market, with the incumbent left with a minority. The recommended response is for the incumbent to create its own separate group to take on the disruptor. This, however, creates a series of new issues, which will subsequently be discussed.

McGill (2008) argues that financial sector companies have survived prior disruptive shocks better than those from other sectors because of their sector breadth and the advantages of utilizing these within a large vertical corporation. I would argue, however, that because the looming disruptive waves involve the transformation of data use, the core skill, nearly every sector of insurance will be impacted, so breadth will not be a defense.

Management during disruptive changes requires a different culture and staff than during incremental changes. Because disruptive technologies create new markets, they tend to find their main uses and new customers over time as they evolve by trial and error rather than as the innovators initially visualized. Therefore, with waves of disruption the new norm, flexibility to follow startling new changes is becoming more important than careful management or efficiency. Improving the ability to assess possible disruptive innovations is critical.

Johne and Davies (2000) examined the upheaval in the UK general insurance market caused by online distributors and found that CEOs at surviving firms used more aggressive responses to the disruption threat than CEOs at non-survivors. In particular, there was more destruction of existing control structures and the removal of middle managers who were unable to adjust fast enough. This was followed by support of staff involved in innovation and experimentation.

McKinsey (2017) shows that the digitization reaction has barely started in most industries and yet has already reduced revenue by an average of 7.3%. Importantly, though, the digital leaders are three times more likely to generate market-leading profit margins than digital laggards are. The main impact of the looming waves of disruption is therefore likely to require survivors to position themselves among the technological leaders or at least the fast followers.

Existing Insurer Capacities

Despite the looming issues around disruptive technology which I have described, KPMG (2015a) found that 51% of US insurance executives knew little about the issues surrounding IT and were not predicting major changes. Only 22% of insurers had thought about the issues or were making plans. Company CIOs are significantly more worried about the lack of action than CEOs. PWC (2015b) found that change management was only the sixth top concern, and that most respondents had a very limited understanding of the issues.

Accenture (2013) found that 95% of insurance CEOs surveyed were not sure that they had the right operating model for today's world, let alone the future. Bain (2013) argues that while insurers are rolling out a range of digital initiatives, in most cases these involve a string of unconnected initiatives layered onto a legacy IT system and a traditional mind-set. Very few current insurers even understand the coming scale of change required, let alone are starting to restructure their businesses to the extent which will be required.

While this ignorance started to change around 2015, with KPMG (2016) finding that insurance CEOs now regarded technological disruption as their major future issue, Bain (2015) found that about 50% do not have a plan for digital transformation and 60% of those with a plan are missing key elements. Few of the surveyed insurance CEOs had confidence that they had a workable transformation plan. None of the companies who have achieved some success have managed to achieve best practice in more than in a few dimensions. You cannot just add a Web site. Very few insurers have tried to reimagine their future. Analysis, thus, shows that the insurance industry is fundamentally unprepared for the future, despite the fact that the insurance landscape of 2026 will look very different to what it looks like now.

KPMG (2016) argues that success in the insurance industry in the future will not come from simply tweaking the Status Quo; insurers will need to change virtually every part of their business if they hope to not just survive, but thrive. They point out that insurers have been trying to transform themselves for decades, firstly to respond to big enterprise systems and then to the internet. Despite this effort and expense, KPMG concluded that little has changed, especially when compared to sectors like banking or financial markets. KPMG does not expect this inability to react to change. KPMG argues that this is because insurers require fundamental transformation and this is very difficult.

KPMG (2016) found that while insurance CEOs are now aware of the threat, most are still not aware of the fundamental extent of the changes required. For example, KPMG found that while 70% of CEOs saw the need for fundamental change, less than a quarter expected their operating model to be disrupted by changes in customer behavior. This is either ignorance or self-delusion, because it is clear that a customer-centric model is required. KPMG found that respondents had little idea of what a 'customer-led business model' meant, despite many consultants pointing this out. Customer behavior should actually be the inspiration behind insurers' efforts to reinvent themselves.

KPMG argues that while a quarter of respondents said they have started a major transformation in the past 2 years, nearly all of these efforts have been inadequate and superficial. They note that there is a big difference between conducting a transformation initiative and actually achieving a transformational outcome. The reality is that insurers will need to achieve change at a far more fundamental level if they hope to reinvent themselves for the future. To truly 'reimagine,' their business insurers will need to transform business and operating models from the ground up. Any attempt to survive by ad hoc changes or minor tweaks will fail in the face of external disruptors. It is the purpose of this book to make it clear the extent to which fundamental reimagining is required.

Services instead of Products

Insurers currently offer what is inherently a service, a promise of future compensation. Yet, insurers have traditionally visualized themselves as selling a fixed, highly specified product, with customers only offered a limited range, with no opportunity for modification, or day-to-day interaction between insurers and customers. Policies were delivered in fancy brochures, and insurers built impressive buildings, in an effort to create an impression of solidness. This packaging of a promise as a physical product was useful when nearly all other types of consumption were physical products, so that consumers found it hard to visualize buying a flow of non-physical services.

By 2010, customers started to move on, and getting used to buying formally physical products like books or music as flows. Borders Group saw themselves as selling physical books within physical stores and were pioneers of software-based inventory control and sales forecasting. They saw the new entrant, Amazon, as merely selling physical books from a physical warehouse aided by a sales Web site. Border thus forecast minimal disruption, which they could cope with by opening their own Web site.[1] They failed to understand that because Amazon could make profit from sales of other products once customers were on their Web site and could add on services via e-book feedback, as well as attracting readers via user-generated reviews or blogs, Amazon had little need to make a

[1]Surprisingly, they outsourced the Web site running and book shipping to Amazon.

profit on physical sales. Amazon thus rapidly undercut Border's prices and drove them bankrupt. Reading via an e-reader which allows annotation and commenting becomes a social activity, in a way physical book can't.[2]

Insurers are at threat of being left behind in the same way. Incumbents are tending to approach the IT challenge by modifying their existing product-based model and by merely adding on digital sales avenues. Both of these fail to understand the utter transformation of their environment and fail to ignite the imagination of their work forces to start creating a range of valuable flow-based services. Instead, insurers need to reimagine insurance as a series of related, customer-modifiable, real-time flows. Given that Amazon is a potential insurance disruptor, insurers need to stop reacting like Borders did.

This transformation could be done by arranging insurance as a series of modular policies, which customers can pick and choose from, with adjustable attributes. Each module can come with omni-channel advice on use as well as customer-created reviews in 'what a user-like-you' thinks. Policies will be linked to telematics, and users will receive real-time feedback on how their activities impact on their risk level. For example, health insurance customers could receive free genetic tests, which when added to telematic feedback will then aid in personalizing medication, as well as creating personalized health articles and tips. Users can be linked into groups of similar users, who can share tips on optimizing health outcomes. Higher-risk customers can have their health metrics tracked in real time so they can be notified of dangerous trends. This will transform insurance from a boring, depressing, one-off purchase, to an engaging series of directly useful value-added services, aimed at optimizing a customer's life cycle healthcare management. During this process, insurers will gain an extremely rich data series which links client activity to health outcomes, as well as a detailed understanding of the best kind of feedback and inducements required to generate desired health outcomes.

[2]E-books have, however, been hobbled by publisher restrictions on extraction and rearranging, in a way which music has not.

Automated Underwriting

The first visible internal change will be within the underwriting sector as this is already transforming. SwissRe (2013) found that 56% of both US and European insurers were started to use automated underwriting. However, very few have moved very far - most current underwriting is still paper and human based, and automated systems are still based on old business models. Only a few are thinking about dynamic underwriting. This lack of urgency will have to dissappear as the waves of disruptive technology build.

It is argued by some commentators that incumbents will have a substantial advantage because they have decades of experience in running risk assessment models based on historical data. External firms have neither the data nor the analysis capacities, so will have to learn these. I would argue that this conclusion is faulty, for two reasons. Firstly, the basis of underwriting will transform to a new paradigm of big data algorithms, and technology firms have more experience with these than insurers do. Secondly, data is not an issue, historical data can be purchased and telematic data will overwhelm it. Unless incumbents immerse their underwriting teams in the new paradigm, they will fall irretrievably behind within 3 or 4 years. They need to start by transforming existing data from all areas of the firm into a common format, which can be data mined.

The best industry expert estimates are that by 2018 up to 90% of all underwriting by insurers will be handled by automated underwriting software. This will occur in conjunction with software-based application/renewal forms which feeds answers into the adminstrative as digital data. They will also be integrated with the collection of client data from as many alternative sources as possible and increasingly integrated with client telematics. This can then be integrated into all other parts of the business.

This will eventually have the impacts of: (i) allowing premiums to be set on a client-specific basis, (ii) allowing premiums to be dynamically adjusted as telematics indicate client behavior is differing, (iii) give the insurer a far deeper data set and a far deeper understanding of client characteristics, and (iv) give the insurer a far deeper understanding of risk causation. This deeper understanding can be fed back into improving the client questionnaire and underwriting modeling. The Geneva Association back in 2013 argued that a paradigm shift from historic to predictive risk assessment was necessary.

However, the most important result of automated underwriting will be to reduce the marginal cost to near zero, as explained earlier. This reduction in cost and the resultant surge in demand will allow a large expansion of underwriting, so that most clients are individually underwritten using a wide array of variables. Until this first automation underwriting step is undertaken, the rest of insurance can't transform itself, as dynamic insurance depends on near-zero cost underwriting joined to automated straight-through processing. The key element will be rules around when human oversight is required. Note that the rapid expansion of underwriting means that jobs are unlikely to be lost overall. However, surviving underwriters will need the IT skills to understand the algorithms and usefully build on the insights provided.

The grouping of clients into risk pools has been the basis of underwriting. In the future, there will not be explicit pools, but an overall risk algorithm. This will involve a range of risk factors, with the weighting of each differing for each client. Client grouping is an administrative technique to make it easier to set rates. Within a world where the cost of individual risk rating is cents, there is no need to group. The algorithm may group clients but as a consequence, not a management tool. This will also an impact on capital reserving and reinsurance, as scenario testing with the algorithm will determine risk capital, rather than the creation of preset client pools.

PWC (2015a) argues that a side effect of this automated underwriting will be the commoditization of insurance provision, as software-based firms enter. In the long run, this will drive down profit levels to the low levels normal in retail sectors. PWC argues that insurers then will be forced to gain their profits from the value-added service activities which they can package alongside the low-margin insurance.

There are many issues to be sorted out. The most crucial is to transfer the skill and experience of existing underwriters into programmable rules, via true/false flow diagrams. The industry saying that 'underwriting is both an art and a science' needs to be carefully considered as only the science can be programmed, and thus areas where exemptions exist need to be defined so decisions can be defaulted to humans.

The use of online applications means that questions can be interactive, with question areas expanded or contracted dependent on prior answers. Thus, there should be little need for additional questions, and fewer questions can be asked of clients who have no current conditions. These questions can be backed by explanations, either in text or short videos, as well as popup Skype boxes, so a staff member can be contacted within the Web page. This will provide data feedback on which terms or areas cause most concern, which will add in the Web site and policy redesign.

The use of big data will bring up many new correlations and useful insights into client behavior, which go well past current insurance score systems. These new insights need to be thought through and clarified as they may have to be explained and justified to clients, to regulators, and to courts. For example, it is well known that credit scores correlate with insurance risk, but an early insight from data is that clients who are more likely to default on their consumer loans are also more likely to die prematurely. Reasons for this can only be speculated, so whether it is causal or just a temporary aberration is unsure, and it is unlikely to hold for all individual cases.

The greater depth and width of data used in new-style underwriting means that new areas can be explored. Examples: (i) which sales agents or sales practices are better at attracting higher-quality clients or encouraging clients to disclose, (iii) which questions on the application form add value, or which questions not currently asked need to be, (iii) whether different channels have differing claim or non-disclosure rates, (iv) what types of social media data are useful, (v) what is the comparative reliability of conditions clients disclosed vs medical evidence for different claim types, (vi) how do differing types of financial data relate to claim rates, (vii) which types of clients non-disclose which types of conditions, in which channel, in which question format.

KPMG (2015b) argues that insurers need to: (i) clean up existing data; (ii) develop a data governance model which allows flexibility and innovation; (iii) create an enterprise data management function whose focus should be on improving data flow and usage; (iv) create a culture of experimentation and enterprise, as the correct answer will not be immediately evident; (v) focus on new ideas rather than what is already known about data, especially new areas of value creation; (vi) focus on profit-driven analytics by trying to eliminate the irrelevant 99% of data; and (vii) focus on asking interesting questions so useful new insights can be discovered, particularly questions which can't be answered by existing data.

The application and underwriting process will be different under a dynamic setting. It needs to be noted that the digital generations will expect instant premiums on application. Insurers will not be able to ask clients to wait, while decisions are required from managers. This can be solved in several ways: (i) The dynamic ability of online questionnaires means that precise questions can be asked, and higher-risk applicants identified; (ii) client disclosures at the time of application are not as important, as insurers can check these subsequently by telematics, or via other data sources; (iii) multiple channels can be integrated, so that if applicants answer a question indicating higher risk, then a Skype or WhatsApp box can open allowing a human underwriter to ask additional questions and visually assess the applicant; (iv) insurers can link in real time to medical or doctor databases; and (v) applicants can use such additional channels to ask about questions. It is well established that the reason for 95% of client non-disclosure is not fraud but ignorance, or not understanding what information is required. Thus, being able to open a box and ask a direct question will clear up the majority of current confusion. Insurers can use innovative new ideas like an App which uses a mobile phone camera to analyze blood.

This dynamic process will then allow non-disclosure laws to be amended to ensure that the onus is on insurers to ask the correct questions at application time and therefore allow insurance to be guaranteed at claims time for all cases except for clear and deliberate client fraud. It will also allow a simplified and rapid application process for 90% of clients, in-depth questioning of the difficult 10%, while giving insurers a more complete risk profile and allow individualized underwriting.

An automated data-driven approach to underwriting will allow insurers to differentiate premiums in real time. Examples of this would be offering different rates when a car is being driven to when it is parked, or a differing rate if a house is occupied than when the owners are on vacation, or varying rates by a customer's adherence to an exercise regime. Privacy issues would be a concern but could be overcome by the insurer establishing a high level of trust.

The extra dimensions added to insurer information on clients will allow deeper insight into client risk and a qualitatively different level of management reporting and decision making and therefore better profitability. The ability to risk-rate clients in real time by activity will allow insurers to proactively engage with clients on a regular basis and provide suggestions to clients on how to reduce risk or lead healthier lives. Insurers could, for example, reduce health insurance premiums for clients whose exercise telematic records more than a set level of consistent physical activity over the last 3 months, and could conversely warn clients whose activity level drops.

A vital part of dynamic insurance will be the creation of a client-individualized 'mobile risk profile.' This is an algorithm which defines a client's risk characteristics based on telematic feedback. This moves with a client, so regardless of the car they drive, health activity they undertake, country they are in, or insurer they use, the profile moves with them. It is thus tied to the person and not any physical object. It could link to the person's digital agent. The profile can interact with telematics or their phone so the client gets feedback on how to improve their risk profile, listing helpful activities, and then, dynamic changes in risk-based premiums can be displayed if those activities are undertaken. I call this 'real-time dynamic risk assessment.'

These types of mobile risk profiles will lead to the possibility of 'lifestyle insurance,' whereby insurers actively and positively engage with clients about their life choices and additional activities like incentives from related companies within their ecosystem, for example, discounts from sports clothing stores, or articles from health writers. This will help to solve the existing issues of non-communication with clients and transform the public's attitude to insurers. Insurers will focus on providing useful services which reduce risk.

The power of the information provided by these new analytical systems will allow a movement away from the current insurer focus on using structured data to make tactical decisions toward using unstructured data to make strategic decisions. This may require the creation of artificial intelligence systems so proactive predictive modeling can be used, including extensive scenario analysis. These will form the heart of future insurance management and will offer a major competitive advantage to those insurers able to integrate their insights into management decision making. Use of real-time dynamic risk assessment will allow management to get weekly or even hourly trends in loss likelihoods. Note this type of dynamic risk assessment is not possible unless underwriting is as automatic as possible so that marginal cost is near zero.

EY (2014) argues that to do this, however, underwriting has to shift away from a focus on internal cost efficiency and refocus on improving the client experience. Thus, the skill set for underwriters will need less computation, which will be automated, and more understanding of client relationship skills. They will be involved in higher-value activities like account planning, solution development, agent partnering, and nuanced risk assessment and decision making. They will be able to, for example, use their new analytics to help agents and advisers select more profitable clients and achieve higher prospect conversion rates.

EY (2014) notes that before 1990 underwriters were the heart of insurance companies and exhibited a broad range of skills, and were the main source of senior managers. However, since then finance executives have provided most senior managers. One reason for this is that as core finance functions were computerized, finance steadily expanded its skills to include planning, analysis, and strategic thinking. Underwriting, conversely, narrowed down its skill set to focus mainly on the binary transactional process. This has to reverse. EY (2014) argues that the risk focus of underwriters and their organizational position make them better placed to manage the required transformation of insurers than finance executives as underwriters are naturally better suited to coordinating the different insurance sectors to ensure that the right clients are selected and managed through their insurance lifecycle. To fulfill this role, the culture of underwriting has to undergo a similar change to that which finance went through in the 1990s. I would argue that insurers who do not rapidly get near the leading edge of innovation of underwriting innovation will fall irretrievably behind.

The ideal future underwriter will need to possess technical skills: with risk assessment, with big data, with software structure, with customer relationship management, with customer profit segmentation, with optimal omni-channel presentation, with using the relevant ecosystem to enhance the relationship between dynamic premiums and incentives provided to clients to induce them to make appropriate decisions, with innovation creation, and with strategic development. This needs to be intuitive as well as technical. The basis of all of these areas will be the new sources of information provided by big data analytics and telematics.

Ideal underwriters will need to leverage their access to this information as well as their understanding of desirable customer types to improve the quality of lead identification and quantification processes, to improve promotional campaigns and cross-selling, to improve account retention, to assess the risk-premium elasticity trade-off, to assess the comparable profitability of client risk segments, to create client social media interest groups, and to assess performance in innovative new ways. They will operate integrated sales-underwriting-propensity models to obtain ideal profit profiles and assess customer channels to improve client satisfaction. Note that a larger focus will be on external interactions with customers and the ecosystems rather than internal efficiency.

EY (2014) argues that future underwriters will need: (i) the ability to synthesize and analyze a wide range of data, (ii) the cognitive skills to recognize a broader and more dynamic business rules context, (iii) the technical skills to leverage a high level of automation to gather insightful insights, and (iv) the communications skills to engage and convince a wider variety of stakeholders. The actual risk pricing of individual clients will be automated in 90% of cases and thus will not be an essential skill.

EY (2014) thus argues that the skill set required of an underwriter in the future will be so different from the traditional skill set that many current underwriters may not be able to sufficiently transform themselves, and that new talent from non-traditional areas will be required. Newer underwriters will need big data analytical-based degrees and probably MBAs to obtain the strategic insight. This increased demand for strategic skills is occurring against a backdrop of an increasing shortage of experienced underwriters. Therefore, EY (2014) argues that one of the keys to insurer survival will be the smart organizational change management and human resource development of the underwriting sector, so that older underwriters are retained to oversee the younger ones.

The future underwriter will be as much a data scientist as a risk assessor. Multiple statistics-based models will be joined to codified, heuristic, underwriting decision tools. Interactive analytical tools will offer 'what if' scenarios and information visualization techniques like heat maps and density illustrations. For commercial clients, a far more in-depth experience can be offered with risk minimization advice based on innovative data and subject-expert advice.

These types of deep-data-analysis systems are already being used in other industries, which has the advantage for existing insurers that they merely need to adopt them, and the disadvantage that external firms which already skilled in these systems are entry threats.

Insurers who are successful will need an underwriting team which has a culture of continuous innovation and experimentation. It is vital to note that the pace of innovation will increase at an exponential rate, as explained in the introduction - that is, the rate of increase of innovation will increase. Thus, insurers who do not rapidly get near the leading edge of innovation will rapidly fall behind. As underwriting innovations will both exponentially cut the cost of client acquisition and exponentially increase client stickiness, insurers will face increasing pressure to innovate.

Traditionally, companies have followed a three-step new product creation process of (a) design a product, (b) make the product, and then (c) sell the product. A low-marginal-cost automated underwriting process enables this to be reversed as (a) sell the product, (b) design the product, and then (c) build the product. Customization to the needs of customers is the heart of this, even if those needs change as customers demand new features as they gradually adjust to the new consumption framework. This is thus not a one-off change but a cultural shift to a differing style of underwriting.

Therefore, I would argue that instead of being a dying sector the future is bright for underwriters who see this technological transformation as a challenge worth seizing. Given that a number of major insurers will fail to respond and thus face bankruptcy, smart underwriters need to ensure their employer is one of those who are proactively engaging or prepare to move to an employer who is. Smart underwriters can use the new techniques and information to enhance their key role in insurance and join the strategic decision-making process. Note that unlike most other areas discussed in this report, the disruptive impact of IT change on underwriting has already started to arrive - the future is now.

Automated Claims

While the insurance industry worldwide has made intensive efforts to speed up claims payments, there is a growing gap between the speed at which insurers think claims can be paid and the speed at which the digital generations now expect. Accenture (2013) found that 74% of policyholders said that their top source of 'extreme frustration' with insurers was having to contact them multiple times for the same reason. Clearly, a large number of pain issues arise with current insurer systems. In particular, millennials think in terms of days or even inter-day, while insurers think in terms of weeks or months. Millennials will experience growing frustration unless a transformation occurs in claims management. Claims administration needs to be real time and near-zero cost.

The only solution is automation via telematics. The intensive use of telematics and administrative software will mean that most activities in the claims process will be automated, with little direct human involvement. For example, if two network-linked cars crash, the telematics will provide a detailed history of each car's actions prior to the crash, and the two insurers' computers will thus be able to determine who is at fault, agree on a sequence of actions, and then contact bank computers to arrange payments, all within microseconds. They can also inform emergency services, tow trucks, crash repair firms, friends of the car drivers, change appointments, arrange auto-taxis, etc., before the dust has settled, without asking the clients many, if any, questions.

If a network-linked TV is stolen, the TV itself can inform the insurer of this and provide its new address, and inform the police. If the TV breaks down, it can provide a full report on why and give details of the part required to the repair shop's computer. If a health telematic detects an impending illness, it can send the required medical details to the insurer and contact local emergency health providers, as well as the clients' friends, possibly before the patient is aware of any issue. The hospital's computer will keep the insurer's computer updated with all current results and procedures. This means that there will be no papers shuffled or manual administration. Nearly, all contacts will be made by software, including writing e-mails or text alerts and making phone calls. Managers can oversee claims in real time and get in-depth details.

The role of the claims staff will then be to oversee the software systems, to ensure that procedures are working as required, to ensure that jobs are actually undertaken to the specified quality, to intervene if the complexity of issues exceeds preset parameters, to ensure the client is informed and happy, and to create innovative new products or procedures. Note that these are not jobs for IT experts but for claims experts as they are concerned with claims procedures and client relationships. The huge increase in data will allow detailed analysis of issues with claims and liaison with underwriters to determine if particular types of clients claim in unexpected ways. Claims data can be automatically linked back to underwriting algorithms.

This automation process can also be in terms of smart software. An example of this is CoreLogic & Symbility Solutions, who have jointly created tablet-based software which allows a house assessor to quickly map a house, note damage, estimate repair cost, and send the required forms via the internet, to be handled by admin staff anywhere in the world. This has cut the time to assess a house by 90%, eliminated nearly all the paper work, and allows scaling in an emergency. There will be no need for skilled engineering professionals to be physically present, as they can watch the assessment from their office computer.

Automation has huge advantages for customers and insurer–customer relationships. Currently, it is difficult for customers to make insurance clams, as they have to positively contact the insurer, make the circumstances of their claim clear, including providing required evidence, understand if their claim fits complex policy terms, work with assessors and claims staff, and then contact the insurer multiple times to ascertain if each stage of the claims process has been undertaken. The customer generally finds the process, even if efficiently run, to be lengthy, confusing, and alienating. This human and step-based process creates high costs for the insurer and has no place in a modern digital society. Digital natives expect same day results with easy access and are often profoundly shocked by the slowness and obliqueness of current insurer claims.

The current claims process is antique - slow and excruciating to customers. An automated process in contrast is speedy and efficient, as evidence can be gathered by telematics, or imputed electronically by claims staff, processed in seconds, and made clear to clients. Client interaction can predominately electronic, with each client able to access an App which shows where their claim is in real time. Because this information links to software, there is no need for humans to update it. There is no need for large call centers, or even Web sites as information will be pushed to clients' mobile phones on a real-time basis. Standard claims should be able to be processed same day. Because loss assessors and adjusters, as well as repairs contractors/health systems, and advisers/brokers, are all linked together into an integrated system, the client can get a complete picture of the claims process.

Research has shown that the customer claim experience is a vital determinate of perceptions of insurer reputation. Use of telematics will enable valid claims to be paid a lot faster and provide strong evidence for decisions when claims are rejected. Aviva Insurance's intensive use of data analytics has reduced fraudulent claims by half a million UK pounds a month and enhanced its reputation.

Insurers can use the integrated data to assess where delays or excessive costs occur and make changes. They can link the claims data to that gathered from their underwriting or wider ecosystem data to ascertain which types of clients prefer which type of contact at differing stages of the claims process or rank them in terms of ease of claims processing, or which styles increase client happiness. They can link the claims process into their social media system or wider business ecosystem and provide the client with useful information or offer cross-selling opportunities.

They can market the speed and ease of their claims process as a competitive advantage. Claims data analysis can then be integrated with underwriting data and client response data to create personalized life cycle advice to minimize adverse events.

The need to undertake a cultural and technological change in claims is, however, hindered by the decline in experienced claims adjusters, with over 70% of US adjusters aged over 45. A world of experience is being lost at a time when a younger generation of programmers needs to access that skill to be able to create robust automated claims systems.

Cultural Change

The biggest concept which insurers need to understand about digital transformation is that the transformation is not about the technology or the data - it is fundamentally about transforming the organizational culture so the company can integrate the new technology-based opportunities. McKinsey (2016c) argues that the biggest challenge in adopting an analytics approach and making the evolution from a 'knowing culture' to a 'learning culture' is not cost, but is largely lack of imagination and excess of inertia.

The major mistake companies trying to cope with the digital challenge make is to regard it as a IT project to be handled by the chief technology officer, instead of an organizational culture challenge which has to embedded into all parts of the company.

As explained earlier, IBM (2006) argues that insurers have traditionally focused on product and process optimization, rather than innovation. This has created a point-solution mentality which causes insurers to treat the symptoms of persistent problems while ignoring root causes. This has to change. Instead of working hard to improve current processes, insurers need to drastically transform their businesses.

The insurance industry does not have a technology problem; it has a problem in the use of technology due to corporate culture and internal politics. Bain (2015) argues that insurers need to: (i) build advanced analytical systems, (ii) create effective digital distribution, (iii) create customer centricity, and (iv) digitize internal operations and sharply reduce cost. One of the major issues associated with this transformation is inhibitions caused by the traditional culture and organization of the insurance companies. KPMG (2014) argues that the incompatibility of multiple legacy systems is a symptom not a root problem. Insurers tend to be policy-centric with all the systems geared to a specific product with a minimal view of customers. This creates siloes between business lines and an unwillingness to share data or internal functions.

Insurers need to reorganize and move away from current practices. They need to move from traditional lengthy business planning to more flexible, less exact, more data-led, and more iterative approaches. They need to learn how to launch new products or services while testing and obtaining feedback and responding to that feedback in a continuous process. Time to market for new products needs to be shortened and made more flexible, so multiple combinations can be trialed. They need to simplify products while also customizing and diversifying product ranges. They need to be prepared to offer trial products to customers and service them through a multitude of service channels.

Murli Buluswar, in McKinsey (2016c), argues that the effective use of analytics is dependent on a cultural change and that most insurers fail this challenge due to fear of the unknown. He argues that it's a mind-set change from an 'expert-based mind-set' to a 'learning-based, flexible mind-set'. The issue with experts in the future world is that knowledge is likely to change at a deep level, so that the paradigm which the expert has used to arrange their thinking is no longer valid. Given that it took time and effort to learn the old one, it is hard for most people to accept that they have to adopt a new paradigm. Knowing how to rethink and reimagine will be more important than knowing stuff. The company will have to refocus company culture toward creating a dynamic learning environment. Yet, how many incumbent insurers currently have a 'culture executive' or a 'learning executive'? The Facebook manual famously notes that 'If we don't create the thing that kills Facebook, someone else will. "Embracing change" isn't enough. It has to be so hardwired into who we are so that even talking about it seems redundant.'

New entrants from sectors which already have flexible product cycles are more likely to be able to manage a more flexible approach to production than traditional insurers stuck within legacy organization systems. These changes mean that traditional insurers' focus on exactitude needs to be replaced by a focus on speed and flexibility. Insurers who follow the traditional focus on cost control and taking the time to get a product just right before it is released run the danger of the market having changed substantially in the meantime.

KPMG (2016) notes that large business organizations tend to be good at minor, tweaking, changes which focus on improving existing business and operating models. Insurers are keen on optimizing the sub-optimal. However, they do poorly at fundamental transformation, the type of enterprise-wide strategic change which truly reinvents the company. There is a big difference between the skills required to encourage digitization and those required to guide a successful transformation. You need a really strong change management capacity, and that is rarely available from existing managers, as they have skills in achieving efficiency in a stable environment, not in disrupting that environment.

This is because there are typically far too many embedded incumbent managers who fear they will lose from a change and because transformation requires a much broader view, and a much more strategic approach, than most insurers have needed for past initiatives. It is also very hard to see the value of benefits from an exponential process during the initial stages - all that can be seen are the immediate losses. Given the inherent fuzziness of transformation, many of the initial changes will fail to produce sufficient advantages and therefore will give ammunition to those who argue against the need for change. KPMG argues that for these reasons most incumbent transformation efforts will fail. What may be required is the introduction of new senior managers with transformation experience, or skilled consultants.

If an insurer wants to reinvent itself, they can't just look at what insurer competitors are doing, but instead need to look at what external firms are doing in disruptive sectors. Many companies also fail because they have tended to appoint employees like themselves. This means that even a transformation team will all have the same world view and therefore will be unable to visualize the broad range of possible futures. An insurer will need to create a diverse company culture with many different viewpoints, focused especially on employees who can break incumbent employees out of their existing mind-sets. Discomfort has to be maximized.

This transformation process has to be embedded in every aspect of the insurer's operations, not just underwriting or customer response. All administration areas need to be consulted on requirements so all information and decisions are available to all who need it. Marketing needs to be comfortable with big data and social network analytics, and be able to communicate closely with the data analysts so that the correct metrics can be created and found in the huge mass of data. Customer contact staff needs to be at ease across multi-channels and have instant access to whatever they require to answer questions. Brokers and intermediaries need access to all the information and tools they require in a manner which enhances the customer experience. These tools need to be flexible so they can be instantly changed based on customer reaction. Pricing needs to be instant and dynamic.

Product siloes need to be replaced by a customer-orientated divisions so that each segment of customers can receive the type of experience which makes them enthusiastic and feel engaged. All decisions need to be seen through the viewpoint of the fairness for the customer - whether they understand the product, whether they can afford it, and whether it is likely to deliver value for money. Customer experiences need to be mapped so opportunities to improve the customer experience can be found and enhanced by additional products. Products and services need to be developed and tested with customers and social networks. Social media trends need to be tracked and used for customer debate. Metrics need to be developed which track customer satisfaction, level of understanding, product usefulness, and likelihood to recommend or rate highly.

Flexibility and speed of response are essential. Experimentation is required where new products or services are trialed and modified. Separate divisions focused on new products or new business processes could be created. It can be useful to initially focus on quick wins so enthusiasm and trust in the process can be developed.

It is also important to note that while the data and analytics should be very complex, the IT interface to staff or customers has to be as simple as possible, so that information is presented to staff in a high-quality fashion, and so it can be easily comprehended and acted on. Interfaces need to be developed by experts in human–computer interactions and in graphical displays. This way every member of a team can avoid feeling overwhelmed.

The initial problem is that substantial reorganizations are very costly and disruptive of current productivity, without immediately generating additional revenue. It is hard to argue for costly change now, for the sake of future survival, unless there is an immediate threat. Leaders are needed who have the capacity to understand a longer-term strategic vision and the ability to implement it. Boards and CEOs need to understand exactly how far their current culture is from the culture required for future survival, the 'cultural gap', and be willing to push for the required changes. If boards wait until the gap is large enough to allow external entrants to disrupt the market, then they have probably waited too long.

Fortunately, there are a number of data integration opportunities which can be more easily trialed and which can help to signpost the transformation path. One is to create a data visualization system which sits on top of existing disparate databases and can be used to extract key data and create a data analytics system. These can trial different data sets or models so that real value insights can be found to be shown to the board. Another immediate priority should be to create an experimental company, where new ideas can be trialed and problems discovered before they are spread company wide. The main danger here is these short-term measures reinforce the mind-set that the solution is technological based rather than cultural, so their purpose should primarily be used to create buy-in from the senior leadership team.

Transformation Pathways

EY (2013) suggests that the path to transformation in the near term involves:

Step 1: the now

1. *Creating a clearly defined digital strategy*: This involves identifying the ideal future insurer model and mapping how to get there. This predominately involves looking at examples outside the industry and recognizing that it may not be possible to create sector leadership in every dimension.
2. *Identifying initiatives which deliver the most*: This involves creating data and analytical capacities so that insurers can identify customer expectations, matching these with current inadequacies and therefore identifying where to focus management effort and spending.
3. *Helping distribution partners develop digital capacities*: This involves examination of all the channels customers may choose to use and ensuring a high-quality, omni-channel experience. Therefore, intermediaries and agents need to have the capacity to deliver the required customer experience as part of an overall process.
4. *Frame the investment argument*: This involves shifting management focus from short-term to long-term decision making and from internal efficiency to customer-centric. The conflict between the need for transformation and the CFO agenda needs to be made explicit, as well as the conflict between customer retention and acquisition.
5. *Build analytical capacities*: This involves developing physical and staff resources, as well as reorienting rate-making and marketing staff to a big data focus. The focus has to be on the best use of the analytics rather just its creation, particularly how to use analytics to create deep insights into customer priorities.
6. *Develop mobile functionality*: Customer interaction via mobile phone Apps is the new norm.
7. *Take social media seriously*: Any insurer who is not constantly on social media will not exist in the eyes of digital natives.
8. *Embed continual innovation into the company culture*: Change is the norm, so the transformation cannot be seen as a once-off but continuous. This involves identifying cultural constraints, utilizing external influences to overcome them, and aligning KPIs with innovation.

Step 2: near term

1. *Combine cultural change with technological change*: The response to the technological challenge is more about company culture than technology.
2. *Embrace cloud computing*: Digital information needs to be always and everywhere available. Given the skyrocketing demands of big data, insurers need to be able to rapidly upscale capacity. It is mission-critical that data outrages do not occur.
3. *Create a sustainable culture of collaboration and innovation*: It is impossible to impose significant cultural change by top-down edict. Staff needs to be brought through an evolutionary process, so cultural change is embedded. The idea that flexibility and experimentation are more important than accuracy or cost control needs to be embedded into management. Company-wide calls for innovative possibilities need to be made.

KPMG (2016) argues that insurers can define their future business and operating models by breaking the transformation analysis into levels of value and examining these over differing time frames; 3–5 years, 5–10 years, longer than 10 years:

1. *Financial ambitions*: What are the future financial outcomes, structuring, investment, and capital allocations.
2. *Markets*: What are the best future markets and do the current portfolios of business maximize the chance of achieving those targets.
3. *Propositions and brands*: How should the portfolio of propositions and brands evolve over time.
4. *Clients and channels*: What changes to the operating model puts the client at the heart of the business.
5. *Core business operations*: What business processes will deliver the financial outcomes required within a high-performance model.
6. *Operational and technology infrastructure*: What are the required priority technological structures.
7. *Organizational structures*: Are there the proper oversight structures to drive change and ensure responsibilities are met.
8. *People and culture*: What leadership is required at various levels to drive the transformation with a high level of passion.

9. *Measures and Incentives*: How will change be measured, in terms of what issues.

It is vital to note that while regulatory issues have delayed change in the insurance sector, this will not save insurers. This is because the insurance sector is inherently internationalizing. Therefore, while regulation remains national, external disruptors will find it very easy to cross borders - on the Web there are no borders. This means that if regulations in a particular country incentivize national insurers to delay transformation, those insurers will fall more and more behind the international leaders and the increasing productivity gap will make it increasingly attractive for international disruptors to enter via Web sites. Incumbents will not be in a position to respond.

It is thus in the long-term interests of insurers to induce national regulators to proactively respond with state-of-the-art regulation, so that national insurers become the disruptors rather than the victims.

Legacy Systems

Many of the top financial service firms are large, complex, organizations which were created from multiple mergers and acquisitions. They thus have siloed personal structures, fragmented administrative processes, and mashed together IT systems, relying on incompatible data types. This ensures that correct information is hard to obtain and decision making is protracted.

One key to future success insurer is thus to get rid of legacy systems and the complexity and bureaucracy associated with the traditional systems. They must create simplified, scalable, technology based on big data, real-time feedback, and dynamic responses to customer expectations. They have to support the kind of real-time multi-channel interactions, predictive analytics, and mobile service delivery options which the millennials and subsequent generations expect.

Insurers have to be aware that competition will not just come from existing insurers but will also come from firms which have already created those innovative and socially linked characteristics in other sectors.

These firms are not burdened by legacy IT systems and business processes, are tech-savvy, and have substantial social capital, as well as existing intimate knowledge of customer characteristics. For example, Google has already entered the US general insurance market. It is, thus, vital for insurance managers to not dismiss the threat of a disruptive technology just because no other insurer has yet trialed it.

The new entrant could have the bulk of its staff based in foreign country. Youi, for example, has recently entered the NZ market with a minimal local presence and has shown that a firm does not have to be locally based to be effective. Any insurer CEO who doubts the possible threat only needs to contemplate the example of Kodak dying because of the entry of firms from a previously unrelated sector. Could the firm which destroys your insurance business be an airline based in Malaysia or a Chinese Web platform?

Thus, a key to future success is to work with firms from other sectors which have existing superior software skills, especially in customer contact, and to supply insurance products via these firms' Web systems. While most insurers are moving into direct online sales, their attempts have in general so far been weak and have not exhibited the attention to customization and rapid feedback which is now expected. Direct Web sales are also hardly leading edge. Very few insurers are exhibiting any indication that they have the skills to move into a qualitatively different era in terms of client servicing.

It is important for insurers to understand how disruption has occurred in different sectors. For example, Amazon created the first wave of its digital disruption by using a Web site to offer a catalogue 10x larger than the largest physical store and 10% cheaper. They created the second wave by enabling a community via allowing bloggers to post reviews and encouraging the public to post ratings. It then used the behavior of this community to gain insights and develop collaborate algorithms. It understood that the bigger its network, the richer its data, the better is the customer experience. It is currently creating the third, larger, wave by broadening its product range to include anything deliverable by truck or net, by distributing for smaller merchants, and by building the world's largest cloud computing service. Amazon has worked on building scale in data and analytical techniques. It has been proactive, not waiting for change, and not protected existing income streams from new opportunities. It has understood that it is not an online book seller, but a business based on data analysis.

Amazon beat traditional bricks-and-mortar stores because it built digital from the ground up, rather than try to add bits of digital onto traditional systems. Insurers will struggle because they generally fail to understand that going digital involves changing the entire structure of their business processes, and not just adding a shiny front-end Web site. It is more about internal management than physical technology. Insurers need to bring in outside expertise, but they cannot just insert them into current structures or their talent will be stifled and they will leave. There needs to be management support or the appointment, of say, a 'digital manager' will achieve nothing as the rest of the staff may think it's that person's job and they don't also have to change.

One of the main issues with IT system improvements is that generally IT departments are already overwhelmed. Gartner surveys show that typically 80–85% of an IT department's budgets are spent on essential maintenance and that requests for new services or changes substantially exceed what can be done in the remaining 15–20%. Gartner shows that the 'new request' IT backlog for US companies typically increases by 10–20% per year, and since resources are not there to handle this, it is creating a compounding backlog. Gartner estimates that each IT application cost about 40% of its purchase cost to maintain. The budget allocation for new projects has typically been decreasing because the time required for maintenance has increased faster than budget allocations. This has resulted in management being disappointed with IT department performance and has discouraged any plans for radical change in IT services.

Management tends to response to demands for urgent changes in IT systems by one of four methods:

1. *Buy and customize a packaged application*: This is often the fastest solution. However, typically, these packages deliver standardized processes which are normally different to what the firm requires. Thus, customization is typically required, and the packages are not built for change so customizing is difficult and expensive. Adding this

requirement onto an already overworked IT department is a recipe for further failure, adds to the routine maintenance workload, and multiplies incompatible systems.
2. *Build a custom solution in-house*: Building a large and complex system is often very expensive and complex given current techniques and tools. It also tends to be prone to increasing failure rates as the size increases. The in-house systems are typically not built for change so amendments are difficult, and because it is non-standard, the company is hostage to the original systems' integrators. Over time ad-hoc expansion multiplies maintenance workloads and adds overwhelming complexity.
3. *Select and rent a cloud-based solution*: Software-as-a-service companies now offer partly customizable software and supply external hardware. However, this does not address issues with interfaces, workflows, and data repositories.
4. *Do nothing*: This is the typical response of an overworked IT department, whereby new requests are logged in and put into an endless waiting list.

The real reason for this growing IT mess is that it is very expensive and time-consuming to create and amend large software systems, and this increases nonlinearly with size. Some reasons for this in a typical company are as follows:

1. Reverse-engineering hundreds of thousands of lines of code to find the exact place to make changes is complex and requires experienced staff.
2. Validating these changes across all applications and sub-systems is extremely complex, and dependences grow exponentially with size.
3. After changes have been made and validated, deploying a new version into production is complex and error prone.
4. Integrating existing and new diverse systems is complex and problematic.
5. Under deadline pressure, non-functional requirements are often forgotten or ignored.
6. After going live, no audit or troubleshooting capacities are in place.

The solution to these issues requires a substantial budget and personal increase, external expert support, and an integrated agile software engineering process aimed at gradually streamlining and integrating systems so maintenance reduces proportionally over time. The end objective has to be an IT process aimed at innovative, user-friendly, products which transform insurer productivity. None of this is easy.

Integration with Customers

Insurer customer engagement is regarded by experts as one of the top crisis issues, with 80%+ insurers having stated programs of investments in improvements. The customer disconnect crisis, however, is not due to insurer failure, but due to the changing expectations of customers and generational change. Insurance customers are becoming disconnected from the insurer's value proposition, confused, and tend not show understanding of any aspects of the value proposition apart from price. They are becoming increasingly hard to sell to, with only a limited proportion actively seeking cover. Profit margins are dropping as insurers compete on price, yet find that customer stickiness is dropping, so that expenses on client acquisition are not recovered. What modern customers want is simplicity, accessibility, platform neutrality, social connectedness, and a clear explanation of a product's value. Very few insurers are meeting these demands.

PWC (2014) argues that insurers' focus on risk, ratings, and products mean that their understanding of customers lags substantially behind that of other industries and leaves them highly vulnerable to disruptive entry by techno-literate firms with high social capital. Morgan Stanley/BCG (2014) argues that unless insurers drastically increase the frequency and quality of their interactions with clients, insurers will be very vulnerable to disruptive entry by service providers who have an established high level of client interactivity.

For the 'no-wait-generation,' the speed of response needs to be qualitatively changed. Millennials expect a response to a simple query within one hour and to a complex query within 3 or 4 hours. Any phone not answered within 2 minutes is an aggravation. Any insurer who talks longer than one day to respond to a query will not get that customer coming back. The expectations of digital natives are in minutes, not hours. Why can't a claim be paid in 10 minutes? Customers expect the person or system they have contact with, to have the answers, and not respond 'I'll get back to you' - any respectable customer relations IT system will give each staff member all the information and authority they need to satisfy a customer.

Responses to customers and changes to online information systems need to occur inter-day, yet many large insurers take months to make simple changes. Morgan Stanley/BCG (2014) cites an example of an insurer taking 180 days and 35 signatures to change a file on the company Web page. Inflexible companies will be at a severe competitive disadvantage, as the speed of response is starting to become more important than accuracy. Many insurers still have policy application processes which take weeks to complete rather than minutes. A dangerous customer expectation gap is opening up, which can be filled by external firms from sectors who are used to fulfilling the new generations' higher customer expectations.

Modern customers also expect multiple channels to be available, Web pages, branches, phone advisers, etc., and expect these to integrate, so whatever information is given to a Web site is available to any other staff/adviser; information should only be given once. While the use of physical branches is dropping, customers expect these to be available for when they need them. Capgemini/Efma (2016) found that while baby boomers were happy with insurer contact via e-mail and Web sites, younger generations expected multi-channel access and lack of this was a major factor in switching decisions. They also found that while younger generations were engaging with insurers up to 2 or 3 times as often as baby boomers, they were unhappier than baby boomers with the level of engagement. This means that even though insurers worldwide are trying to improve their customer responsiveness, customer expectations are rising faster than insurers can change. Technology gives insurers the ability to proactively service customers. If a customer has to call an insurer to find out what is going on with any part of their policy that should be considered a failure by the insurer.

In general, it is still difficult for a customer to get information on insurance products, on policy quality issues, on how other customers liked the product, on claims processes, and on the process of their claim. Typically, customers have to use call centers and often experience delays of three or four minutes. The call center staff member often can't answer issues and has no real-time information as to where in the process the claim is. Customers compare this to other sectors, like Amazon, where obtaining information on products is simple, independent product reviews are available, payment is simple, each stage of delivery is tracked, and returns are assured if the product is not to their liking. They can get very aggrieved that insurance seems to be from a by-gone age. How many insurer Web sites offer advice on what insurance products the customer does not need?

Customer loyalty is also dropping, with MyCustomer (2015) finding that 57% of UK respondents consider switching their car or house insurance every year. They also found that only 32% of customers reported positive customer experiences. Thus, very few customers are excited or engaged with their insurer and are very open to considering an external disruptor.

Insurers are aware of their customer disenchantment issues, yet, despite active investment, seem unable to close the engagement gap. Adding an App or two won't cut it; insurers need to drastically transform the customer experience. Yet, many insurers still seem impressed with themselves for having a Web site! Insurers need to move into the twenty-first century. In particular, insurers cannot expect customers to come to them; they need to attract the customers to them. They need to be more interesting and relevant - show that their product enhances customers' lives and is not a grudge purchase. They need regular, enhancing, and relevant contact with customers, across all channels. This contact needs to be interactive, and adaptive, responding to customer concerns in real time. While insurer response may involve some customer segmentation by channel, it is vital to recognize that most customers will expect to use multiple channels.

The customer journey from initial awareness of the use of an insurance product, to purchase, to claim, needs to be systematically reworked, so that insurers are reoriented and redesigned around the customer, and not around reducing actuarial risk. McKinsey (2016a) argues that this redesign requires four dimensions:

1. *Installing customer empathy*: Good design requires real empathy that goes beyond what customers think they want, and responds to underlying needs, not the stated needs. Detailed customer feedback is required.
2. *Getting comfortable with an iterative approach*: Good design methodology requires an initial release of 'imperfect' products, which are iteratively improved. This enables customer feedback to be incorporated and drastically speeds up response time. In this framework, products are never complete.
3. *Replacing functional siloes with agile cross-functional teams*: Because insurers have been structured around competency areas (e.g., risk, underwriting, sales), no one really owns the full customer experience or is accountable to customers. This can only be overcome by use of agile, cross-functional, teams which are project orientated.
4. *Braiding business and IT*: Traditionally, business has led IT, setting requirements and parameters. In the future, IT will be too important to be left to either the CTO or the COO, and thus, business processes and IT need to be braided together. All IT solutions need detailed feedback from all areas of the business, as well as from potential customers.

This redesign process has to end up evolving a customer journey which is exciting, engaging, and ongoing. This leads to four outputs: (i) deep customer understanding, so that you can predict what they value and respond to it; (ii) embracing empathy, so the right people with the right skill sets are in the right place; (iii) real-time response, which combines design, strategy, and technology; and (iv) quickness, so that the company responds rapidly to changes.

The goal should be to create relevant, engaging, interactions at every contact point, regardless of mode, to understand the context of each interaction, to provide genuine two-way dialog, and to provide consistent high-quality service. Each stage should be tracked by data metrics, so that breakdown points can be found and trials conducted on how to increase customer happiness. Low cost is far less important than engagement satisfaction.

Customer engagement needs to be customized, so that the style of engagement, reminder frequency, social network links, etc., are amended as the particular customer desires. This could be based on feedback metrics or could be set by the customer. This is a vital issue - very few insurers think about letting customers themselves define the terms of interactions. Traditionally, insurers have controlled information, rather than allowed a two-way flow. This is contrary to the assumptions of the younger generations.

Very few insurance incumbents have tried to examine their business process from a customer perspective; they are still locked into a products-and-processes model. Most incumbents cannot even provide Apps which allow a customer to update account information in an active manner (so answers change subsequent questions) or cross-populate other customer data fields. Very few offer millennial stables such as one-click-buying, set-and-forget-reordering, open-customer-reviews, and personalized suggestions based on prior purchases or Web serving or social media. These are basic level functions, not advanced, but seem beyond current incumbents.

Insurers also have minimal information on their customers. For example, social media giants will be automatically aware if customers undergo significant insurance trigger events (like buying a house, getting married, or having a baby), while insurance incumbents have no idea. A simple App which allows a customer to change all customer details for all companies within a business ecosystem after a life event, for example, a change of address, is still speculative for insurance incumbents, yet is regarded as base standard by digital natives.

Personalized, context-specific, interactions require the combination of customer insights, digital content creation, with delivery via omni-channels. This gives customers the sense that insurers know who they are, what their needs are, how they relate to the product or company, where they are in the life cycle, and what occurred in previous interactions, whatever the channel, wherever it occurred inside the ecosystem. This is a product both of end-to-end IT systems and interactive CRM systems.

Martinez (2016) argues that it is vital in internet advertising to understand where the power in customer data lies: Is it with the network supplier, 'the publisher', or is it with the provider of the click-through ads, 'the advertiser'? Each of these two parties collects a different type of information about browsers, and thus, the two data sets have quite different monetary values. In general, value has been shifting toward advertiser data, so if an eyeball provider, like an insurer, isn't savvy enough to create sophisticated browser targeting and tracking software, then it will find it very hard to arbitrage any value from its ecosystem partners. Currently, most insurers do not have Web site CPM or the ability to track conversion rates.

The largest issue is that insurers are not generally aware of how far behind the leading edge of customer engagement software or customer expectations they are. They need to radically reimagine their role and recreate their IT processes to close the engagement gap. The upside is that experiences with active engagement InsurTech show substantially increased sales across a range of products and a substantial increase in customer stickiness.

Potential external disruptors have advanced customer relationship and insight systems and therefore will find it easier to add insurance as a product than incumbents will find it to drastically redesign their business processes. Incumbents will struggle more in this area than others.

Big Data and Artificial Intelligence

While some large companies have tried to create effective customer insight functions, so that it doesn't end up as just another traditional market research operation, most have struggled. One reason for this is that elevating customer insight into a strategic position requires strong and persistent efforts from top managers. Another reason is that customer behavior is rapidly changing, with younger generations approaching product purchase quite differently. The largest source of data relating to customer changes is those derived from big data sources, yet most insurers have yet to move from struggling to understand this toward making mastery of big data a competitive advantage.

The availability of big data is exploding, yet the possibilities of its use have been little explored in the insurance industry so far. A major issue with big data is its size and unstructured nature. To the uninitiated most will seem to be noise. Only inadequate standardized systems have been developed so far to allow insurers to extract the useful aspects of this overwhelming data, so innovators will have to invest in creating bespoke analytical systems.

It is also useful to move from a simple closed analytical underwriting model, which has a set of equations, toward a more forward-looking model, which uses scenarios and structured cause–effect chains to give a deeper understanding of loss possibilities. This is because in a rapidly changing world, the causes of major losses may be events which have not yet occurred, rather than events which are known. Within this, insurers need to sort out the 'known unknowns' from the 'unknown knowns.'

Using machine learning methods on big data involves a move away from a 'deductive approach' - where you apply rules learned from a sample to particular clients, toward an 'inductive approach' - where you use detailed data on clients to learn general rules. It also involves regarding data as a 'real-time flow' rather than static, closed, pool. Siegel (2016) argues that this requires focusing on data dynamics, the characteristics which cause change, rather than on stationary casual factors; 'how do the behavioral characteristics of current clients differ from the clients you had two years ago? Are they more or less likely to claim or cancel?'

Insurers can use big data to increase their customer base in two ways: (i) by selling more to existing customers and (ii) by selling to new customers. A vital aspect of this will be effective data-driven customer insight systems. These use predictive models to anticipate evolutions in customer behavior. Careful analysis of big data helps this process by giving agents feedback on which types of customers and which style of interactions result in higher prospect to sales conversion, in lower lapse rates, in larger policy size, and in more reliable customer information. Big data also allows companies to differentiate agents on these criteria. The reduced cost of underwriting due to automation will enable insurers to penetrate lower down the income chain, to the lower middle-income market, which has traditionally been seen as too expensive to service.

A vital part of the response by insurance survivors has to be the creation of effective AI systems using adaptable learning algorithms. One of the key reasons for this is that possible competitors like Google have taken the deliberate policy of transforming themselves into a 'machine-learning-first company.' Although these Silicon Valley pioneers have always used AI, they have recently become obsessed by it. For years, AI was considered a specialty, limited to an elite few; now, IT thought leaders argue that it is becoming the core of future disruptors.

The core skills required to master AI differ substantially from the skills traditionally required from programmers. In particular, AI does not involve deciding on work flows and output equations before the start but setting up a system to create its own answers. Creating AI systems thus involves (i) identifying the right data, (ii) choosing the right algorithmic approach, (iii) creating the right conditions for success, and (iv) and then trusting the system to do the work correctly.

While AI systems won't replace humans, they will radically change human life. The use of superior AI systems will allow insurers to mine big data derived from telematics and ecosystems to discover activity-risk correlations which are not obvious to actuaries, and to cut marginal cost substantially. AI will be a key component of internal administrative systems, especially their ability to respond to customers via auto-generation of e-mails or phone calls or social media posts (using text and vocal recognition skills) as well as responding actively to telematic feedback.

The AI analysis systems need to be led by business and not technical managers, so that practical applications and insights are discovered. This role of linking the data to the business is critical and involves a rare talent of understanding both data and business.

Expertise in AI will allow insurers to integrate their products into the telematic-based products used by other firms in their ecosystem, enhancing these products and extracting vital data. An insurer who has no ability to offer ecosystem partners this integration ability will not be attractive ecosystem members and will likely lose their place. The difference in approach means that insurers' teams of programmers may need extensive retraining. This can be difficult as skilled and experienced AI trainers are scarce, and once trained, data analytical staff will be offered large inducements to move to more exciting companies.

It is vital to understand that use of big data insights within an expanded IT administrative system does not just allow replacement of repetitive activities, but their major gain is that new insights will allow humans to work more efficiently. For example, (i) pricing can become segmented and targeted, as analytics allow deeper understanding of the value of products to different customers and the resultant price elasticities; (ii) management can work out the optimal size and composition of teams, and the optimal number of tasks particular types of workers should be involved in at any one time; (iii) management can work out what types of sales approaches work best for which types of clients; and (iv) management can work out which types of data dashboards provide staff with the critical information and how different types of customers react to this.

Technology is going to be an important part of insurers' ability to capture and analyze new sources of customer data and develop deeper relationships. Yet, the real differentiator is how effectively this information is turned into insights and a readiness to lead the innovations in the marketplace. Using big data analytics to develop a better understanding of customers also enables insurers to develop products or services which radically enhance the customer experience.

The use of these data streams can also enhance insurers' integration with customers' lives by offering data-based services. For example, car insurers can link their in-car dynamics insurance systems to traffic systems and provide minute-by-minute feedback on traffic density conditions over differing routes to the customer's destination. Health insurers can link the food a family buys to blood-chemistry outcomes. One of the keys for insurers to become a customer-centric company is a focus on the integration of big data into client-facing activities, delivered via a radical reduction in per-service administrative costs.

It needs to be remembered that data security will be mission-critical, as any serious breach of customer confidentiality could lead to law suits, regulator action, and insurer bankruptcy. Cloud systems and data linkages are also not infallible and can suffer outrages. For a dynamic rating system, this could lead to major issues. Thus, multiple backups and access systems will be required, as will power backups, alongside state-of-the-art security protocols and a proactive data security team.

A major issue with multinationals using big data about people is that its use is subject to regulation, and this will differ for every country the firm operates in. Given that the only way to maximize data use is on an international basis, across all jurisdictions, international agreements are required. This needs to include legally enforceable guarantees for protection of privacy and non-discriminatory application. This can be extremely difficult if over a hundred different units within a firm over twenty countries are constantly interacting with the data lake.

Internal Systems

Many of the issues which insurers face can be traced to either to poor legacy IT and inflexible management systems, which fail to give staff company-wide information on a customer, or to inadequately fine-tuned data, or to a failure to positively engage with customers. McKinsey (2016b) found that only 14% of companies with transformative plans had been effective in trying to achieve the aims of their data and analytics programs. Those 14%, however, had found that their market share and revenues had increased more than they had expected. Of those who struggled, their major obstacles were not technological but difficulties in securing effective internal management support and difficulties in designing an effective organizational structure. CEOs and boards seemed more able to focus on the physical aspects of the creation of a new IT system than on either the analytical side or the need for a new style of management. All the high-performing companies had CEOs who were engaged and supportive of the required cultural changes.

EY (2013) also finds that the main factors holding insurers back from digital transformation are internal - legacy technology, slow pace of IT system implementation, and business cultural constraints. They found that 47% of insurers surveyed had no clear digital business case and for those that did have plans, those plans only covered low-level issues like integrating budgets with HR planning. The majority of insurers felt they had inflexible and inappropriate operating models and management systems. Only 5% of insurance middle management felt that the senior management understood the change required and led by example. While 30% envisage this improving, no insurers had senior management which seemed to comprehend the scale and urgency of the transformation needed. McKinsey (2016b) argues that the biggest hurdles to an effective analytics program have not been a lack of strategy or tools; it has been a lack of leadership support and communication, ill-fitting structures, and trouble finding the right people for the job. Unless the mind-set of the senior management of current insurers changes, they will continue to lag further and further behind other sectors and thus remain extremely vulnerable to entry by external disruptors.

The siloed, product line, basis of traditional insurer management means that insurers tend to have different IT systems for each business line and different systems for underwriting, for customer relation management, for claims management, and for sales. There is no IT link with related firms like suppliers or brokers. This means that client information often has to be inputted multiple times, staff often have only a partial view, queries and claim cannot be handled fast, effective data analytics are impossible, and the top management does not have a comprehensive overview of key metrics.

The main reason why insurers have been laggards in IT is because most insurers have traditionally had a risk-adverse culture focused on cost control and accuracy of data predictions. Failure in a project has been seen as career death - there is no 'Fail Often, Fail Fast, Fail Forward,' approach. However, the future will require experimentation and a willing to allow systems and staff to fail at these trials. A 'controlled failure' has to be seen as a career-enhancing rather that a career-limiting move. As well, since more data is vital the traditional idea that 'those who hold the data hold the power' has to change to the idea that 'those who share the data have the most power.'

Banks have been more innovative in use of digital systems, information, and customer engagement and thus threaten to take market share from traditional insurers. Unfortunately, internal insurer attitudes to data sharing are inbred into insurer company culture as well as legally regulated so change could be too slow to enable insurers to meet the challenge of outsiders with a sharing culture.

A substantial increase in IT investment is required. EY (2013) found that insurers currently only spend about 10% of their business and IT budgets on digital developments and IT budget share is barely enough to maintain existing systems. Very few insurers spend 2% of their budget on R&D, yet to compete this will have to exceed 4%. Investments in IT systems and staff retraining will have to be multiplied by orders of magnitude, as the most common reason for the failure of technological transformation projects is a lack of adequate investment. Unfortunately, EY (2013) found that a majority of insurer managers have no clear idea of where existing spend goes. Only about 15% of insurers are trialing cultural change projects. The vast majority of insurers are still focused on internal change issues rather than rapidly changing customer expectations.

One of the major obstacles is that the future is arriving so fast that proposed threats often seem very unlikely and so are outside the scope of any 'reasonable' threat review. Why would Kodak have thought about the electronics sector when they examined threats to their film business? Given that 90% of possible threats will prove to be busts, it is also very hard to establish clear plans for reaction. Therefore, threat reviews need to be open to blue-sky thinking and 'unreasonable' ideas. As wide and diverse a range of employees as possible should be included, including external thought leaders. Insurers will need to transform their work forces with a culturally different style of staff and a management structure which focuses on customer response and flexibility rather than accuracy or cost. Businesses then need to maximize their flexibility so unexpected threats can be countered.

One way to create major internal cultural change is to shift to a social media style internal communication system. This means that, instead of internal communications being person to person via e-mail or phone, with a strong top-down bias, webs of information are established, with the ability of many employees actively sought. The internal social platforms are then used to access information, with a focus on collaboration via social tools. McKinsey (2012) argues that this can improve staff productivity by up to 25% and increases innovation and flexibility as new ideas are discussed by a selected wider circle of experienced staff, rather than imposed by upper management. These internal social networks will form the exoskeleton of the company and will result in richer, more engaged, and more flexible company structures which don't rely on command and control hierarchies to maintain coherence.

The key reason for slow change among insurers has not been a lack of foresight or a lack of investment, but has been inadequate thought about what the implications of 'what-has-yet-to-occur' which is difficult as the impact of WHYTO will always be uncertain and not posing a definite threat. To counter this requires a change to a flexible style of management which is opposite to traditional insurance risk-reduction modes. This has to start with the CEO, as most employees are paid to optimize the present, not to prepare for the future.

An example of the use of internal social networks is Canada's TD Bank Group, which after a series of mergers found itself internally disjointed. Launched in November 2001, TD's internal 'enterprise social network' has 4000 communities and thousands of blogs and wikis. It is used to communicate within company-wide networks of teams, to share expertise, to offer advice, to collaborate on projects, and to find relevant knowledge from employee profiles. TD found that the social network cut down drastically on phone calls, e-mails, and meetings. In particular, unwanted or irrelevant e-mails or meetings were largely eliminated. Most importantly, the network gives management the chance to lead and supervise in new, more flexible, ways. For example, sales managers can communicate with sales staff directly without going through branch managers. Status boards keep groups up-to-date. The collective intelligence of nationwide groups can be accessed and internal cohesion enhanced without gathering staff for conferences. It recognizes that the best ideas can sometimes come from junior staff, even cleaners or warehouse packers.

Implementing major technological, managerial, and cultural change is extremely complex and is frequently unsuccessful. A substantial issue is that investment in new systems has to occur while existing systems are maintained, even though the new systems may cannibalize the old. There are often major management hindrances. Eastman Kodak did not fail to transform because of lack of technical capacity - they invented the digital camera, or lack of customer demand - people still took photos. Kodak failed predominately because it did not market its new technology for fear of harming its old business. This held back change for a while but meant that when change did occur Kodak was swept away by it, rather than leading it. Insurers will only survive the coming disruption, will only lead it, if they acquire a senior leadership team which is dedicated to internal and external transformation and has the expertise to implement this.

Traditionally, however, insurers have a culture of confidentiality and discretion that works against the blossoming of a free-wheeling social network, whether external or internal. Regulations also limit the extent and scope of insurer communications with clients. So far, most insurers have limited social technology investments to minor areas like marketing functions and have not attempted to embed deep collaboration - they are still *talking to* clients and staff rather than *talking with* clients and staff. They still tend to view adverse customer or stakeholder feedback as an area to be restricted, rather than a quality growth opportunity. Insurance laggards fail to recognize that in today's world online communities will engage in discussion and reviews of their products regardless of what they company does - the only question is; Is this discussion happening with the company proactively involved or is it happening with the company excluded?

Given that these approaches require a substantially different style of management, and will take time to learn, insurers who delay experiments in learning the skills will find themselves rapidly falling behind rivals.

Based on these findings, the majority of insurers will probably not cope with the coming perfect storm of disruption, with at least half of existing insurers likely to face rapidly shrinking market share. Only about 10% of existing insurers are making the transformation changes required to ensure sector leadership. The leaders of the insurance sector in the future are likely to be external firms with outstanding skills in areas, like customer relationships, which insurance products can be added on to. Note that adding insurance as a product to a strong external disruptor is easier than transforming an existing weak insurer. It is arguably likely that the leading insurer of 2030 has yet to enter insurance.

An example of an outside entrant is the Malaysian Tune Group, which has used its subsidiary's, Air Asia, extensive IT-based customer data to enable the administration and distribution of insurance. It started in 2011 in travel insurance and then moved into life and non-life products, selling over 7 million polices by 2013, across Malaysia, Indonesia, Thailand, Singapore, and China. It currently has over 2000 agents, is busy opening physical branches, and is negotiating to buy major existing regional insurers. By 2016, a mere 5 years after it started, it is the leading SE Asian digital insurance franchise. Which SE Asian insurer foresaw that a discount airline would become a major threat?

Note that there are large financial implications for insurers in moving toward a more flexible, real-time feedback model. Insurers are used to the stability of fixed 12-month premiums so the use of dynamic short-term premiums could create uncertain fluctuations in cash flow which could be destabilizing. This will be easier dealt with by external firms which have existing large and uncorrelated cash flows.

End-to-End IT Systems

The heart of future insurance companies will be a high-quality integrated IT system, which aggregates, analyses, and provides data to users in a high-quality friendly format. Insurance has always been a data-intensive business and the future world of a tidal wave of big data will reinforce this trend. Survivors will be those who can undertake this IT transformation faster and more effectively than their competitors, including external disruptors.

Historically, companies have favored an incremental approach to IT changes, addressing the immediate point of pain and then handling subsequent issue as they arise. It has been viewed as just another shared service, to be allocated a budget appropriate to the urgent issues needing a solution. This causes issues as technology teams in different parts of the company independently address issues in discrete systems, hence creating islands of solutions, breeding complexity, and fragmented and redundant systems. For example, most insurer documents and communications are created via MS Word templates, yet these are difficult to extract data from, do not allow flexible formatting to differing platforms, do not allow easy integration with differing data formats, and use-activity is hard to track. These templates need to be in more digital friendly formats, which allow encryption and activity tracking. These systems need to allow two-way interactions, so customer inputted data or corrections are noted system-wide.

Neirotto and Paolucci (2007) show that most IT system investments in insurance have failed to deliver what was intended, with little correlation between IT investments and resultant improvements in competitive advantage. They argue that this has been because insurer IT investments have not been implemented with an adequate strategic vision. This is an issue as Breznik (2012) shows that successful strategic IT investment is a growing source of competitive advantage.

In the future, an insurer's IT system needs to be viewed as the company DNA, its core, around which everything else is built. This inherently means that the IT transformation is too important to be left to the CIO and the coders. The inputs and outputs need to be understandable intuitively by everyone in the company including customers. The human–computer interaction and data visualization aspects are vital. A superior system will enable workers to complete tasks faster and cheaper than competitors, and customers will judge the quality of an insurer's service primarily based on the ease of use and adaptability of its omni-channel interfaces.

It needs to be remembered that that cost of a legacy system is not the cost of the physical system, but the cost of the inefficient processes which surround that legacy system, as well as the opportunity cost of what the legacy system doesn't allow you to do.

A blockchain payment systems joined to smart contracts and electronic notarization will enable the simplification of administration chains, cut costs to pennies, and provide clear evidence and transparency of which actions have been taken, as well as providing a data evidence chain to follow the payment process. This will be the basis of the micro-payments which will underlie dynamic insurance. It will also enable mobile phone-based micro-insurance[3] in emerging markets or for younger customers.

[3]For example, it is common in Africa for a micro-insurer to offer a $150 life policy costing a few cents each week added to the mobile phone bill. Why not do this for renter's insurance?

Bain (2013) argues that the keys to successful IT transformation are: (i) getting the basics right - so that customer access speeds and reliability match that of social media firms; (ii) use a 'service-orientated architecture' to extend existing systems in modules, rather than try to replace the entire current system; (iii) focus on the highest priority areas first, so to get some wins; (iv) integrate technology awareness and systems into all business units, so IT is not just an issue for one department; (v) think primarily from a customer viewpoint, by understanding what their priorities are; (vi) track technological trends, and trial which innovations could be useful, and become fast followers of trends; and (vii) segment customers and defend high-value ones while discouraging low-value ones, offering the latest services to high-value customers. Tim Yorke[4] argued that the way we get away from legacy is to stop it being the monolith and putting architecture in places that allow you to plug things into an architecture that is flexible.

The rebuild of the IT system needs to occur in an end-to-end fashion with usability and flexibility as the core concepts. Three key strategic steps are required: (i) defining the end IT system, (ii) deciding which elements of the existing system have to change, and (iii) determining the sequence and scope of the change. The end IT system has to be defined in terms of the tasks it is required to achieve, divided into essentials and nice-to-haves. Example questions would be 'what information is required to actively excite customers about their insurance product?' or 'how is information best presented to actively engaged customers?' or 'where and how is data best stored so it is available to those who require it?'

The end objective of the rebuild of IT systems has to be to drastically reduce distribution costs and cut the marginal cost of offering clients choices to near zero. The system must have inherent flexibility as the transformation is not a one-off threat, but a change to a faster rate of change, a transformation which has no endpoint.

[4]Tim Yorke, COO, ERS, Insurance Post, Aug' 16.

The survivors will need a firm vision of a future of insurance which involves dynamic, flexible, modularized, customer-friendly products. This needs to be able to handle an ever-swelling tide of customer data, in a way which enhances the customer experience. Customers need to be provided with products which excite and a customer experience which matches what they experience from their favorite social media channel. Ad hoc amendments to existing systems will not achieve this.

Cost, Scale, and Platforms

A vital aspect of the required changes which insurance survivors need to undergo is reducing the marginal cost of transactions close to zero. Customization and dynamic premiums are not possible if the cost of each transaction is measured in hundreds of dollars and not in cents. The advantage of an end-to-end intensive IT system is that it allows this level of marginal cost to be achievable. The issue with these intensive IT solutions is that they have a high establishment and maintenance cost, defined as fixed cost. This type of high-fixed cost, low-marginal-cost environment obviously means that the larger a firm is, the lower average cost becomes. Added to this is the requirement of massive data sets before AI systems work efficiently. Hyperscaling is thus important as there is a massive scale advantage.

Against this scale advantage is the issue of IT complexity. It is a well-known problem that large IT transformation projects typically fail due to complexity; the larger the firm is, the more complex are the inter-relations, the program requirements, and the reform politics. Smaller, simpler, firms can thus create IT systems which are more efficient and can reform these faster. Since these new systems should have costs as low as 10% of the old systems, and given the increasing rate of disruption, flexibility and speed could be more important than scale and end-point cost. Thus, a key survival skill for insurers will be the ability to remake their IT system periodically.

It needs to be emphasized that in the future, the IT system will not just a stand-alone inside-company system. Successful insurers will need to work with a wide range of other firms in a business ecosystem, as discussed in a subsequent section. At the heart, this ecosystem will be an IT 'platform,' which links all the firms in a continual flow of data. The insurer's internal IT system will have to link seamlessly with this platform. The firms who control these platforms will dominate the future.

Flexible Programming

The two key requirements for future insurance business systems will be 'control' and 'flexibility.' Control is needed because mistakes in insurance can have major cost implications. Flexibility is needed to cope with ongoing transformation. Because programming large systems can be overwhelmingly complex, however, most systems of programming traditionally use a set step process of (i) ascertaining system requirements, (ii) defining system parameters, (iii) defining data, (iv) defining user-interfaces, (v) coding, (vi) testing and error handling, and then (vii) implementation.

Two major problems can occur during IT project creation to disrupt this sequence: (i) the external environment changes, so system requirements change, and (ii) as the implementation process progresses, the understanding of non-IT staff grows so they think up a series of new innovations. These are both valid reasons for amending system specifications. The problem is that a key business lesson is that IT projects tend to fail when the process is interrupted by changes in system requirements. Programming of large-scale IT projects is very complex as all elements are linked so that changes in one area can cause unexpected errors in another area. Programmers, therefore, prefer to complete the project to original specifications and then subsequently make ad hoc changes. This is done by dealing with requests one at a time, with extensive testing before each change is implemented.

Yet continuing with the original project when it is obvious that the external environment has changed can also often be a waste of money. This is particularly true if required changes are to the underlying business logic, so that ad hoc changes to a now ill-specified system open it to instability and inefficiency caused by a stable core system being disrupted by a growing mass of add-ons. The extreme difficulty of implementing large IT projects is why incumbent insurers are at a disadvantage against IT savvy external disruptors who have an up-to-date internal system. These new systems are based on newer inherently agile programming approaches.

One of the main defining characteristics of insurance survivors will therefore be expertise in IT system speed-to-market and system flexibility, combining control and flexibility.

Progress (2014) argues that one way to achieve this agility is by (i) breaking up IT projects into modules and (ii) using a 'business-rules management system' (BRMS). This is a decision system which separates the key business decisions from the rest of the programming activities. The essential problem is that for a programmer, key business requirements are no more important in coding than, say, data retrieval protocols. Progress (2014) argues that what a BRMS does is to separate out the key business aspects and by using an intuitively easy dashboard screen, put the ability to change these rules under the control of key managers or the relevant line manager. This enables business users to author, validate, test, and deploy rule sets as decision-making services with minimal IT knowledge. This places control in the hands of business users and sharply reduces time-to-deployment, hence creating IT flexibility. For example, for a quote calculation, the inputs and outputs would be agreed on by the managers and the programmers. Then, the premium calculation is defined as a set of business rules, within the stand-alone BRMS. This means that the managers know how to define the rule and the programmers know how to request a decision. This BRMS is then linked to all other areas of the IT system. The BRMS separation means that managers can change the premium calculation without impacting on other programming activities, as the only change would be in the premium outcome. This allows ongoing business flexibility while allowing the programmers to focus on usability, reliability, and performance.

BRMS systems should present decision rules in standard language to managers and allow extensive pre-deployment testing. This enables managers to play around with systems outputs in terms which users understand, and allows selected users from a wide range of areas to trial changes and see if they misunderstand uses. It is thus vital that the interface is user-friendly. The ability to make substantial changes to IT systems while the system is active has a transformative power for insurers.

An illustration of the problems inflexible software systems can cause can be seen from issues encountered with the New Zealand health insurer, Southern Cross's employer health policy. This policy is set up so it covers the employee and their family, with the employee as the 'policy holder.' Any claim has to be made by the policy holder, and all communication has to go via the policy holder. As there can only be one policy holder, Southern Cross' systems cannot cope with both of a couple, husband and wife, working for the same employer. The result of this inflexibility is a 1950s' Kafkian nightmare world, whereby if the husband is the policy holder, then the wife has to ask her husband to make claims, OK all procedures, and handle all correspondence. The wife is treated on the same level of competence as the children. Southern Cross are aware of this issue, but (i) the IT issues involved in making a change to the modern world are beyond them, and (ii) individual staff have no incentive to take charge of an issue and ensure it is solved. Thus, the 1950s continues to live on. Compare this to Tesla, who when notified of an issue, immediately accept responsibility, proactively work out a software fix, and upload that to all cars before 99% of owners are even aware the problem exists.

Digital Laggards

Most insurers are failing to meet the challenges described above. EY (2013) finds that nearly all insurers are currently digital laggards, trailing substantially behind most sectors in their use of digital channels and are not in-the-play in terms of interactive customer relationship software. International surveys consistently find that insurers are regarded by customers as the most backward service sector in terms of customer experience. KPMG (2016) thus argues that incumbent insurance companies are now in an epic battle to transform themselves to avoid becoming disintermediated by new digital competitors.

EY (2013) also finds that while insurers have aspirational digital ambitions, these are predominately unrealistic, as insurers do not have the flexible management systems, the staff, or the experience to compete with digital leaders; especially, as those digital leaders are themselves enhancing their expertise at a rapid pace, insurers are chasing a rapidly moving target and thus increasingly open to technological disruptive entry by those digital-savvy firms. In particular, expertise in inter-active social networks and use of mobile screens are weak, even though strength in these areas is vital to future success.

PWC (2014) argues that insurers are trying to meet the challenge by primarily focusing on e-commerce: that is, doing what they are already doing, but digitally. For example, nearly all incumbent insurers have inflexible, form-based, administration procedures. Insurance forms tend to be paper forms which have been digitalized, rather than rethought. While there may be legal reasons for forms to go back and forth, in 90% of cases, the procedure can be simplified, and forms made interactive. Insurers need to rethink chains of procedures from a customer viewpoint.

Only a few insurance leaders are taking the next step of utilizing their data capacity to develop deeper, more personal, and longer-lasting customer relationships, allowing them to move away from price. PWC (2014)'s survey finds that customers are more willing to engage with insurers than the products and Apps which insurers are currently offering allow them to. For example, 67% are willing to use telematics to cut premiums.

Customer relationships are also lagging. Morgan Stanley/BCG (2015) finds that currently insurers typically have one or less interactions with customers per year, and typically when contact is made, normally at claim time, the experience is disappointing. Their research shows that in terms of customer satisfaction with the online experience, insurance is one of the lowest ranked industries, 13th from 16 industries. The style of insurer–customer interaction makes this disappointment inevitable. This dissatisfaction is particularly high for small and medium business owners. Customer satisfaction decreases as they move from purchase to maintenance to claims to renewal. Therefore, the insurance market is extremely vulnerable to disruptive entry by firms with expertise in intensive and superior customer satisfaction.

Insurers have put substantial effort into market research and surveys. Despite this, they are currently struggling to understand the fine detail of the difficulties which customers are experiencing and the complexity of the experience from the customer angle. Surveys persistently show that customers rate the digital experience provided by insurers far lower than the insurers rate the experience they think they provide - insurers typically do not understand how backward their customer experience is. The current approach is not working; insurers are increasing being regarded by the younger generation as IT dinosaurs.

For example, many insurers have created a slick Web site, added a Twitter app and a Facebook page, and then have been stuck for what to do next. KPMG (2014) shows that while 69% of insurers say they have a digital strategy beyond a Web page, only 37% say it is aligned to the company's strategic objectives; 90% have only a limited idea about how to move beyond a 'push product' approach toward two-way active interaction. The few who have tried two-way communication are often burnt by internet trolls and stuck on how to handle this. They are uncertain about how to create regular contacts with their mostly older client base in a way which is useful to clients and thus welcomed by them rather than being seen as a distraction in busy lives. This shows that these insurers are missing the bigger picture that organizational change is needed. They are unaware that insurers must move beyond talking to customers to talking with customers. These are basic issues.

Transforming the company using a big data intensive approach would be a good start to solving issues. An example of how insurers could meet future challenges is the way the use of customer telematics can enable insurers to access the real-time feedback to integrate themselves into customer's lives, so they become irreplaceable partners and can offer value-added services. PWC (2015a) envisages areas like insurers being instantly aware if clients' vehicles or machinery breaks down and thus arranging repair crews, or being aware if clients are exercising and improving their health and thus reducing premiums, or being aware of driving errors and increasing premiums.

Another example is the use of survey or social media comments, where currently insurers devote substantial attention to have staff manually reading through. These can give rich insights into customer experience and is an area of future competitive advantage for the survivors. Yet in an era of increasing online commentary and rapid response expectations, it is simply not possible to manually analyze more than a sample. Comments need to be analyzed by language-based software, with staff only altered to key aspects or trends. Software should be able to respond by itself to the majority of generic issues. Yet, very few insurers worldwide have robust social media data AI capacity.

Omni-Channel Response

Floreddu and Cabiddu (2014) define an omni-channel response as simply meaning 'enabling a broader range of channels for establishing personalized relationships with customers.' However, it really means more than this, as an effective response to the threat of social media entrants requires a revolution in the way insurance customers are treated and the way information inside an insurer is collected and organized.

An omni-channel response does not mean new approaches simply layered on top of old; instead, the channels have to be integrated into a seamless fashion, so that customers can access any information or service they need via any channel. Any staff who needs an aspect of customer information, whether call center or actuarial or claims adjusters or marketing, needs that information in the most appropriate manner with key details emphasized. This means that if a customer initiates an inquiry via e-mail, then explores via the Web page, sends a text, and then phones a call center, all the queries and information the customer has provided, and the topics they are interested in, are available to the call center worker.

McKinsey (2012) notes that reliance on personal visits or phone calls or newspapers for product sales has just about died, and radio and TV viewing is increasingly restricted to the older generation. The insurer response has to be more than merely setting up Facebook or Twitter accounts; it is active engagement in a wide array of social media platforms. For example, if a customer is on the Web, they may prefer to engage with a person via Skype window in the Web page than a phone call. This is particularly important in India and Asia, where over 50% of customers share purchase recommendations via social media.

The focus should be on finding out the customer's problem and actively solving it, rather than actively pursuing a sale. This needs to be as efficient and low cost as possible. For example, 90% of quotes need no human involvement so should be instantly assessable once customer details have been imputed, whether this is via an agency, or the internet, or Facebook, or text, or phone app, or quote aggregator, or a broker. A field agent should be able to sell an underwritten policy, or process a claim, on a mobile device at one meeting, as long as standard parameters are met. Most insurance types should be able to be purchased, amended, and claims made via any channel. For example, NTUC Income, a Singaporean insurer, allows customers do all three via a phone app.

When a potential customer calls a contact center or into a branch, all the information which they imputed online should be available to the agents so there is never a need for customers to provide any information more than once. In a health insurance claim, for example, the doctor should be able to upload and sign documents online, the client should be able to Skype the claims adjuster and area specialist simultaneously, and thus have any claim paid within 2 or 3 minutes of the insurer being aware of it. This is only possible if all claims administration and checking are done instantaneously via software.

Poor customer experiences are increasingly destructive as customers have the means via social media to distribute their complaints to more than their friends. While previously companies facing bad news stories could delay and diffuse its effect, this is very hard to do with social media spreading news and opinions about it. Required response times to adverse news or complaints are now in minutes or hours, not days.

Millennials and later generations, in particular, are exhibiting a strong tendency to switch suppliers based on reputation or social media feedback. While the proportion of customers who currently use social networks to make product decisions is currently low, McKinsey (2012) argues that this will rapidly increase. Yet, only a few insurers encourage online unaltered reviews of their products and performance.

Social Dynamics

An increasingly important aspect of social networks is the ability of people to form groups with like-minded individuals across the globe, even if they have never personally met them. The social bonding in these groups has been shown to be strong, and thus, they have a powerful influence on product decisions. Any positive or negative service experience to one member is thus likely to have a wide-spread ripple impact. Some of these can involve members with high-level skills in particular areas who may thus become highly influential opinion makers. Failure to actively engage with these opinion makers can be disastrous, yet insurers are traditionally very cautious about engaging in debates about their products or customer relationships even within traditional avenues and almost never debate within the newer media. They need to adopt the new approach of being extremely open with information and actively engaging with society. They can only successfully do that if they have quality products and robust procedures which they are proud of. It is all about customer trust and producer reputation. Social media and online review sites can be powerful tools but because of the tendency of social media to attract a lunatic fringe, successful use can be difficult.

Producer reputation is thus growing in importance, yet is still not actively managed by insurers. An issue is that insurers may have find their social capital eroding without any way of tracking which potential customers are alienated, as currently insurer data systems can do little more than identify which customers had a bad experience. Insurers have little data on non-customers and why they choose to not purchase. Verint (2016) reports that the majority of customers who have a positive experience with an insurer will not give the insurer feedback, but will tell friends or write a positive review. The behavior of a client's social network is very powerful. For example, research has shown that if a person switches mobile phone providers, their friends are 7x more likely to also switch.

Data systems need to be able to identify exactly which areas of the process caused the issue and determine whether this is due to customer differentiation or generic failings. These need to be achieved in real time (inter-daily), with the results distributed on social media, so potential customers who are following the complaint are impressed rather than discouraged. Modern analytics can achieve this, yet are little explored by 90% of existing insurers. The data will soon be available, and if incumbents do not proactively use it, then external disruptors will.

Effective client engagement software systems also have the potential to drastically reduce client contact costs. There are significant scale economies to these systems, so there is a strong first-mover advantage, with innovators likely to attract younger, lower-risk, higher-profit customers, thereby trapping firms with lagging legacy systems in a downward spiral of shrinking non-digital customer base with increasingly higher risk and higher cost.

Effective insurer customer engagement systems have the potential to revolutionize the fortunes of successful companies. The key is to turn the currently typical unengaged insurance customers into engaged customers, who benefit from frequent positive insurer contact and who promote the benefits of the insurer within their social network. Bain (2015) argues that promoting-insurance-customers stay longer, buy more, bring in extra customers, and cost less to service. Their lifetime value is worth more than seven times the value of disengaged customers. Once insurers take the next step of using feedback from, and proactive engagement with, these promoting customers to change their products and processes, the value of these promoting customers doubles that figure.

Active Engagement

Active engagement with customers is thus vital. Yet, most insurers typically only interact with their customers at initial sales, at renewal, or at claim time. These give customers a very shallow and negative impression of the product, as their experience is restricted to the insurer demanding money or asking tough questions. This naturally leads to most consumers having a negative impression of insurers. The Edelman Trust Barometer for 2010 found that only 41% of customers trusted insurers 'to do what is right,' versus 71% for technology firms. The major reason for this different was a lack of positive engagements, with 90% of insurer engagements found to be stressful or negative. Surveys of those who have made major claims find that about 70% felt that the insurer 'did not care.' This is despite the industry rapidly paying 95% of all claims. What is missing in insurer–customer contact is not efficiency but empathy.

In contrast, digitally savvy companies monitor their customers on a continual basis over a wide range of channels. For example, a travel booking Web site, like hotels.com, uses its software to monitor a customer's travel progress and send updates by e-mail about possible travel issues, or to send useful hints. They heavily encourage customer feedback about hotel experiences and have a generous refund policy if issues arise. A single five-day trip may generate five or more customer contact opportunities, and knowledge learnt from customer feedback will be fed back into future contacts. The customer leaves with the impression of a company which engages and cares. Contrast this with a typical insurer - who may have non-positive contact once a year with a customer. These disengaged customers are receiving frequent, positive, contacts from a range of firms in other sectors, firms which could easily add insurance as an additional product.

This nonexistence of a sequence of frequent, positive, customer contacts is the basis of the current failure of the insurance experience. It is the main reason why customers feel disengaged from insurance, and why insurance is regarded as a product to 'be sold, not brought.' Insurers need to adopt a new mission - 'to make insurance joyful.'

One lesson from banking is that once customers could view their account balances online, they interacted with the bank Web site on a far more frequent basis than expected. One of the keys to a successful digital transformation for insurers is thus the use of social media and big data to create a sequence of continuous, enhancing, positive customer contacts. These contacts should be relevant and useful to the client, and include discounts or promotions tied to life events and loyalty programs, so that they are welcomed by the client as useful, interesting, and educational.

Insurers need to create some activity which incentivizes customers to interact frequently. Real-time dynamic premium pricing systems could achieve this. Research has shown that customers get an emotional reward for even small price changes resulting for their beneficial actions. These frequent contacts can be linked to news, to education, and to pricing specials. Innovative new idea could be trialed, like offering a 40% reduction in this weekend's driving premiums to those who achieve a set safe driving level for the telematics. These could be linked to specials from businesses in the wider ecosystem. This embeds the active customer engagement. A useful part of this engagement comes from friendly empathic staff. Therefore, management engagement inside the company is also vital. It also needs to be remembered that distributers are digital clients as well.

This type of engaged contact will also help at claim time. Many life and health insurers only assess client data at application time. Much data is second hand - basically insurers know very little about each client. The use of telematics and other data sources on a continuing basis qualitatively transforms the insurer knowledge base, enabling personalized underwriting and personalized advice on reducing their risks. Higher-risk clients can have their health condition monitored, and if they do not follow treatment protocol, insurers can increase premiums or withdraw cover.

Innovators

An example of an engaged innovator is AllLife Insurance which offers affordable life and disability cover to those suffering from existing conditions, who most insurers regard as uninsurable. By getting clients to agree to intensive monitoring and strict medical protocol, AllLife has both improved client health outcomes and increased profit, and is currently growing at 50% per annum.

Another example of an engaged innovator is the South African insurer, Discovery, whose health focused product, Vitality, which gives incentives for healthy living in ways which align with customer priorities. Discovery has consequently experienced rapid growth, while lowering customer risk profiles and cost. Vitality collects a significant volume and variety of client data, including wearable devices, and has discovered new links between client activities and health risks. It has discount arrangements with gyms and monitors client purchases of health food.

Clients are sorted into groups and are given vitality points on a real-time basis based on health-promoting activities, with higher groups offered substantial discounts on insurance and health-related products. Clients are given news on health-related areas. These innovations have for the higher groups reduced lapse rates by 52% and reduced mortality rates by 34%. Discovery has used its leading-edge software and engagement systems to expand rapidly, with joint ventures in the UK, the USA, China, Singapore, Australia, and recently Europe.

Competitive Advantage and Dynamic Capacities

One of the fundamental issues is how an insurer can achieve and sustain competitive advantage within a modern fast-moving business environment where ownership of scarce or rare resources is now insufficient. Teece et al. (1997) define 'dynamic capacity' as 'the firm's ability to integrate, build, and reconfigure internal and external competencies to address rapidly changing environments.' This ability to react dynamically is now more important than any existing advantage which the firm may hold over competitors. This is especially true in a case where potential competitors may arise from outside the sector, so management may be unaware of comparable strengths and weaknesses, thus the threat may arise unexpectedly.

Floreddu and Cabiddu (2014) disaggregate dynamic capacity into the capacities (i) to sense and shape opportunities, (ii) to seize opportunities, and (iii) to maintain competitiveness through enhancing, combining, protecting, and reconfiguring the tangible and intangible assets. This is essentially a firm's cultural capacity to visualize a different future of as-yet-to-occur challenges and rearrange physical and personal resources to meet those challenges in a manner which exceed the capacity of future competitors. The leading-edge use of IT and other technologies is a vital part of dynamic approaches, but they are tools, not core capacities. The core capacity is cultural.

Floreddu and Cabiddu do, however, argue that effective IT systems and innovative IT staff add substantially to a firm's dynamic capacity. To create an effective omni-channel response, they argue that firms need to evaluate existing IT resources, data, competences, and capacities to deploy different channels, what marketing activities implement to support the omni-channel strategy mix, and competitor capacities. IT resources need to be understood in terms of activities rather than jobs and modularized so that reconfiguration is easier to implement. Given that IT-based information flow will be at the heart of surviving insurers, required future skill sets need to be identified and capacity sourced.

Omni-channel approaches require a change from data collection and management focused separately in each channel, to a customer-centric approach with data from all channels integrated. This should also give managers a richer data resource on customer behavior and start to allow insurers to switch to a two-way rather than a one-way dialogue with customers.

Peer-to-Peer Insurance

Peer-to-peer insurance is a new and growing area. It involves groups of customers jointly insuring each other. There are many types of peer-to-peer insurance. The first type is often created by a third party, like an insurance broker who helps form customers into small groups, generally via a Web site. A part of the insurance premiums flow into a group fund, the other part to an insurance company. Minor claims by a member are firstly paid out of this group fund. For claims above the deductible limit, the insurer pays out. If there are less than expected claims, the member either gets refunds or a credit toward the next policy year. The broker is paid via a commission.

The second, more recent, type is similar to the broker model except that as the peer-to-peer provider is the actual insurance company. If the pool is insufficient to pay for the claims of its members, the insurer pays the excess from its retained premiums and reinsurance. If there are lower than expected claims, the 'excess' is given back to the pool or to a cause the pool members care about. The insurer takes a flat fee for running the operations of the insurance enterprise. A third type is where a group is set up by the members themselves, via a social or Web-based network.

The only real requirement behind these groups is that all group members must have the same type of insurance or something in common, such as being members of the same club or believing in the same charity.

In structure, peer-to-peer insurance is very similar to traditional mutual insurers. The main difference is the use of automated software, and Web distribution has substantially reduced administration costs. In that sense, while the growth of peer-to-peer insurers may reduce traditional insurer market share, the innovation does not involve any substantial alteration of the insurance market as a whole.

Some P2P insurers, however, are making use of intensive end-to-end software systems to rapidly expand. They also use big data and behavioral algorithms, speed of processing, and easy-to-use client interface, to make themselves feel natural to digital natives.

Cyber-Insurance

One of the future growth areas is cyber-insurance. PWC (2015a) notes that cyber security policies will be a rapid growth area, with insurers able to gain service-based revenue from monitoring cyber-attacks and proactively responding. The majority of corporations are only starting to recognize their vulnerability to cyber-attack even though there are currently 10,000 attacks a day worldwide. These attacks are starting to transform from minor incidental damage to major deliberate attempts to delete and destroy operating systems.

Defense against these attacks is well outside the capacity of most firms. For example, software producers post details of problems with their software on their Web sites, alongside the required upgrade patch. Reading these notices gives hackers explicit instruction on the vulnerability and thus how to exploit it. Software producers expect companies to download the patch asap. Currently, hackers will attack half of all computers within 28 days of a patch being released. Despite this being low-tech hacking, surveys repeatedly show that less than 30% of firms regularly download these patches, so that 70% are vulnerable. Research shows that 95% of firms do not have the capacity to proactively react to high-tech cyber-attacks.

The damage cyber-attacks cause, their cost, and the intensive nature of the response required are a huge opportunity to an insurer who can offer specialist expertise in data security and can alert clients in real time to attacks. It needs to be noted that as both industrial and service sectors integrate their entire production systems into complex software systems, hackers will not only be able to access data, they will also be able to disrupt production. Autonomous networked cars are at high risk and could be used in terrorist attacks. Even households will be vulnerable once house appliances are integrated, as net-linked appliances have very basic security and most owner leave them on the default password.

This market is substantial and is growing at over 30% per annum, so it is a useful source of new revenue. The advantages to insurers of being able to convince clients to allow real-time integration of the clients' telematic systems with the insurer's security alert systems are immense, as not only can the insurer take immediate action to stop failures as they occur, but also the access to a rich stream of real-time data on failure will allow them to gain new insights into causes of failure, and thus prevent them.

Even if insurers get a strong market share however, cyber-insurance is very difficult to price as it is a very new area and strongly subject to contagion and the possibility of catastrophes/black swans. It is like earthquake insurance in that there could be a long period of calm and low claims, leading to low premiums, and then an out-of-scale loss due to a worldwide software virus. Therefore, reinsurance will be vital in this area.

The major issue for insurers in this area is that success in this area demands extremely high levels of IT skills and very fast response times. Customers are far more interested in a company which can offer pro-active real-time protection than one which merely offers compensation after the event. Many new, currently unimagined, issues will arise, so insurers will have to possess a very high level of IT skill to stay up-to-date. Surveys find that most insurance managers are scared of the difficulties involved in combating hacking, rather than excited by its business opportunities. Actuaries regard the area as the preserve of techies. It is thus more likely that IT firms will dominate this area than insurance firms will.

Business Ecosystems

Insurers who respond aggressively and proactively to the opportunities offered by big data, telematics, real-time dynamics, and complex system analytics will leap ahead of their competitors who do not, as the per-transaction costs will drop by multiples. Note that this involves linking the insurer's data analytical system into customers' Webs of telematic items in a way which is very foreign to how insurers currently operate.

A key aspect of this is using analytical predictive systems to move away from compensating clients when things go wrong, toward predicting when things will go wrong and acting to stop problems. This is the kind of value-added services which will create the profits which will disappear from existing areas. While overall per-customer profit margins may shrink, innovators will compensate by an expanding market share, as well as expansion into new higher margin areas.

There are two aspects to this reinvention: (i) cutting distributions costs from over 100% of initial year premiums to closer to 5% and (ii) integrating the products into everyday life so they are seen as relevant. While this reinvention will probably occur initially in car insurance, it will rapidly spread out into all product lines.

Another aspect is the recognition that the range of specialist skills required to achieve sector leading expertise in each area will expand past what a typical single insurer can be expected to create. Insurers will thus have to make strategic decisions to specialize in a narrower range of skill set and to source skills they can't provide themselves from permanent partners in related areas. The success of insurers at integrating themselves into a wider at this network will be a defining feature of survival.

Morgan Stanley/BCG (2015) thus argues that an increasingly important competitive concept will be that of an interconnected 'digital ecosystem' of related companies, who interact to create combined services and generate value, rather than as large vertically integrated stand-alone bodies. This is not a new idea, as Iansiti and Levien (2004)'s survey shows, and originates well before the internet. They show that the use of ecosystems is a vital aspect of Walmart's and Microsoft's success. Despite this, the majority of management education focuses on the internal operations of a single company rather than how to integrate a network of assets, the majority of which your company does not own.

What is new is thinking of a network in terms of data flow, rather than physical product flow. The ecosystem is enabled by a central standardized software/technical platform, a 'keystone,' which connects producer and customer devices, applications, data, products, and services. This keystone is created by a platform owner, who allows producers and data services to interact in a customer-centric manner, and whose IT platform integrates the ecosystem. Note the key role of telecom providers in linking the telematic device to the cloud, so a continuous stream of data is downloaded. The size of these ecosystems will allow a degree of hyperscaling not possible for an individual firm.

An important competitive aspect of the future, therefore, will be that insurers will have to be a part of an interconnected digital ecosystem of related companies. An example would be a car platform which links automobile manufacturers to software providers, to telecommunications providers, to breakdown rescue services, to vehicle service providers, to insurers, etc., so customers can be offered an inclusive, yet customized product for autonomous cars. Google's current push to use the Open Automotive Alliance to establish Android as the automotive base system is an initial example of this. Working within an ecosystem is now standard for manufacturers. Car manufacturers' proportion of the parts they make has dropped from about 80% in the 1980s to about 35% now. Insurers need to undertake a similar outsourcing/insourcing analysis. Figure 5.1 shows possible insurance ecosystems.

The role of an insurer is thus to source and work with the leading platform innovators. The role of the platform supplier is to enable harmonious integration, to provide a high level of low-cost customer service, and to provide a wide range of real-time data to partners to enable continuous product and platform improvement. There have to be common data protocols and common application programing interfaces.

The key advantages of an ecosystem for insurers are that customer service can be provided by a firm with higher levels of customer relationship skills and social capital than insurers have traditionally demonstrated, as well as data feedback from a wider range of customer engagement areas than an insurance-only product would provide.

In terms of telematics, cooperation with related product suppliers has obvious cost advantages as telematics can either be jointly installed or have a dual purpose. Currently, it is hard for insurers to justify the

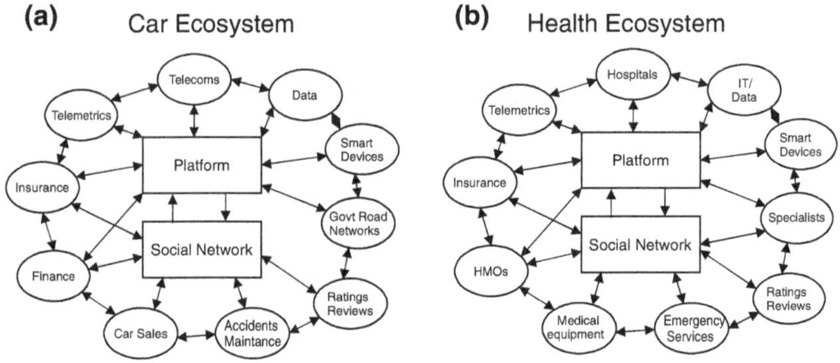

Fig. 5.1 Possible insurance ecosystems

cost of installing telematics in terms of reducing claim cost by itself. However, within an ecosystem, where data used by all parties, the costs per ecosystem member reduces to economical levels, once the profits from cross-selling by all members are factored in.

Ecosystem-wide integration requires that IT design is no longer about building or buying software systems on premises and ensuring the system links to a few external partners. It will be about understanding and integrating the end-to-end customer experience across the whole ecosystem regardless of the firm actually involved. Thus, an individual firm's IT system has to be viewed as just a specialized part of a greater whole, based around secure but open IT protocols.

The entire ecosystem has to seem seamless and integrated from a customer viewpoint, so they can move rapidly from product search to reviews, to sales, to media, to financing, to insurance, to maintenance, to claims, all on the same screen with no discernible difference between companies. The platform provider has to ensure this customer interface is high quality and user-friendly. The platform has to run 24/7 globally for millions of customers.

These systems will have to be designed from the start to be mutable, able to be adjusted as new innovations arise. The greatest error insurers can make to allow themselves to be integrated into an increasingly ad hoc spaghetti IT system. Strategic decisions will thus have to take precedence over strictly technical decisions.

This data integration is a challenge to insurers, as they have traditionally operated as closed systems with firewalls and encryption for reasons of security. Data has been used only internally and not shared with customers, nor have customers or other stakeholders been able to self-input or edit data. Creating the ability to integrate with the data systems of ecosystem partners, and myriad external data sources, while maintaining data security, will be a substantial challenge. This is too important to be left to CIOs.

The disadvantages of digital ecosystems to insurers who hesitate are obvious as others will rush to fill any obvious product gaps, and insurers who do not find a secure place in the leading digital ecosystems will find themselves increasingly disconnected from customers and limited to low profit-margin roles which others find unattractive. They are also likely to be left with higher-risk customers as the high-quality data which embedded digital ecosystem insurers obtain allows them to offer differentiated premiums to lower-risk customers, as well as substantially lowering cost via software-based customer contact and underwriting. There are substantial economies of both scale and scope with IT and big data so that successful first movers may develop unstoppable momentum. The initial leading ecosystems may grow to dominate.

The experience of Ant Financial is instructive. It is an affiliate of Alibaba, China's largest Web, e-commerce, and mobile device company. Ant Financial leveraged off Alibaba's huge client base to establish first a mobile payments system, then credit, wealth management, and international financial services, before introducing insurance. Ant started by offering merchandise-return insurance and has moved onto to health policies, and peer-to-peer lending as well as structured finance. These services are integrated and software based, with very low per-product costs. The combined client data created by Ant's wide product range and Alibaba's range of e-commerce, entertainment, healthcare services, etc., also allows Ant to leverage off an unprecedented width and depth of knowledge about clients to offer customized products and premiums in an inter-active manner. It needs to be noted that Asian internet platforms are moving into a range of services, especially financial, in a way in which western platforms are not. Therefore, the main platform disruptors are likely to originate in Asia.

It is an open strategic question as to whether insurers should establish their own ecosystems. It is unlikely that insurers will have sufficient client trust or software integration expertise to either front the platform or build it. However, insurers will have a competitive advantage in areas like selecting clients with the high profit margins, segmenting clients into group based on data-derived characteristics, supplying capital, and integrating across multiple segments. The kind of client profiling and segmentation offered by firms like Bought-by-Many is an example of a profitable direction for insurers. The main hindrance for insurers is that their legacy systems and instincts work against a model of deep-data personalized prices and premiums. Insurers will also face the problems that data across an ecosystem may be specified in quite different ways and will require substantial work to integrate.

Most current platform providers are not inherently interested in providing insurance; they just take the opportunistic view that it is one of many possible products they could provide via their platforms. If they can provide it cheaper and easier than existing insurers can, then they will invest. However, they will be happy to integrate existing insurers into their platform if those insurers show themselves able to live within the new digital world.

Note that the platform supplier cannot unduly exploit their power position, or the ecosystem decays, leading to a Yahoo style collapse. The nurturing and maintenance of partners are vital so system health is maximized.

Insurers will have to very clearly define the advantages and skill sets which they can bring to an ecosystem so they can sell themselves as the preferred partner to the leading platforms. Among possible skill sets would be experience with pricing product from intensive client data, existing client relationships, and brand name. Platform suppliers will assess applicant insurers on their ability to supply customized product at a low price and the ability to establish and maintain a very high level of client trust and engagement. Platform suppliers, who will probably originate in IT-based sectors, will have a very low level of tolerance for hindrances caused by legacy systems or instances of poor client service or inflexibility in coping with rapid change. They will expect an insurance partner to already have a state-of-the-art IT system which can easily be integrated into the ecosystem platform so the insurer can actively use the new flow of data and can immediately provide an exciting, dynamic, customer-friendly product which matches the high expectations of the platform's digital native customers.

Insurance pricing and approvals will have to occur in real time, less than one minute, based on data sourced from the entire ecosystem. This is easier to achieve than insurers currently assume because the premium does not have to be static, set at the start based on the insurer obtaining all possible information. Instead, because of constant telematic data feedback, premiums can be dynamic, with an indicative premium initially offered, which is then adjusted later based on revealed client characteristics from feedback.

To be able to achieve this, insurer IT systems need to operate at different levels; they must be intuitively accessible to customers, they must operate in real time, core systems must evolve and improve while rapidly absorbing innovations, new ideas must be rapidly trialed and implemented or rejected, costs in all areas reduced, while core business and cash flow is not unduly impacted. This will require both heavy IT investments and substantial cultural changes in insurance management systems.

It needs to be noted that many of the new online insurers have been established with the long-term aim of being sold to platforms, rather than expanding as stand-alone insurers. It may be hard for existing pre-digital (dinosaur) insurers to convince platforms owners that they would make a better partner in the new world than the savvy digital insurers.

It is vital to note that within a wave theory of innovations, successful embedding into an ecosystem can only be a short-term solution. When next wave of innovation occurs, customers within the ecosystem will probably not be aware of or prize the attributes of the new innovation. The failure of both incumbents and their best customers to respond forces innovators to seek new customers which often results in the majority of companies within the incumbent's ecosystem failing. The issue for an incumbent is that it is not just a matter of one incumbent switching, as they will either have to convince the new innovation ecosystem to slot them in, or convince the existing ecosystem to switch. Failing that, an insurer needs to attempt to jump ecosystems, to a platform which offers newly superior technology.

A key attribute of insurance survivors will thus be managing this network of partners, ensuring that the entire network out-performs and the insurer continues to provide the product, data, and process attributes which makes it an attractive network partner. The inter-connectedness of the ecosystem means that the insurer will have to assess the performance of partners to ensure they provide leading-edge attributes and take action if the failure of these partners starts to create issues.

Data within an ecosystem is an issue. IP, liability, privacy, profit sharing, regulatory/compliance all are more complex with a seamless ecosystem, when the customer may not be aware of which company they are interacting with. Software licensing & data ownership and CRM issues arise. The reputation of each member may depend on the CRM of other partners. The ecosystem needs an agreed set of standards, skills certification, and vender performance management. Flexibility and fast reaction need the ability to trial beta systems and accept product/system failure as part of that. Agreed compensation protocols will be required.

Social Capital

Insurance purchase can be an emotional experience for customers and can tie in with major life events. Insurance is an intangible product and often complex for consumers. Thus, consumers have a tendency to either delay purchase or rely on advisors or brand trust, rather than do their own research and evaluation. Effective use of social media to identify these trigger events and induce customer purchase can thus be more useful in insurance than other products, yet insurers are laggards in social media use. As previously explained, this leads to the idea that 'insurance has to be sold' as consumers, even though they recognize the importance of the products, feel disengaged from the process. Insurance is also different from most products as nothing of value is given at the time of purchase, only a promise of good behavior at a later date.

Thus, a key to future insurer success is to recognize the importance for insurers of customer trust and thus social capital. This trust is not created by advertising but by actions and presentation style. Nahai (2013) shows how customers judge their level of trust in Web sites based on a range of specific subconscious indicators. Insurance Web sites do poorly on nearly all of these indicators. Very few insurers have, for example, used crowd-sourcing to generate ideas for policy features, an idea common in technology firms. Danske Bank in Denmark did try this with new product ideas and gained substantial feedback, which improved the product and its mobile phone interface. Insurers will have to invest heavily to keep up-to-date with the latest trends in Web and customer relationships software, while offering a client-focused interface which is sophisticated enough to appeal to the IT savvy and easy to use so it appeals to the less IT savvy. Morgan Stanley/BCG (2014) found that 55% of customers would switch based on a better online experience.

Floreddu et al. (2014) point out the growing importance of social media in determining corporate reputation and the increase in avenues available to aggrieved customers. They use the example of Dave Carroll who after 12 months unsuccessfully requesting that United Airlines replace a guitar they broke wrote a song ('United breaks Guitar') which he posted on YouTube. This received over 1 million views in the first 4 days and led to United's share price dropping by almost 10%. United then replaced his guitar and have since taken great care to handle customer complaints with speed. When the next broken guitar complaint occurred, they flew the complainant to China to consult with the maker - an exercise which cost about $50,000, but gained them invaluable social media credit.

Halliburton and Poenaru (2010) reported that only 13% of customers trust advertising, whereas 90% trusted recommendations from friends and 70% trusted online customer reviews. They also found that key internet commentators were vital. Unless insurers are proactively engaging with customers and key stakeholders they don't have a future.

People don't now place much importance on advertisements or statements of a company, as they do on what their family, friends, and social networks say. The main origination source for customers in the future will probably be social networks. Morgan Stanley/BCG (2014) shows that 68% of under 50-year-olds currently source a substantial proportion of the information they require for product decisions from social networks, and this is steadily rising, and 54% will use social media peer recommendations when buying insurance in the immediate future. Of particular interest is that 72% have, or will, researched social media comments on customers' claims experiences before they decide on an insurer. This is strongest in the rapidly growing markets of Asia. Thus, establishing high social capital is the key to future success for insurers.

Existing insurers, however, despite having established brand names, tend to score very low in surveys of social capital. Internet retailers, social Web networks, mobile phone operators, and even banks consistently rank higher than insurers in social capital surveys. This gives new entrants from the IT sector, firms who have high social capital, a distinct competitive advantage. Unless insurers transform this area, they are extremely vulnerable to disruptive market entry. Companies which act like AllState did in the 2007 Pincheira case will find that their level of social trust plummets at an unsustainable rate and given the growing need for positive feedback, will find their client base disappearing. Reputation is not what you say but what you do day to day - 'do you meet or exceed customer expectations?'

The basic element of social capital is trust, and to establish this, insurers need to be seen as 'authentic' on an intuitive level by potential customers. Digital natives will be more skeptical of the insurance promise than prior generations and more prone to flight at any hint of non-authenticness. Insurers need to generate brands based on more than intensive advertising in disappearing media formats. Authenticness is a fuzzy concept, and potential customers will use a range of quite subtle clues to assess it. Outbound sales and inbound claims need to be integrated, as Perdue University (2014) showed that the swift resolution of a complaint is often the most effective time for additional sales.

A key issue for insurers here is the degree of 'client stickiness,' which is the extent to which clients stick with existing suppliers and do not periodically shop around. Traditionally, personal insurance has had a high degree of stickiness, while general insurance had been lower, but still moderate. Insurers have thus not had to work hard to retain existing customers and have focused their advertising on attracting new customers. One of the key customer benefits of digital platforms is the extent to which it drops the costs to customers of both product comparison and supplier switching, in term of both cost and time. Therefore, products which are presented on a digital platform have sharply reduced levels of stickiness. In many markets, insurers have tried to slow this process by refusing to cooperate with aggregator Web sites. However, the attractiveness of these sites to the newly digital-savvy public means that this strategy only delays the required changes and makes the market more attractive for an outside disruptive entrant. Refusing to engage with platforms is a dead end. The key question should be; Does a quality ecosystem platform exist?

To be successful in a world of social capital, insurers will have to collect a qualitatively wider and deeper range of data so that they can gain true insights into the lives of clients. Insurers do have an advantage over possible entrants as customers are used to providing a wider range of personal data than for other producers. In the world of real-time data, however, the type of data required is qualitatively more personal, and therefore, deep trust is required in the holder of that data. There is clear potential for this data to be misused, and even a single example of misuse could devastate an insurer's social capital.

An issue with current insurers is that they collect client data for reasons which do not relate to the products provided. An example would be requiring a client's full name, phone number, and street address before a sample quote can be provided, without justifying why the street address or phone number affects the quote. Insurers also tend to ask standardized information from each customer, even if they already know the information, or if the information is irrelevant for that client. In a digital era, insurers will need to provide up-front a clear reason for each item of information, and why it is in the customer's interest to provide it. Any hint of information being collected for the company's own benefit, rather than the client's, will destroy social capital. Getting clients to spend time providing unnecessary information also sends the message that the insurer is disrespecting the potential customer's time.

Companies have to view social media as a positive way to communicate with customers, not as a threat. However, speed is vital - it used to be said that the first 24 hours of an adverse story were vital, but now it's the first 24 minutes.

Insurers will have to accept that digital native clients will review and rate their services and Web platforms online in detail and insurers which do not offer a very sophisticated, efficient, and friendly service, will be rated down, and will struggle to attract new clients. Firms will rise or fall in ratings fast, so that long-established businesses can disappear in a few years. Firms which try to discourage ratings will effectively disappear from the view of digital natives, whereas firms who encourage ratings and respond to feedback will find demand strongly increasing. Using social networks to advertise to related groups will multiple this tendency. McKinsey (2012) argues that use of social network links can, through client acquisition and fraud detection, generate insurer value of up to 26% of the cost base in call centers.

It is vital for insurers to realize that customers are likely to be already creating social media network discussions around the insurer's reputation and customer service, based on existing social media sites. If an insurer is not aware of this, then the social capital of the insurer may already be negative. Insurers cannot hide their head and ignore it. Neither can insurers expect to engage with social media once their reputation or client trust is lost, as commentary will simply move to closed sites. Proactive engagement is necessary from the start so enough trust is retained to allow aggrieved customers to engage with the insurer.

Customer engagement will thus become a key insurer skill. As discussed before, this partly means creating frequent communications with customers which are not just related to annual renewal notices or claims. It is vital, however, that this communication is useful to the customer and welcomed by them. This is easier in some areas than other, but once telematics are widely used, it is possible in all areas. Health and life insurers can offer health news as well as feedback on customer efforts. Car insurers can offer dynamic premiums based on current driving, or traffic info. For example, insurers could link car telematics to the central panel LCD and change premiums minute by minute based on driving, thereby encouraging best-practice driving. House insurers can link with household telematics, appliance suppliers, and interior designers to offer household news about appliance innovations, grocery specials, or design ideas. Insurers, however, do not have a wide enough range of skills to engage with customers by themselves. The key component is thus the selection of market-leading media partners and the creation of a dynamic business ecosystem, where an attractive package can be created.

Insurers will have to actively monitor their social capital and have proactive programs to increase it. Insurers will have to offer a 24/7 service across a range of social platforms and modes. They will have to actively engage with clients and promote publicly available customer feedback. This openness goes against the grain of current insurance companies, who tend to conduct market research in secret and not make adverse feedback public. This is no longer viable, as it signals fear and generates mistrust.

Communication also has to be two way, instead of the traditional insurer response to a crisis of issuing bland reassurances and not actively listening to grievances. In a digital age, successful companies will have to positively invite public feedback, negative as well as positive, as they will be judged by potential clients on their response to that feedback. Digital natives are impressed by companies who actively engage in public debate and provide reasonable justifications for decisions. In a digital age where firms have lost control of market research data, adverse feedback can no longer be hidden, but has to be rapidly handled. Customers understand that not all feedback will be positive and will judge based on overall trends. Insurers who are successful in terms of Web site usability, security, cheapness, Web site and response speed, customer support and feedback implementation will give customers positive reasons to move from their current insurer. Any insurer, however, who is consistently rated low can expect to lose any new customers.

It will be particularly important that insurers are seen to respond rapidly and positively to claims as reviews around claims experiences are the key factor in establishing favorable overall social capital. One key to this is to ensure that customer engagement occurs over the full range of insurer activities and not just around claims. Insurers may have to strategically manage flexibility around claims payouts, as a tight claims policy will immediately be spread via social media and will rapidly be reflected in shrinking new business. Given that it is easier to lose a reputation than gain one, a short-term tightening reaction to a spike in claims has the potential to adversely and severely impact on market share.

Insurers will thus have to understand that in a digital world claims refusal will be substantially different, with each claims refusal which is based on a 'difficult-to-understand-interpretation-of-abstract-terms' likely to be widely discussed and reviewed on social media, with multiple customers able to comment on each claim refusal. Even one clear example of what is seen as 'unreasonable behavior' will impact very negatively on insurer reputation, as the speed and breadth of adverse social commentary multiples reputation losses. A repeated pattern of 'unreasonable' claim refusal will have the potential to destroy an insurer's social capital. Given the dynamic nature of future policies, insurers with a bad social media rating may lose customers and cash flow very fast.

Because bad press from poor claims responses will impact on the reputation of the wider ecosystem, affected insurers may lose their place in prized ecosystems as other parties will fear contagion of their reputations. While mistakes can be forgiven by social media discussions, any systematic adverse pattern of behavior will be quickly and widely discussed. Insurers will have to understand that the creation and retention of client trust are the basis of future success.

Aggregator sites will evolve which allow customers to mix and match insurable activities. For example, one insurer may offer cheaper rates when the car is in the garage, another offers the best rate during commuting, and a third offers the best rate for the summer vacation drive. Companies may decide to offer 'specials' for Friday's commute to those who switch for that morning from competitors. Note that firms which create effective aggregation software will sit at the center of the ecosystem and thus collect customer data, will hold immense power over insurers, who will be relegated to mere product suppliers, always at risk to disintermediators who specialize in one insurance activity.

Insurance Policies

Most current insurance policies are technically complex, with the exact definition of terms having substantial weighting in terms of costs. Therefore, it can be vital that customers take time to read and understand policy detail, and possibly seek expert advice. This is necessary in a world where insurance is a permanent and serious purchase, where policy terms and premiums are static.

However, in the future world of digital real-time polices, the overwhelming bulk of customers will have neither the time nor the inclination to carefully read and understand small print - very few online customers read the 'terms and conditions' in a mobile phone tick box. Heavily reliance on policy terminology is also unrealistic from a customer viewpoint if polices terms and premiums are dynamic, ever-changing based on telematic feedback.

Customization of insurance to the needs of individuals is also vital. As non-Americans understand, Starbucks coffee is low quality and high cost. The reason why Starbucks is so popular is that customers can specify a range of choices, so they can get exactly what they want - not 'Starbucks coffee' but 'John's Coffee.' In this kind of customer expectation world, insurers cannot continue to offer 'life insurance,' where the terms and conditions are standard across multiple customers. The future has to be an individualized policy, whereby customers can amend terms and conditions and thus premiums, until they get 'John's Life Insurance.' Yet, it is unrealistic from an insurers' cost viewpoint if policies are customized to individual clients.

The only solution in the more dynamic future is for policies to be offered as modules, with terms vastly simplified and standardized. There, however, also needs to be some flexibility within conditions or added options, so customers can go on a Web site and play around with adding or subtracting, and watching how the premiums change, until they are satisfied with their customized version.

The meaning or terms also have to be very clear. It is vital that what the average customer expects a term to mean is what the term is interpreted by the claims side to mean. It is vital that what the insurer seems to an average person to be offering is what they are actually offering, not what the underwriter thought the term meant. Polices will have to be explained in clear and simple terms and be able to stand up to a systematic public comparison with those of competitors. Insurers who do not distribute their policies online and allow them to be compared and reviewed in detail on social media will disappear from customer view.

Digital natives will not accept insurer's defining policy terms based on legal rulings or long-established industry practice if these seem unreasonable. Thus, insurers will have to establish policy terms based on what seems reasonable to a wide range of the public. Premiums will have to be costed on the basis of a high level of customer goodwill and an understanding that long-term reputation and social capital are substantially more important than short-term gain by a strict claims policy. Since claims clarity and goodwill versus competitors will be reviewed and compared online, insurers will have to ensure their policies and claims responses are at a level they can be proud of.

Premiums will need to be individualized and policies modularized and made dynamic. An additional factor is that because feedback from telematics will give customers a good idea of their risk level from each activity, customers will no longer be prepared to be lumped into a pool of higher-risk individuals. This feedback will be dynamic, and some customers may find this exciting.

Policy diversity across insurers thus needs to be reduced and plain English terminology adopted. This has to occur alongside increased customization, flexibility, and real-time information flow. For example, a major problem with some Web-based policy application systems is that customers often don't understand the choices or terminology within an excessively lengthy questionnaire, so use advisers to guide them through the process, defeating the purpose.

This policy customization is not possible if humans are involved in setting up or administrating policies, as the marginal cost is too high. The advantage of a software-intensive underwriting and administrative insurer is that the marginal cost of allowing individualization drops to a viable level. There is a strong first-mover advantage to this software-intensive system as human-based competitors will find themselves unable to compete and faced with falling revenues alongside rising costs of software investments.

References

Accenture. (2013). *Running Business for Growth*. Insurance-blogs.

Adner, R. (2002). When are technologies disruptive? A demand-based view of the emergence of competition. *Strategic Management Journal, 23*(8), 667–688.

Bain & Company (2013). *For Insurance Companies, the day of digital reckoning.*

Bain & Company. (2015). *Global digital insurance benchmarking report 2015: Pathways to success in a digital world.*

Boston Consulting Group. (2016). *How digital switchers are disrupting US auto insurers*, July 26.

Breznik, L. (2012). Can information technology be a source of competitive advantage? *Economic and Business Review, 14*(3), 251–269.

Capgemini/Efma. (2016). *World Insurance report*.

Christensen, C. M. (1997 & 2011). *The Innovator's Dilemma* (4th ed.). Harper Business/Harvard Business School: USA.

EY. (2013). *Insurance in a digital world: The time is now*. Ernst-Young: New York.

EY. (2014). *The future of underwriting: A transformation driven by talent and technology*. Ernst-Young: New York.

Floreddu, P. B., & Cabiddu, F. (2014). *Multi-channel strategy and sustainable competitive advantage: A dynamic capacity approach* (Working Paper). University di Cagliari.

Floreddu, P. B., Cabiddu, F., & Evaristo, R. (2014). Inside your social media ring: How to optimize online corporate reputation. *Business Horizons, 57*, 737–745.

Halliburton, C., & Poenaru, A. (2010). The role of trust in consumer relationships. *ESCP Europe Business School.*

Iansiti, M., & Levien, R. (2004). *The keystone advantage: What the new dynamics of business ecosystems mean for strategy, innovation, and stability*. Boston, USA: Harvard Business School Press.

IBM. (2006). *Insurance 2020: Innovating beyond old models.* USA: IBM Institute for Business Value.

Johne, A., & Davies, R. (2000). Innovation in medium-sized insurance companies: How marketing adds value. *International Journal of Bank Management, 18*(1), 6–14.

KPMG. (2014). *An industry transforming: Insurers and intermediaries in a fast changing, digital world.* White paper.

KPMG. (2015a). *Automobile insurance in the era of autonomous vehicles: Survey results*, June.

KPMG. (2015b). Big data: The big factor driving competitive advantage. *Frontiers in Finance.*

KPMG. (2016). *Empowered for the future: Insurance reinvented.* KPMG International.
Markides, C. (2006). Disruptive innovation: In need of better theory. *The Journal of Product Innovation Management, 23,* 1.
Martinez, A. G. (2016). *Chaos monkeys: Inside the Silicon Valley money machine.* London, UK: Ebury Press.
McGill, R. (2008). *Technology management in financial services.* London: Palgrave-Mcmillan.
McKinsey. (2012). *The social economy: Unlocking value and productivity through social technologies: Consumer financial services.* McKinsey Global Institute.
McKinsey. (2016a). *Transforming life insurance with design thinking*, May.
McKinsey. (2016b). *A digital crack in banking's business model*, April.
McKinsey. (2016c). *How companies are using big data and analytics*, April.
McKinsey. (2017). *A future that works: Automation, employment, and productivity*, January.
Morgan-Stanley/BCG. (2014). *Insurance and technology: Evolution and revolution in a digital world.* USA: Boston Consulting Group.
Morgan-Stanley/BCG. (2015). *Insurance and technology: The emerging role of ecosystems in insurance.* USA: Boston Consulting Group.
MyCustomer/Microsoft. (2015). *Customer experience in the insurance sector: Insight Report.* UK.
Nahai, N. (2013). *Webs of influence: The psychology of online persuasion.* FT Press.
Neirotti, P., & Paolucci, E. (2007). Assessing the strategic value of information technology: An analysis on the insurance sector. *Information and Management, 44,* 568–582.
Peters, T. J., & Waterman, R. H. (1982). *In search of excellence.* New York, USA: Harper & Row.
Progress Corticon. (2014). *Flexibility and control in insurance operations.* White Paper. www.progess.com.
PWC. (2014). *Insurance 2020: The digital prize—taking customer connection to a new level.*
PWC. (2015a). *Insurance 2020 & beyond: Necessity is the mother of reinvention.*
PWC. (2015b). *Insurance banana skins.*
Siegal, E. (2016). *Predictive analytics: The power to predict who will click, buy, lie, or die.* USA: Wiley.
SwissRe. (2013). *Automated underwriting: Threat or opportunity?* New York.
Teece, D. J., Pisano, G. G., & Shuen, A. (1997). Dynamic capacities and strategic management. *Strategic Management Journal, 18*(3), 509–533.
Verint. (2016). *Customer-Centricity in financial services: The rules of engagement.* White Paper, USA.

6

Impact by Type of Insurance

Autonomous Vehicles

The majority of the insurance industry managers are under the impression that rise of autonomous driving will not impact on car insurance until 2030 or later. This is not true, however, as fully (100%) automated cars are not required before technological advances severely disrupt the car insurance market. Semi-autonomous car technology will have a substantial impact far sooner. One impact is that premiums will drop substantially as there is mounting evidence that even semi-autonomous drive cars are safer than manual-only cars.[1] As of August 2016, all the crashes advanced semi-autonomous cars have been involved in have been caused by human drivers either running into an auto-drive, or in one case, a human deciding to put the Google car in manual mode.[2]

[1]US National Highway Traffic Safety Administration data show that as of 2016, semi-autonomous cars had a 60% lower crash rate than fully manual cars.

[2]Note that the Aug 2016 crash of a Tesla car did not involve an autonomous car, but a car with advanced cruise control capacity, which required constant human supervision.

M. Naylor, *Insurance Transformed*, Palgrave Studies in Financial Services Technology,
DOI 10.1007/978-3-319-63835-5_6

Since advances in vehicle automation depend on perfection in a range of physical technologies, like sensors, rather than just software, overall advance may occur slower than software-only technology. The pace of autonomous technology is, however, faster than many insurers recognize.

One reason is that while media has been focused on fully autonomous Google cars, a range of other manufacturers have made substantial progress in semi-autonomous cars. Note that these are 90% autonomous cars but have the advantage over Google cars, as there is no need to intensively pre-map roads like Google does. In April 2015, an Audi with Delphi technology drove from San Francisco to New York, 3400 miles of road it had never driven on before. Its human driver only took control on 1% of the densest city roads. 2016 and 2017 saw the start of extensive trials of cars which will incorporate 80% of the technologies required to be fully autonomous, including highway adoptive auto-cruise (speeding up and slowing down with traffic, passing other vehicles when necessary, and alerting the driver when their exit is near so they can take over), autonomous braking, the ability to handle stop-start traffic jam driving, and self-parking. While a driver will be required to be at the wheel, the car may be in auto mode 80% of the time. Most elements of this range of technology will probably be introduced into the 2018 generation top-of-the-range Mercedes, BMW, and Audi cars.

Car manufacturers are deliberately introducing these innovations in steps, to allow customers to get used to them. There will thus not be a big moment when cars go from 100% human control to 100% automated; instead, cars will go from 40% to 60% to 80% to 100% over the next decade or so. This self-drive ability will be extended to suburban streets by 2020. Fully autonomous cars will follow with some commentators arguing this will involve up to 50% of all cars sold by 2025. Similar features are being installed in trucks. It is very likely that black boxes to record crash details will be required in all cars. The EU made basic black boxes compulsory on all new cars from 2016.

One aspect of these cars which commentators have so far not explored is their ability to be in constant Wi-fi communication with other cars and with a centralized data center. SwissRe (2016) argues that by 2020, more than 2/3rds of cars sold will have some form of connectivity, or 260 million extra cars a year. There are two kinds of connectivity: (i) *tethered*, which involves a 3rd part device such as a mobile phone and (ii) *embedded*, which transmits from a device which is part of the car. Most current networking works via tethered devices, but since most new cars will feature screens with Internet, embedded networks will soon become the norm. All Tesla cars have embedded networks. A substantial proportion of commercial trucking fleets is already networked as operators find that data on vehicle location, on driving time, etc., offer significant scheduling advantages. Therefore, most of the innovations in this area will probably be trialed on trucking fleets.

Since embedded connections have two-way capacity, there will soon be a vast stream of driving and road data available to all those companies within the car ecosystem. This will allow insurers to analyze risk in far great detail, but will also accelerate advanced driver assistance systems and autonomous driving software. Because of this data, by 2020, new cars should be able to handle autonomous driving in most expressway and stop-start driving environments, as well as self-parking.

The impact of networking will be substantial. Currently, an autonomous car is maneuvering along a road by itself forced to recognize other cars and road dimensions and conditions with very limited external feedback. The current situation of one autonomous car traveling down a dumb highway is thus like a blind man moving by trying to find the footpath edges and bumps by echolocation. It is extremely difficult for even a smart car to tell a rumpled newspaper from a rock, to identify a faded pedestrian crossing, or to spot a temporary roadworks sign. Battered road signs can be hard to distinguish.

A major hindrance in auto-drive development was that prior system, like the Google system, requires cars to retain huge data-bases of road layouts and finds it hard to deal with roads which have not been intensively pre-mapped. Gomes (2014) thus argued that these mapping and computer requirements meant that nationwide autonomous cars may never be possible. Google currently needs to employ people to spot road signs, etc., from its road videos. This is impossible for a large country.

The real breakthrough with autonomous cars will therefore occur when they are networked so that they can communicate with each other, with road side objects, and with a central IT database. This is because networking removes existing stand-alone limitations, as real-time feedback from sensors will mean that even when automated cars are manually driven, they will map roads and add to the collective data base. With each car-mile driven, more data is added, so roads get extensively mapped. And, as long as one autonomous car drives along an unmapped road, then all subsequent cars will be able to access a data base to receive details on that road. Tesla cars are networked, so Tesla continually collects road data from every car as it drives along, so their road data is constantly growing and takes note of changes in road conditions. Once a substantial percentage of cars have network capacities, the cars can start to talk to each other. If we add to this 'smart roads' which have embedded telematics in street lights, traffic lights, pedestrian crossing, in the lane-maker bumps, or metal incorporated into road paint, then cars will receive continual feedback on what it needs to know. The first car through a roadworks diversion can explain to the rest of the cars how to handle it. Road workers can put down Wi-fi-chipped cones which will map out for cars exactly how to drive around the road works. Rural roads or off-grid tracks can be added to the data base.

There is the possibility of issues with initial navigation systems if roads are predominantly dumb. It has become not uncommon for humans using software-based navigation systems to blindly follow the navigation advice even if it is obviously faulty. The issues could be worse with a car, which may be less aware of surroundings and no way of rescuing itself if it gets lost. However, once smart roads are created and cars networked, then real-time feedback from other cars, as well as a database of all cars which have made the journey previously, should avoid these issues, except in very rare cases, for which protocol can be established.

Thus, the real breakthrough with autonomous cars will not be the ability of cars to sense their surroundings, staggering as this is in engineering terms, but their ability to communicate with each other, and with telematics, to collectively gather information on roads and the movements of other vehicles. The future situation will be like the man gaining sight, as telematics will light up the road way, roadside objects, traffic lights, and the position of all other cars.

Networked cars can continually pass on info to each other in real time on car position, road conditions, exchanging data on current position and speed, where they are going, mutually arrange directions so they can travel faster and closer, and receive information from cars miles ahead as to road or traffic conditions or roadworks, over as many future miles as is required so that each car has a far better idea of the road and other cars than any human driver. Cars can then even coordinate with each other over traffic information to enable the group of cars to mutually choose traffic routes which minimize total traffic. The cars will talk to traffic lights and traffic management systems, sending flocks of cars through lights, or re-routing down less busy streets. The highway system will be able to move cars as coordinated groups, like flocks of birds. Traffic police will be able to issue general instructions to all cars in an area, if a diversion is needed, and to stop cars they have suspicions about. The collective wisdom of cars will vastly exceed what each individual car could achieve.

These cars will be, thanks to radar and networked roadside markers, able to operate just as safely at night, or in fog, or storms, as they will not be solely dependent on visible light as human drivers are. They will talk to parking space sensors before they arrive, will be allocated an empty space, will drive to it autonomously, and then charged for it. Each car will not need extensive onboard maps or large computing power, as these can be stored in the cloud.

It is useful to note the huge size of data which new model cars produce. A car can have 1000 sensors, the processing capacity of 20 PCs, and produce about 25 GB of data per hour. This will increase at an exponential rate, especially once cars start to network. The complexity of car software is rapidly exceeding the complexity of the mechanical engineering, so that an auto-drive electric car is essentially a computer on wheels. This complexity has left some automobile manufacturers struggling, e.g., the components in Ford cars are supplied by a range of contractors, each with their own software systems. This means that even though Fords are heavily computerized, Ford is struggling to leverage this due to difficulties in integrating the parts into an in-car network.

Over time, this huge data base of real-time information on the movements of cars will allow algorithms to be created to make autonomous cars far safer than any human driver. The system will treat cars driven by human drivers, or non-networked cars, as dangerous and warn all other networked cars to establish wide leeways around them. Note that fast computers, visual sensors, big data, Wi-fi, telematics, cloud-computing, and advanced software will combine in a way, whereby the sum of the parts vastly exceeds each individual contribution. There are significant scale and scope economies, with possibilities exponentially expanding as the percentage of people and devices connected rise. Exponential rates of improvement in auto-drive software imply that by 2020, human drivers may be 10x as unsafe as 90% self-drive cars and over 100x less safe by 2025.

It is vital to note that autonomous driving is not the only car software innovation made possible by networking. An example is the Tesla S model which is externally linked to the Internet. Since all parts of the Tesla S are connected to an internal computer, this allows Tesla engineers to spot a problem and solve it by uploading a software fix. Tesla engineers can download data from all the cars, discover common issues, and invent improvements, without leaving their office. Sensors inside the car will continually monitor performance, for example, using an exhaust sensor to monitor fuel burn and then adjusting engine parameters to improve performance. Wear rates of different parts can be tracked and changes made to manufacturing. Software can alert owners when parts are near to failure and book maintenance, which a self-drive car could drive itself to.

Once a car is networked, then required software upgrades can take place by push-downloads without the owner being aware of it. This means that Tesla owners discover that their cars receive continuous upgrades in capacity without them having to do anything. For owners, their experience of owning car becomes like a software product - with continual improvement expected. This will be particularly useful once electric cars are common, as these are easier to modify remotely. For example, Tesla has been able to substantially increase the capacity of its car battery cells by software updates sent remotely. Insurers need to be able to link into this car software network, or they will be left with no market.

In another direction, Mercedes-Benz already allows their car to inform home-software that the owner is coming home, so that heating and other home appliances like the coffee maker or oven can be turned on. This link could be used in other ways, for example, the fridge or food cupboard could send a shopping list to the mobile phone, and the car can then communicate with local shops to find the best specials and deliver the driver to the optimal combination of shops.

The elderly, disabled, or children could be driven rather than have to rely on the courtesy of others. Those who drink would have no issues getting home. Some of the autonomous vehicles may look nothing like today's cars. For example, if a vehicle is delivering pizza or groceries, why would it need seats or height? - it could be built like a smallish box. A self-drive taxi may only need space for one or two people.

Automobile Insurance

There are many issues for insurance companies around autonomous cars. The biggest is that once networked autonomous cars are freely available, KPMG (2015) estimates that there will be at least an 80% drop in crash rates. Car crashes kill more than 30,000 people in the USA annually. Think of all the factors that affect a human driver: physical (tired), emotional (angry), psychological (confused), or intellectual (distracted) factors all come into play when a person gets behind the wheel. Based on current experience, the US NTSB estimates that since 93% of all car crashes are caused by human error, so it is possible that crash rates for auto-drive cars could drop by more than 90%, even if autonomous cars are not 100% crash-free. Semi-autonomous Tesla's have so far had a crash rate 5% of other cars. Volvo has an aim of eliminating car crashes caused by the Volvo by 2020. Theft will disappear, as these cars will also be nearly impossible to steal, as they will both require voice and face recognition to start and can be programed to lock the doors and deliver the thief to the nearest police. This leaves only damage caused by external factors like things bumping into the car or weather.

The result of this is that car insurance premiums will fall drastically. All State's 2015 annual report admitted that automated cars could destroy their auto-insurance business. Those want to drive manually will pay a hefty surcharge, probably 10 or 20x the automated premium, so drivers will choose to forego self-driving if possible. Even before autonomous cars are used, telematics will enable insurers to identify the bad driving habits of each driver and reeducate them, as well as identifying the worst drivers, who create an abnormally high number of crashes, and use high premiums to discourage them from manually driving. Override controls could be used to disable cars when drivers exhibit dangerous patterns of behavior, or enforce time restrictions on learner drivers. Car insurance in an era of very few accidents is a terminal industry.

International Transport Forum/OECD (2015) predicts that use of auto-taxis will cut the number of cars used in major cities by up to 80%, and that private vehicle ownership will only exist in less populated rural areas. While this decline in per unit premiums may be off-set somewhat by a rise in vehicle value, in general, it is likely that a severe drop in premiums will impact heavily on insurer cash flow. Activities like supporting sales branches could become unviable.

As noted earlier, commentary has been mainly focused on 100% autonomous cars, and since these may be a decade or more away, insurers have felt no sense of urgency. However, the key factor for insurers is the arrival of 80% autonomous cars, and these started to arrive for high-end models in 2017. Most manufacturers have already conducted extensive trials. Since these 80% cars will have far lower crash rates, declines in cash flow will impact on insurers from 2017 onward at the premium end of the market.

Even using conservative assumptions, KPMG (2015) estimates that by 2040, car insurance premium cash flow will be no more than 40% of the current size. This is probably too conservative as SwissRe (2016) found that current-tech adoptive-driving systems will, by 2020, reduce crash rates by 45%. Note that this includes both driving and parking incidents. More advanced systems are expected to reduce crash rates by up to 90%, with most remaining crashes involving crashes caused by 3rd party low-tech cars. Therefore, I would argue that using reasonable assumptions, the impact on premium cash flow will be probably more intense and a lot faster, with premiums dropping by over 80% by 2030. Before this, the turning point, where intense and probably destructive completion starts, is likely to occur before 2025, conceivably from around 2022. Changes to car insurance will be enhanced once cars are networked, and a separation can be made between insurance when the car is parked and insurance when it is driven, as well as the introduction of real-time dynamic insurance. Note that since the weak link will be human drivers, car insurers can be expected to offer substantial discounts (up to 90%) to drivers who keep the car in autonomous mode. The dynamics of this is discussed in more detail in a subsequent chapter.

Three probable outcomes arise from the above changes: (i) *Accident frequency will decline* to where the difference among driving behaviors becomes negligible, and it is difficult to charge a meaningful premium for insurance. (ii) *Insurance will take the form of commercial product liability* instead of personal driver liability as we let software do the driving. (iii) *Vehicle utilization will rise and cars on the road will decline* as one car can serve the driving needs of multiple travelers per day.

Given that crashes caused by the autonomous cars will likely be the fault of software or the telematics, product providers may well have to cover costs under normal product guarantee laws, or will provide very cheap life-of-the-car insurance at purchase time. Volvo and Tesla have already announced plans to offer buyers automatic car insurance with purchase, with Audi and Mercedes indicating similar plans. Issues with product-based insurance are discussed in a subsequent chapter.

It needs to be remembered that the automobile industry itself is on the cusp of its own disruption tsunami. At the center of this is Tesla and Elon Musk. While Tesla is currently very small, Musk is promising to produce 1M cars a year by 2020 and predicts they'll be larger than Ford by 2025. By 2020, the Tesla model 3 will be the same purchase price as a gasoline car, yet energy costs will be 5% (or less if paired with home solar charging). Musk expects, that by 2020 or soon after, to increase recharge distance to 620 miles/1000 km, exceeding gasoline cars, along with Level 4 autonomy. All Tesla cars come with the hardware required, so level 5 timing becomes an issue of how fast AI can be evolved.

Within a business ecosystem, the power will reside with the firm which receives the continuous steam of driving data, which will be the key to underwriting risk. Unless insurers take charge of this stream, they will be reduced to suppliers of risk algorithms for dynamic insurance. Samsung is investing heavily in the autonomous car parts suppliers and can be expected to be a major platform center, sub-contacting insurers to provide product/system-based insurance for the entire group of cars.

Insurers want access to a database of telematics data to help them set personalized premiums for individual drivers, but arrangements governing how that information is gathered, managed, and accessed could be subject to scrutiny by competition regulators. Telematics data can constitute personal data, and therefore fall subject to data protection laws, on the basis that it records the activities of individual drivers, or a number of individuals. Insurers will need to be able to make sense of this data via a model with predictive capabilities based on frequency of driving, hard braking, sharp turns, time of the day, and a handful of other factors to determine the personalized premium for each customer based on risk profile. UBI programs offer many advantages to insurers, consumers, and society. Underwriters also need to be aware of specifics of ADAS systems and insist that repairs are qualified and sensor alignments are checked regularly.

Linking insurance premiums more closely to actual individual vehicle or fleet performance allows insurers to more accurately price premiums. This increases affordability for lower-risk drivers, many of whom are also lower-income drivers. It also gives higher-risk drivers the ability to control their premium costs by incentivizing them to reduce miles driven and adopt safer driving habits. Fewer miles and safer driving also aid in reducing accidents, congestion, and vehicle emissions, which benefits society. Note that there are two differing concepts; pay-how-you-drive (PHD), where rates change based on risk, and pay-when-you-drive (PWD), where rates change based on usage. Both of these would be used to set dynamic insurance rates.

Car insurance is thus the test area of the new IT revolution, the 'canary in the coal mine'. The key variable is the speed of the spread of the 80% or 90% technology. BCG (2015b) estimates that the per unit cost of 90% technology, predominantly sensors, will initially be about $6000 extra per car, while car premiums may drop by $400 per year. While manufacturers may initially restrict the technology to high-end cars as a sales incentive, the desire to spread the upfront cost over as many units as possible guarantees its spread to middle-level cars by 2020. Costs will drop rapidly as volume builds so that all but the lowest end cars will have the technology built-in by 2024. Young drivers in the UK, who are charged an average of £2300 per annum premium, are already switching to telematic-based policies. Note, that in contrast to the high cost of the current method of installing black boxes in cars, future cars will come with sensors pre-installed.

Some commentators have argued that the high cost of sensor systems will limit their appeal. However, since networked cars will be able to form conveys (closely packed cars moving at high speed) on expressways, they are likely to get priority lanes and get passengers to work far faster. Alternatively, these auto-cars can network with each other and work out mutually advantageous commuting routes. These substantially faster commuting times for auto-use will be attractive to customers and make them willing to pay a premium. Note that all cars produced since 2006 include an OBD chip which records miles driven speeds, speed of turns, braking, and gas consumption. Linking to this is sufficient to allow insurers to offer driving based discounts, so black box installation is not necessary. Progressive already offers insurance based on this to its customers.

The scope for stand-alone car insurers will rapidly shrink, with their main future business backing product guarantees by manufacturers. At this point, stand-alone car insurance is a niche product, as for most drivers it will either be a software-linked product or a lifestyle choice for the few remaining drivers who choose to manual drive despite the high premiums.

BCG (2014) argues that the major mistake insurers are currently making in the telematics area is that of inadequate levels of investment. A small product portfolio in this area heavily restricts insurer flexibility as there is not much they can do without large enough scale to gain a competitive advantage. BCG (2013) states that correct use of car telematics changes key elements in the insurer value chain and is positive for insurers as (i) it enables insurers to select and price individuals more accurate, offering innovative solutions to low-risk groups, (ii) it enables accurate and rapid assessment of claims, (iii) it enables insurers to predict loss incidents, and (iv) it enables insurers to differentiate their value proposition and protect their customer base from direct offerings. It is urgent that insurers gain experience with telematics in the auto area as this is vital learning for insurers to cope with telematic expansion into other areas of insurance. A very good starting area for gaining experience with big data derived from traffic telematics is integration with commercial vehicle operators who are already using real-time location and usage data. Some insurers have already created this ecosystem link. The future of cash flow for car insurers will be from the provision of web/telematic-based car services, rather than from risk-based premiums.

It is useful to understand that within the wider car ecosystem, there will be growing sources of cash flow, though these will tend to arise from offering dynamic services, rather than a static risk-based insurance product. Insurance survivors will those companies who can transition toward an engaged customer dynamic relationship, whereby they became an active part in customers' lifes via data-based services. The problem for insurers is that, in general, they do not currently have adequate skills or social capital to be able to compete against IT firms who already have active engagement with customers.

Imagine that you step into a self-driving car of the future. The car's heads-up monitor issues an alert: 'I sense that you've been drinking. I probably don't need your driving assistance, but there's always a slim chance I may, in the event of an unexpected emergency. If you want to operate this vehicle under the influence of alcohol, your insurance rate for the next 12 hours will increase to $2 per hour. Press here to accept this.'

Insurers will have to switch away from linking their insurance to one product to a general client activity. Thus, instead of insuring a client's car, they insure the client whenever they use a share car, even if that car is always different. This switch to a mainly share fleet will require the use of a 'mobile client risk profile' which is a software-based tool actively monitors the telematic feedback from whatever car the client is driving. Thus, premiums are based on a driver, and their habits, and not linked to any particular car. Note that this implies that monitoring client use needs to be automated, as clients can't be expected to inform the insurers whenever they use a share car and exactly what they do with it. This is especially true for autonomous cars, as users may send these on a trip without physically being in them - like picking up children. Insurers whose costs are not low enough to provide this type of micro-cover will not last long.

McKinsey (2016) argues that insurers will need to complete a range of tasks before they can move into offering successful dynamic auto-insurance products. They need to (i) identify and engage with an ecosystem to create the appropriate system of telematics, (ii) create appropriate and sophisticated analytical tools to integrate data from disparate sources, analyze it, and provide useful feedback, (iii) create user-friendly customer interfaces, (iv) enlarge the customer data pool, (v) digitalize interactions, and (vi) rapidly expand the depth and scope of internal capacity. The vast increase in sensor feedback data, and the ability to adjust driving parameters based on feedback from other cars, will mean that insurers will have a far more in-depth understanding of conditions which led to crashes. They will then be able to set dynamically adjusting premiums, based on those conditions.

There are major risk-pricing issues if the majority of driving decisions are taken by software rather than a human driver. For example, do you set premiums based on the risk rating of the software or the ability of drivers to oversee it and take control if things are going wrong?

There does not seem to be an issue of customer reluctance to purchase these semi-auto-drive cars. It is interesting to note that on social media discussions of current 80% autonomous highway mode cars, the predominant feedback was 'why only on highways?' BCG (2015b) found that only 22% of those they surveyed were averse to buy a self-drive car, and it would only take relatively minor evidence of lower crash rates and therefore lower premiums, to convince most car owners to switch. Capgemini/Efma (2016) shows that the younger generations anticipate that they will self-drive cars in far higher numbers than insurers expect. Evidence from auto-taxi trials shows that female passengers strongly prefer taxis without a human driver and would pay more.

This indicates that the general public is generally accepting of autonomous drive vehicles, supporting the auto-manufacturers' strategy of introducing the technology in stages. After all, adaptive cruise control and self-parking are now accepted as normal so the next step to autonomous highway cruising is small, and the next step to autonomous city driving is small, and so on. It is insurance companies which are lagging, and they will either have to catch up or lose their market to new entrants. If we add to this the possibility of differing policy options like pay-as-you-go premiums as well as rapid claim handling due to telematic feedback, then insurers who are not market leaders or fast followers will be facing bankruptcy.

An additional issue is reduced private car ownership. ITM/OECD (2015) postulates that there is likely to be a move in larger cities away from car ownership toward rental or toward shared cars. SwissRe (2016) points out that car ownership rates in large western cities are already dropping. Many urban drivers would car share if they could find certified safe fellow-passengers going from around their home to around their work place. This is an easily solved software information issue, for which apps are already being developed. Auto-taxies are currently being trialed and will be introduced widely by 2020. The removal of the driver ensures that they will have low marginal costs, especially if shared, well below the cost of driving yourself. BCG (2015a) estimated that auto-taxis with that least two occupants would be 35% less costly than current taxis and comparable with mass transit. Uber estimates costs will be more than 50% below current taxi rates. BCG thus argues that within cities, auto-taxis or car-sharing will become common, resulting in declining rates of private ownership - why own an expensive vehicle which just sits in an expensive car park 95% of the time?

Current estimates by industry analysts are that by 2025, 25% or more of all cars could be owned by fleet owners such as Uber or Lyft, predominately autonomous drive. These fleet owners will have the capacity to largely self-insurance, especially if the predominate cause of accidents are software related. For insurers, this ownership switch to fleets run by a firm like Uber is a concern as it will lead to sharply lower margin bulk deals. Elon Musk argues that by 2030, the low margin cost of driver-less drones means that individual ownership of a cars for urban dwellers will seem like owning a horse[3]; something done for leisure enjoyment. John Zimmer of Lyft argues that this transition could occur by 2025.[4]

[3]https://www.businessinsider.com.au/elon-musk-owning-a-car-in-20-years-like-owning-a-horse-2015-11?r=US&IR=T.

[4]https://medium.com/@johnzimmer/the-third-transportation-revolution-27860f05fa91#.kxmuehhxd.

House/Contents Insurance

The use of big data and analytical techniques means that house insurance will be able to be priced to individual houses, using data like house building materials, distance to neighbors, proximity to schools or transport routes, soil conditions, flooding risk, etc. House telematics can be linked to insurance company computers to report intruders, or fires, etc., to accurate track risks in real time. Houses will have finger print or voice-activated security linked to doors or windows. Sensors linked to electrical wiring can shut down electricity flow if overheating and a potential fire is detected. This will lead to less claims and thus lower premiums. Aviva has mapped ground conditions in every UK city, allowing them to risk-rank house by house.

House contents insurance also faces a substantial drop in premium income, as nearly all products will come with networked chips, thus enabling the owner or police to track the location of stolen goods in real time, and remotely disable them. This will make burglary unprofitable. The end result is that burglary rates will plummet, fires will be controlled faster, and customers will be discouraged from building in higher-risk location. This will substantially reduce insurance premium cash flow.

Estimates in general predict at least a 60% drop in risk for a connected house. Of course, house upgrades occur at a far slower rate than car renewal, but as insurers fight over an increasingly smaller premium flow, profit margins will fall faster than risk levels. The overall impact on premiums cash flow will be less than that of car insurance, as the risks like flood or earthquakes will remain mostly unchanged.

However, given that general insurers tend to obtain 40–60% of their income from car insurance rather than house/contents, then as car insurance becomes a shrinking overall income pool, competition can be expected to increase for house customers, thus reducing profit margins in all products to near zero. Given that the expense ratio for P&C insurers in the USA (costs and claim over premiums) has increased from 96.2% in 2013 to 100.3% by 2016, any reduction in premiums due to InsurTech would leave many P&C insurers financially non-viable. On the upside, effective real-time customer relationship systems combined with house level data will allow innovative new customer contacts and potential income from sale of data-based services. For example, clients can be alerted about bush fires, flooding, or tornados likely to affect their house. Alerts about a recent spike in local burglaries can be packaged with education from a related home security firm.

The increasing use of household robots will add an expensive new item to be insured, and thus, a valuable new area of premium flow in the short run. Insurers may be able to compensate for lower-risk premiums by working with their business ecosystem to provide additional services like linking with security monitoring firms to capture telematic data for all kinds of risks houses face and respond to those in real time. This can include health telematics so an appropriate response by an ambulance etc., can be arranged. The insurer will only gain from this if they are proactive and use their skills in data interpretation to set themselves up as the co-coordinating center of this response network, rather than just a supplier of a decreasing value product.

Disruption in this sector can be expected to occur by 2020. Neos Insurance in the UK is already offering house and contents insurance alongside a suite of smart-house telematic-based services. Their profit comes from service fees as their focus is on preventing adverse events and reducing insurance need.

Life Insurance

PWC (2014) argues that life insurance products have tended to be overly complex and expensive to distribute, and this has restricted sales to well-off market segments or older customers, keep client contact to an occasional payment, and has ensured low conversion rates and building client resentment.

Yoder and Rao (2015) argue that the main reasons for the percentage of western populations holding life cover dropping over time has been (i) decreasing percent of the population aged 25–40, which has decreased the market, (ii) a sharp decrease in death rates below age 70, which led younger couples to devalue the need for premature death cover, (iii) increasingly product complexity and, (iv) a shift from products being sold via workplaces toward selling to individuals. These have led to an increase in the difficulty of selling products which has necessitated the creation of a network of brokers and agents to explain the products to clients. The commissions which this network requires have led to unfavorable distribution economics, both reducing insurer profits and reducing demand from clients.

Yoder and Rao then argue that Generations X and Y expect simple products, transparent pricing, quick delivery, and being able to deal with product suppliers where and when they want. Insurers have been far slower than other product suppliers in recognizing this change in consumer expectations and argue that this has led to three interconnected downward vicious cycles. The first is that the need for advisers leads to slower service, to decrease in product transparency, to increased product complexity, and therefore a need for advisers. The second is that increased distribution costs lead to decreased insurer profitability which leads to decreased life sales which lead to slower service and which finally leads to increased distribution costs. The third is that increased distribution costs lead to customer reluctance which leads to a need for insurance 'to be sold not bought' which leads to the need for advisers which lead to increased costs. They contrast these cycles with the mutual fund sector which has grown strongly and has experienced a virtuous cycle of simple products, decreasing distribution costs, sales without promotion, commissions dropping below 1%, increased sales volumes, and rising profits.

Yoder and Rao thus argue that life insurance, and the associated income replacement and trauma products, needs to be reimagined. They need to be made simpler, easier, and faster to obtain, with cheap and transparent pricing and distribution costs. They need to be made more relevant to the lives of young couples who see premature death as extremely unlikely. Life insurers need to reduce administration costs to near zero and offer simpler higher quality products. This can be done by allowing customers to self-create policies by combining blocks of products into a suite. The focus has to be on engaging more deeply with customers so purchases are made with greater understanding, so a lifecycle services approach can be created. Data analysis has already proved to be highly predictive for death rates, especially during the last two years of life. One US insurer is using its predictive end-of-life data model to provide estate/tax/trust/counseling/palliative care services. Similarly, telematics could potentially have a large impact on life and health insurance, engaging clients with insurance services, adding useful new sources of insurer income, and providing a stream of valuable data.

One suggestion Yoder and Rao make is to shift emphasis from death toward promoting health and quality of life. Wearable bionics can then track blood contents and fitness levels, scan for signs of sickness, and alert clients to potential problems. Discounts can be given for health-related activities, warnings given if clients engage in unhealthy activities. They argue that this shift will change client perceptions about the insurer, integrate them as a part of weekly life, and encourage younger people to take out policies. Even though health telematics are still crude, several companies have tried this approach with significant success in terms of client reaction.

Yoder and Rao (2015) argue these advances, combined with automated distribution and underwriting, will decrease costs and induce younger, more affluent, clients to see cover as relevant and therefore proactively seek out cover further lowering distribution costs. It will allow clients to be individually underwritten and grouped into small market segments. It will allow detailed data analysis so that deep understanding can be gained around the relationship between client activities and well-being and sickness.

Feeding the insights back to clients so they can understand how their life choices impact on their health will both improve client life choices and create the sense of connectedness which the insurance sector is currently lacking, and provides a clear value-proposition to clients. Note, however, that insurers will find it difficult to get clients to agree to share a real-time stream of personal information unless they can establish both inherent trust and a clear benefit. From the subsequent reaction of clients to this increased information, insurers can then build behavioral models of how to incentive clients to reduce their risk profile, possibly by trialing differing methods with separate groups. The increasing richness of the data will build a virtuous cycle, whereby insurance is sought, not sold.

McKinsey (2015) argues that competition will ensure that most of the benefits of the changes will flow to clients in terms of lower premiums or increased access to health information. Insurers who do participate will face large investments in data collection tools and software. Insurers who do not participate will rapidly lose market share among the non-chronically sick, and will face eventual bankruptcy.

Health Insurance

Health insurance has also been heavily criticized for offering an overly complex and unnecessarily diverse product range. This results in a high lapse rate and subsequent high product distribution costs. Energesse (2015) argues that the major reason for policy churn in Australia is the customer confusion caused by customers being offered a choice between more than 25,000 different policies. High lapse rates (over 20% of customers per annum with some insurers) mean high lost revenue and a significant financial impact on insurers due to the relatively tight net profit margins. In addition, insurers and customers waste a significant amount of time negotiating and resolving issues related to poor purchasing and claims experiences. Foster (2012) found that while 80% of companies claim that they deliver superior customer service, only 8% of customers agree. Given that 70% of customers decide to buy based on how they feel they are treated, this is a major industry issue.

Energesse (2015) found that the highest lapse rates for health insurance occur within 6 months of purchase, and that the number one reason for purchase was price. They argue that this is caused by two factors: (i) customers find health insurance products confusing and do not understand the value of the product. It is thus a grudge purchase dominated by fear. In the medium-term customers try to rationalize their purchase and suffer regret, as they realize the product does not meet their actual needs. (ii) Insurers are thus forced to compete on price so have developed products with complex exclusions and restrictions. Customers do not initially understand these, but in the medium term, they either realize the product's poor quality or feel uneasy at the non-understandable complexity. This creates a vicious cycle in customer retention and experience, whereby customers struggle to understand benefits, so they switch to cheaper products or options, which then do not provide the required outcomes at claim time, which then sour them on the concept of health insurance.

Energesse argues that the real reason for poor customer experiences can be summarized into these four major themes: (i) customer perceptions of confusion and lack of value, (ii) regulatory and competitive forces, (iii) sub-optimal systems, processes, and data management and, (iv) health system dynamics.

There are some key factors inhibiting client perception of value. One factor is that health insurance has unusual delayed gratification, so that many customers do not understand their product choice until claim time, when it is too late to switch providers. The second factor is that since only 5–10% of customers ever make a claim, most customers perceive very limited value. The third factor is there are few opportunities for the insurer to engage deeply with the customer. The fourth factor is that payments tend to be made direct to health providers so that customers may not be aware of the costs of their treatment. These factors mean that today's customers perceive lower levels of customer service from health insurers than they do from other companies which they deal with. There is thus a substantial likelihood of customer switch if those companies offer insurance. The current structure of the insurer–client relationship means that there are very opportunities created for the insurer to impress the client with superior engagement. This has to change, as was discussed in an earlier chapter.

These issues can only get worse given the drive toward individualization of underwriting and increased customization. The only solution to these issues is for health insurers to reinvent their administration systems, and offer simpler, higher quality products. As with life cover, the way to do this is to use software as the base administration system and create policies by combining blocks of products into a suite which customers can pick and choice from. The focus has to be on engaging more deeply with customers so purchases are made with greater understanding. There also needs to be greater integration between the software systems of insurers and those of health providers, so that the customer experience is seamless.

Given the complexity of health insurance products, involving humans in giving advice is vital. These staff need to have excellent, complete, information on customers, as well as the ability to transfer client advice to dedicated area specialists. The software then needs to be capable of generating policies, handling claims, as well as interacting with hospital software systems and extracting required information from documents created by a wide range of medical staff and arranging health care. This needs to be in real time, so that transactions can be completed while the customer is being advised. Digital natives expect responses in minutes rather than days, let alone weeks.

An example of health innovation is the agreement in the UK between DeepMind and the Royal Free NHS Trust to use algorithms to assess and monitor kidney function tests and send alerts when blood results are abnormal. In the UK, 10,000 people a year die from preventable acute kidney problems. The App can also be used to monitor sepsis, liver dysfunction, and general organ failure.

Health insurance will be as affected by telematics as other insurance areas, as the growing use of wearable biosensors will allow hospitals and insurers to collect real-time data on the biochemical changes which occur before a person gets sick, and thereby start to predict illness and alert that person to seek appropriate medical help. The positive media news an insurer would receive from such a lifesaving response would be invaluable.

The problems with current measurement methods of patient health is that: (i) they provide only episodic readings, (ii) they can require high-cost physical collection, (iii) patients often fail to adhere to treatments, and (iv) they do not detect problems which occur before a patient exhibits chronic symptoms. Currently, if a doctor thinks there is an issue with your health, (i) they have to see you, (ii) request a blood test, (iii) you have to physically attend a blood test clinic, (iv) the blood sample has to go to a specialist, (v) the results have to be sent to the doctor, and (vi) you have to go to the doctor to discuss treatment options. The test also only shows blood contents at the time of the test. Continuous monitoring via biosensors overcomes all these issues, as they provide dynamic real-time data and sends real-time blood analysis to the doctor's AI program, alerts them if an issue occurs, and tracks blood contents vs activity on a 24/7 basis. This can be linked to sensors in your bathroom scales and what your food cupboard thinks you ate.

McKinsey (2015) argues that the use of biosensors will cut the cost of treating chronic disease by 50%. These sensors include (i) wearables, which collect information via the skin, (ii) implantables or injectables, which collect more intimately, and (iii) non-wearables, which collect information periodically such as Wi-fi-linked scales. These can be unobtrusive - MC-10 and Sano Intelligence already produce patches, 'biostamps,' which stick on your skin and connect to a mobile phone App. These stickers can detect a broad range of metrics, e.g., blood pressure, hydration, glucose, oxygen saturation, temperature, heartbeat, stress, sunburn, sleep levels, wound healing, drug levels, and movement patterns. They are powered by mobile phone transmissions. MC-10 is working on stickers which can be fitted to internal organs. They could also be used to control pill boxs or medicine injectables.

While there are serious regulation issues with implantables or injectables, beta-versions of wearable devices are available now and are expected to exceed 1.3B by 2025. Injectables are in clinical trials and should start to be available by 2020. In the meantime, there has also been work on including sensors in mobile phones which can analyze blood components by scans. Pills bottles will track when medicine is taken, and blood sensors can then track the biochemical response to the medication. Hats can track brain patterns. Mobile phones can record food purchases. More intrusive telematics will face medical trial delays so maybe only be used outside of higher-risk patients before 2028. Nearly, all data, however, can be collected externally; for example, bowel microfauna can be analyzed from a toilet-based sensor. Some sensors are now the size of a full stop.

A market segment to start trials with is patients with critical health needs, who should agree to wear cumbersome sensors. Health specialists can decide which metrics need collecting, and data analysts can then start to analyze the flow of data to both feedback alerts to doctors and to ascertain if trends can be found which predict adverse changes before they occur. Another market segment will be those keen on fitness or professional athletes, who will agree to wear sensors so they can learn from the data analysis. From these experiences, engineers will discover how to make sensors smaller, and data analysts will discover enough useful features to induce the average user to wear them, as well as inducing insurers to pay for them or offer discounts to wearers. Note that this is not the far future as these devices are rapidly approaching a useful state, probably within the next five years.

If we take the case of an elderly woman with congestive heart failure and diabetes: beside her bed there could be a sensor to record her weight as she stands up; bed sensors monitor pressure points to detect early signs of ulcers; Sensors in the floor monitor her walking gait to assess her risk of falling; A patch on her arm monitors her heart rate, blood-oxygen level, blood pressure and glucose levels; Drinking cups and toilet sensors monitor her hydration levels; Sensors in her clothing can monitor if she has collapsed as well as track heart rhythms; Her medication pill has a tiny sensor which tells her arm patch that she has taken it. All these sensors automatically transmit data via her phone App in an encrypted format to the public health system. The data is analyzed for risk factors, and medial help is sent if required. Why should an elderly person be provided with a medical alert which they have to activate after they collapse when sensors can automatically request help before they collapse because health metrics drop below preset levels?

Recent technological conferences have featured experimental but already existing items like (i) bionics which monitor health and are barely visible plasters, which can send out data via the wearer's mobile phone, (ii) exoskeletons, for use in dangerous of heavy lifting situations, which are predicted to cut injury rates by 70%, and (iii) body suits with neuro-interfaces which can exercise limbs of paraplegics in a way which either encourages nerve regrowth or allows limb control directly from the brain.

Horvath (2013) argues that biomarkers involving the epigenome and methylation systems are good predictors of how rapidly a human body is aging in response to environmental and lifestyle factors.[5] Accessing these results will provide accurate mortality profiles, helping underwrite life insurance on a more individualized basis. Insurers could also set rates based on promised change in lifestyle and use periodic tests of these biomarkers as feedback to check if these promises are kept. This provides data to underwriters and is an incentive for customers.

[5] For a summary, see Gibbs (2014).

The range of data that can be collected is widespread: heart rate and patterns, temperature, glucose, blood serum, enzymes, hormones, sleep patterns, body fat, activity levels, mood, blood chemistry, oxygenation, EKG brain functions, and bowel microfauna. Wound dressings can track healing progress. Employers can use watches or wrist straps to detect workers who have used illegal substances or who are drowsy in unsafe environments. All can be tracked in real time, 24/7. The analysis of data should discover trends which predetermine sickness and enable doctors to call in and treat patients before they get sick. Patients who do not take medicine can be alerted and warned.

The analysis of this river of health big data from millions of patients from diverse sources like physical activities, eating patterns, sleep, health metrics, and food purchases, will provide many links to be made between social habits and disease or between the specific genes of a person and the lifestyle they should lead. This will not only allow health care providers to set up alerts for intervention with the client, which maybe immediate or asking the patient to come in, but it will also provide a rich and deep source of data linking everything the client has done prior to the adverse health event, including physical activity or changes in blood chemistry due to food etc., to health outcomes. This will give health researchers the capacity to understand physiological reactions and segment clients by their reaction type. For example, UK insurer, Aviva, has combined data from a range of non-health sources, like shopping or online behavior and has found that these can predict future health outcomes nearly as accurately as blood or urine tests. Patterns of Facebook 'likes' have been found to be a good predictor of a number of health indictors. This illustrates the importance of an insurer exploiting the advantages of data sourced from the wider ecosystem.

The largest collectors of health data are likely to be healthy, rather than sick individuals. The availability of cheap and easy to use sensors embedded in clothing will allow people to quantify their health over their life span. Linking telematics in clothing, household appliances, mobile phones, toilets, computers, etc., will allow people to track their health and their productivity to find patterns: Are they most productive with e-mails on a Wednesday afternoon? What level of coffee intake maximizes decision making while minimizing heart stress? How does that third beer on a Saturday night impact on belly fat? What pattern of weekly eating produces the best gut microfauna? Those who seek fitness can have sensors in their watches or shoes to give feedback from blood or muscles as to improvements and the effect of differing exercise regimes. Each house will own a pill maker, which will use daily data on blood chemistry, heart patterns, gut microfauna patterns, and gene details to produce the optimal daily vitamin. A medical program will provide a monthly health and productivity report.

Medicine can then move away from an annual visit to a doctor who on very limited data provides a 'this-tends-to-cure-people-your-age-&-gender' toward a personalized prescription based on detailed personalized data and a huge data bank of outcomes from similar people internationally. Medical research is based on trials involving as few as 500 heterogeneous people for a very short time frame. Big data would provide data on millions of people on a continuous basis. This would enable data on the 'people-99%-like-you' to be extracted and a personalized cure created. Insurers can offer inducements to clients to follow a personalized optimal health/activity/eating plan and provide regular health information highly applicable to you.

Before this data can be useable, however, it needed to be standardized and its collection automated. In many countries, medical records are still based on paper, so systems will need to be changed so all medical personal data is inputted digitally probably via tablets. Another issue is that currently, most medical records are kept in proprietary formats/data standards, and providers view holding the data as a competitive advantage to be denied to competitors. Yet, the economics of data scale dictate that the network of companies with the largest and most diverse data collection will gain the most insights and be able to price most accurately. Thus, companies who cooperate by forming ecosystems to increase data size will progressively pull ahead of companies who do not collaborate. Linking to public health or hospital data is essential, preferably internationally.

Social capital will be vital so that customer trust can be gained so vital and confidential health data can be gathered. Industry wide methods of secure data storage may need to be created so there is an infrastructure of trusted, neutral, and secure storage. On a positive note, many hospital software systems are currently used to compare the outcomes of treatments across a wide range of patients, so that adding in telematic data will be easier than in other insurance areas. Many hospital risk prediction systems already accurately predict the risk of death or complications from different types of surgery based on personal factors including genetics, as well as other areas like length of time required to recover. Riskprediction.org.uk provides this to the public.

The access to a huge database of health, medical, and lifestyle metrics will enable insurers to analyze treads and predict health problems, or relate health metrics to exercise in a detailed way. Vital here will be access to as much data on client lives as can be obtained, so that data analysts have a complete picture of what aspects of life cause health and ill-health. The successful insurers will have to convince clients to grant them access to a constant steam of real-time lifestyle data. For example; men who skip breakfast have a 27% higher risk of heart attacks, yoga participants have less mental diseases, while those who buy alcohol in the evenings have shorter lives than those who buy alcohol in the afternoons. Note that these types of data outputs are often not directly casual, as a third factor may be causing both to change - those men who skip breakfast have more stressful lives.

The combination of genomics, IT, nanotechnology, biotechnology, and cognitive science will create 'precision medicine,' whereby doctors will be able to tailor treatments to a patient's individual biochemistry, and remotely track in real time how the treatment is evolving and make changes if required.

General Electric (2012) argues that upgraded health systems software connected to smart devices could cut health system costs by over 25%. They add that information inefficiencies in health care exceed 10% of current costs, and as such the sector is ripe for technological disruption. Given that health care accounts for about 10% of global GDP, or US$7.1Trillion in 2011, the impact of a 25% cut is substantial. These substantial possibilities to reduce health care costs and the resultant commercial opportunities is generating a flood of telematic InsurTech investments, estimated to be US$120B p/a by 2020. This will progress fastest in countries with existing quality hospital software systems. This incentive is likely to ensure that health insurance a fast follower behind auto-insurance in the timing of transformation. Insurers in the USA, who spends about 18% of GDP on health, and where hospitals already tend to have quality data systems, are likely to be leaders.

When combined with a multitude of other health innovations in development, per patient spending on health will drop substantially, leading to a drop in health insurance premiums and therefore cash flow. The aging of the population may hold up aggregate spending, though a large share of innovations is focused on diseases of old age. The need for heavy investments in telematics and associated analysis with a stagnant cash flow will be difficult for insurers. They may choose to segment their client base into those prepared to contribute more toward inclusion in the full program and those left within the old system.

Those insurers who do invest will find costs dropping as data is collected remotely, is analyzed by software, adjustments are made to medicine machines by software, emergency teams are sent by software, doctors are consulted remotely, and humans are only involved if the software finds trends exceeding preset parameters. Costs related to precautionary tests will substantially drop. For example; AI image recognition is already having an impact on the diagnosis of CT or X-ray scans for detection of abnormalities, as leading AI systems have proved to be more than 50% better than human specialists at reviewing scans with radically lower cost.

One of the largest impacts of telematics and big data will be on claims. Because insurers will be collecting real-time data on a wide range of factors, they should be aware that an adverse event has occurred in real time and should have automatically collected nearly all the elements required for a claim without the client informing them. If a client falls sick, the health bracelet will tell the insurer that a medical emergency has occurred, and send a record of recent health metrics, while the insurer's computer can arrange emergency assistance, analyze scans, and make payment of health bills without any need for patient involvement. This proactive approach will increase insurer engagement to a qualitatively different level, increase the social capital of the insurer, as well as allow cross-selling of more services.

The key benefit, however, will occur from a switch in insurer focus from 'sickness' to 'health' as they move to predictive pricing. Insurers can offer relevant, real-time, health tips to clients by providing real-time feedback on the metrics gathered from telematics. This will give them the opportunity to interact with healthy customers on a regular basis and be seen as a 'positive' company. There will also be substantial opportunities for sales of data-based value-added services.

Successful insurers will thus have the opportunity to become more involved in clients' lives because of their expertise in real-time information management and analysis. Insurers will have to switch from the current focus on cost and control of benefit payouts to heavy focus on customer responsiveness and creating reason to engage. For example, AXA Singapore's health product arranges and pays for: a person to fetch children to and from school, a nurse to attend to follow up treatments, rehabilitation services, for doctor's home visits, modification to the home to accommodate disability, transportation to the hospital, house cleaning and meals, and psychologist consultations. This establishes the insurer as a positive, helpful, partner in life and grows social capital.

Another growth area will be the use of domestic home-health robots to provide care. These can be used to decrease the need for long hospital stays, or to free other family members, or provide for elderly. Given that these domestic robots will initially be expensive, about the price of a luxury car, insurers can start to add provision or purchase of these as an attractive policy option if specified health conditions occur. These robots will also need intensive servicing and linkage to a health care telematic and monitoring system. Any health insurer who manages to position themselves as the coordinating hub of a health ecosystem will not only receive a significant level of cash flow, but they will also have the chance to cross-sell, to gain intensive data about client physiology, and to create proactive communication avenues with clients who will welcome relevant information.

Successful insurers will also have to be heavily involved in social media and be proactively aware of ratings/review systems. Insurers who manage to switch their focus to being data intensive will find that this will create an access to the rapidly expanding markets in other areas of information management as our world becomes deeply interconnected. Given that society is aging and there is a tendency to increase the proportion of income on health as people get richer, the volume of cash flow from health-related services should rise, which will give health insurers the incentive to invest heavily, as well as give outsiders the incentive to enter.

Note the degree of sensitive personal health information provided by biosensors and other telematics mean that there is an extraordinary high level of client trust required for insurers to successfully create this transformation. This will be a major barrier for existing insurers who are not currently creating a dynamic proactive client communication strategy. Many insurers with established low trust levels due to focus on cost control will find it impossible to establish the required high level of client trust to access the data.

An aspect of this trust issue is that major issues arise if health biosensors are vulnerable to hacking, especially if they are linked to medication systems. Therefore, proving a high level of system security will be vital. Another aspect is that clients will be relying on health telematics to provide appropriate emergency health responses, so that clients are literally placing their lives in health ecosystem response software. Given the low social capital of existing insurers, clients may find it hard to trust their lives to the integrity of the insurer's software and systems, and incumbent insurers may find it hard to build a high enough level of client trust. The sector is thus open to disruptive entrants with technical knowledge and existing high social capital.

Overall, the extremely large size of the health sector and health insurance, combined with what is perceived to be high levels of waste and low-quality IT systems, makes it a very attractive market for disruptors. Regulation, experience, and the scale to negotiate costs would seem to make incumbents attractive partners for disruptors, but their legacy systems and conservative culture discourages disruptors from working with them. There will be a longer delay in market disruption in health, but the likelihood of disruptive external entry is high. First-moving insurers who do survive without adverse incidents will find that the positive media from providing lifesaving real-time services will give them a near unbeatable competitive advantage.

The increasing accuracy of health risk predictive systems raises the issue that some clients with high-risk factors will only be offered restricted insurance or at high rates. This raises important regulatory issues, which are discussed in a subsequent chapter. However, feedback between premiums and lifestyle indicators has the potential to improve overall health outcomes. AllLife, which links premiums to following doctor's advice, has shown that nearly all clients improve their lifestyles.

Commercial Insurance

The use of telematics in commercial transport fleet is already routine, as the real-time data about vehicle usage, vehicle wear, and goods tracking, is useful to transport businesses. Linking these sensors to insurer networks is therefore easier than linking private automobile fleets. Real-time container tracking via telematics is also routine. These existing telematic sensors lead naturally into an automated claims process and flexible underwriting. Dynamic insurance solutions are therefore already being trialed for large commercial transport operators, and will rapidly be expanded into all areas of commercial transport and marine insurance. Morgan-Stanley (2016b) argues that telematics are already disrupting small business insurance, and the impact will be affect 25% of the market by 2020. This can be expected to rise to 60–70% by 2025.

Some commentators argue that because commercial insurance contracts and processes tend to be customized, this is hindrance to the use of process automation. I would argue that this is not true; software can easily be designed for customized systems if AI systems have enough programable rules. In fact, the large size of commercial policies and the existing widespread use of telematics make commercial insurance an ideal test-bed for the creation of modularized customer-selected policy construction and automated processing. The size of these contacts means that small insurance savings add up to substantial amounts so pressure will be on insurers to offer the most modern deals. Insurers who offer proactive monitoring and claims services will be welcomed. Even more welcome will be insurers who use the collected data and AI analytical skill to provide accident/loss/fraud avoidance advice or accident/loss response services.

Note, however, that since firms like Octo-Telematics have been providing this type of data and associated analysis since 2002, covering fleet use, location and use, as well as crash-causation, insurers who seek to enter this market in competition have a fifteen-year lag to overcome.

Commercial transport fleets and associated goods can therefore be seen as the area were procedures and protocols around data, communication, and policies will be explored and defined. Insurers who aim to survive the looming disruptive waves will thus have to proactively seek opportunities to offer dynamic insurance so they can gain experience with real-time data collection, use, and analysis. The ability to respond to adverse situations as they occur, to handle the huge flows of often incompatible data, and to integrate these into a platform will be essential skills to be developed. To do this, they will have to integrate themselves into the transport ecosystems. For example, they will have to work with telematic suppliers to ensure that the correct range of data is collected.

Cyber Security, Drones, and Hacking

The proposals outlined in this chapter assume that insurers will be collecting an immense amount of personal and confidential data about their clients including real-time location and links to the control of items like cars or vital medical equipment. Clients will only agree to this if they have a high level of trust in the insurer's honesty and data security ability.

These databases and links will be very attractive targets for hackers, either to commit mayhem or blackmail. Data security needs to cover both the insurer's IT system and any customer telematics which the insurer could be seen as liable for. Already, multiple monthly cyber-attacks on insurers occur, and this can only exponentially rise as the value of the data rises. Given the high level of client trust required for the data collection, any successful hacking event could immediately destroy the reputation of the insurer, and given the reduced brand stickiness, the insurer may find that their business rapidly disappears. Thus, advanced level data security will have to be the top priority.[6]

The downside to telematics is their vulnerability to hacking. This is especially true for smart household appliances, where research has shown that 90% of owners do not change the default password. This hacking could be malicious to cause damage, to ascertain if the owner is home, or to spy on your activities. While smart appliances are worthless

[6]For a detailed cyber security summary, read Morgan-Stanley (2016a).

to steal (as they can be tracked), blackmail unlocking scams could be common. Insurers may have to start insisting on professional installation. The hacking of health telematics in high-risk patients is extremely concerning as changes to these could cause death. Insurance relating to smart device hacking could thus be a useful growth area, as would be the sale and service of IT firewall systems.

Insurance relating to drones is another growth area. SwissRe (2014) extensively describes the potential uses for drones and argues that they will have a reasonably high rate of insurable risk and therefore attract a useful premium flow. They argue that spending on drones will reach $US11B per annum by 2023.

SwissRe (2014) also argue that drones will become a standard tool for claim assessors as they can survey locations easier and faster than humans can, when a physical presence is required. For example, if insurers pre-arrange a national network of drone bases, then assessors can assess a claims location remotely from thousands of miles away. With an array of built-in sensors and an ability to crawl, drones could cover 90% of assessment tasks. This will be particularly useful for the agricultural sector, where a farmer can show an assessor crop or other damage even in remote locations which have no roads. There will be no need for an assessor to climb ladders or enter dangerous areas. A recent California start-up, DropIn, assesses automobile claims by using claimant mobile phones to conduct interviews and drones to assess the crash site. They use a nationwide network of over 1000 drone operators contracted to respond immediately. Often no operator is needed; for example, AI linked to a drone can assess roof tile damage after a storm with no human involvement by using visual recognition tools.

References

Boston Consulting Group. (2013). Telematics: The test for insurers. *BCG Perspectives*.

Boston Consulting Group. (2014). Bringing big data to life. *BCG Perspectives*.

Boston Consulting Group. (2015a). Robo-taxis and the new mobility. *BCG Perspectives*, April 21.

Boston Consulting Group. (2015b). Revolution in the driver's seat: The road to autonomous vehicles. *BCG Perspectives*, April 21.

Capgemini/Efma. (2016). *World insurance report.*

Energesse. (2015). 'Future Solutions in Customer Experience for Health Insurers White Paper'.

Foster. (2012). *The customer experience index.*

General Electric. (2012*). Industrial Internet: Pushing the Boundaries of Minds and Machines*. P. Evans & M. Annunziata (Eds.). USA.

Gibbs, W. W. (2014). The clock-watcher. *Nature*. 508.7495 (Apr 10, 2014): 168–170.

Gomes. (2014). Driving in circles. *Technology*. October 21.

Horvath, S. (2013). DNA methylation age of human tissues and cell types. *Genome Biology, 14*(10), 3156.

International Transport Forum/OECD. (2015). *Urban Mobility System Upgrade: How shared self-driving cars could change city traffic.*

KPMG. (2015). *Automobile Insurance in the Era of Autonomous Vehicles: Survey results*, June.

McKinsey. (2015). *The Internet of Things: Mapping the Value Beyond the Hype.* McKinsey Global Institute.

McKinsey. (2016). *Shifting Gears: Insurers adjust for connected-car ecosystems*, May.

Morgan-Stanley. (2016a). *Cybersecurity: Rethinking security*. Blue Paper. USA.

Morgan-Stanley. (2016b). Insurance—property & casualty—digital disruption in small business insurance. *North America Insight*, June 29.

PWC. (2014). *Reinventing life insurance.*

SwissRe. (2014). *Insurance and the rise of drones*. New York: SwissRe.

SwissRe. (2016). *The future of motor insurance: How car connectivity and ADAS are impacting the market*. Berlin: SwissRe/Here.

Yoder, J., & Rao A. (2015). *Insurance at a tipping point*. Insurance Thought leadership, PWC, June 20.

7
The Dynamics of Decline

Introduction

Most industry commentators agree that the insurance industry is facing unprecedented innovations. The issues in dispute are: (i) Are the innovations incremental or disruptive, (ii) How long the waves of innovations will take to disrupt current market conditions, and (iii) Can incumbents react in time to survive?

The answers to these questions can only be speculative and will differ for each sector of the insurance market. Analysts need to approach these questions using a range of innovation disruption concepts. When an analyst discusses the future, it is well understood by the industry that any predictions involving exact dates are likely to be wrong. The usefulness of analyst reports is instead found within the conceptual reasoning.

This chapter uses auto-insurance as an example to explore the concepts which underlie the dynamics of decline. These decline dynamic concepts can be applied to other sectors. Cognizant (2017) found that few insurance managers regarded changes in the automobile market as worthy of concern before 2030. I will show that this lack of concern could be based on misunderstandings about dynamics of

M. Naylor, *Insurance Transformed*, Palgrave Studies in Financial Services Technology,
DOI 10.1007/978-3-319-63835-5_7

sector decline as disruptive change often occurs far faster than incumbents expect. Remember that modern mobile phones were only introduced in 2007, yet now dominate our lives. As noted in the Chap. 1, history shows that 3/4rds of social change occurs in the last 1/4 of the disruption time period. Therefore, ascertaining where on the disruption time-line each insurance sectors sits is vital.

The auto-insurance industry is significant. In the USA, it generates $220 billion in annual revenue and supports 277,000 jobs, about the same number of mechanical engineering jobs. For many P&C insurers, auto-insurance is over 50% of their total cash flow. Therefore, understanding its demise is critical.

Profitability vs Premiums

A key concept is that there is a difference between the rate of spread of a technology and changes in profitability, in this case, spread of autonomous cars and the decline of auto-insurance profitability. If high-end cars embed 80% technology by 2018, then this will probably be embedded in middle-end cars by 2021 and low-end cars by 2025. If there are large differences in crash rates or telematic costs drops due to scale, then this may happen faster. This implies that new low-end manual cars (less than 80% auto-drive) will still be on sale in, say 2023, and cars sold then will not be off the road before at least 2030. It is thus likely that the majority of cars on the road in 2025 will still be manual.[1]

Note that there is a 'valley of death' for crash rates between 80% cars and 100% automatic. This is because more than 80%+ cars require so little of the driver, that despite being at the wheel, they are likely to not pay active attention to the road, and instead do other activities. Yet these software systems are not perfect so accidents will still occur. Therefore, there a strong argument that level 4 autonomous cars are

[1]Germany has recently passed a law-banning new cars with internal combustion engines from 2030. This means that all new cars will likely be auto-drive. Given low crash rates, similar laws can be expected to ban manual drive cars.

more dangerous than either level 3 or level 5 cars, and therefore car manufacturers will halt at level 3 and then jump to level 5.

What needs to be clearly understood, however, is that the demise of the car insurance industry is not about percentages of cars with X or Y type of technology, nor is it really about declines in premiums flows. Demise dynamics depends instead on profitability. The general rule is that at the point when premium cash flow starts to decline by 5 or 10% per year, the natural reaction from insurers will be to cut premium profit margin to retain market share. This tends to lead to 'destructive competition,' where in order to increase market share in the hope of holding premium income constant in declining markets, companies compete until profit margins turn negative. This means that car numbers and premium flows could still be at 70–80% of previous levels, but insurance profits may no longer be positive. Profitability falls faster than premium flow, which falls faster than the technological change. This drop in profitability will also impact heavily on insurer stock value. If incumbents cannot convince the market that they have a viable path to the future then stock markets will sell, which will severely handicap insurers' ability to raise the required funds to transform themselves. An example of this is a comparison of the 2017 stock value of Tesla versus Ford.

If we apply this analysis to the suggested rate of technological spread in the first paragraph, this implies sharply decreasing auto-insurance premiums from 2020 on. In addition, since the richest customers will be the owners of the 80% cars, whose level of safety implies low premiums, an increasing proportion of premiums will come from insuring the lower income owners of the remaining manual cars. Insurers who want to remain will thus have to compete for a shrinking pool of decreasing quality clients, or those few who chose to manually drive as a hobby. The winner in this kind of market is the supplier who is prepared to supply at or below cost. The only firms with an incentive to stay in this type market are car producers, or those niche insurers used to providing specialist cover for higher risk clients.

Thus, it is vital to understand that the turning point for car insurers does not occur when 100% autonomous cars arrive on our roads in substantial numbers, which is a decade away, though selected brands will introduce these by 2020. The insurers' turning point occurs when a sufficient number of 80% autonomous cars exist to substantially cut crash rates, and thus cut premiums, and thus cut insurer cash flow, and thus cut profit margins. The demise of auto-insurance profitability is not about the rate that 100% auto-cars are introduced but is instead about the full package of current technology, 80% auto, which is being introduced from 2017. Data shows that 80% technology cuts crash rates by about 40%. If we remove the crashes predominately caused by the other driver, this increases to a 70% drop in crash rates. 90% auto-tech, due by 2020, will cut crash rates by over 80%. Premiums for top-of-range cars may thus fall by corresponding levels. The speed of diffusion of this technology down to the average car is a debatable point, but it's likely to underway by 2023, with an 80% transition by 2035.

At that turning point, those insurers who get more than 40% of their cash flow from car insurance will be forced to either back out of the market and prepare for sale to another owner, or start to compete intensively in an arena of a declining market. Some commentators will argue, correctly, that 'car insurance will still exist for decades.' I'm sure it will; people will still drive manual cars for fun for decades. My response is that horse insurance still exists, but I'm not sure that current insurers visualize their future in that way. In leisure driving market, niche auto-insurers are more likely to survive than the major ones.

Tipping Point

The crash rate of an individual car, however, does not just depend on its own level of technology; it also depends on what percentage of other cars have crash avoidance technology. Therefore, if some cars behave so as to avoid crashes, avoiding cars being driven erratically, then it becomes harder for manual cars to crash. There, overall crash rates do not just depend on the rate of spread of auto-drive technology; it also depends on the overall proportion of cars with crash avoidance technology in a particular area. The existence of an increasing number of 80% cars will mean that crash rates will start to fall faster than the spread of the technology, as these 80% cars increasingly detect and avoid straying manual cars.

This is not a linear process but is a downward S curve. At a certain point called a 'tipping point,' the environment changes rapidly from one where one type of behavior dominates to one where another type of behavior dominates. In a networked environment, manually driven cars can be identified well before the auto-car gets to them and they will be given a wide margin. At this stage, it becomes difficult for manual drivers to find a car to crash into.

Studies show that for this to occur the percentage of 80% cars does not have to be close to 100%, even 50% is enough. Using models derived from diseases and financial crises, it can be argued that there will be a tipping point when about 40–60% of current cars have 80% technology, though a reasonable case can be made for a lower percentage.

While the details of this can be debated, it is clear that crash rates in general will start to drastically drop, well, before fully automatic cars become the predominant vehicle on the roads. There will thus be a 'tipping point' in crash rates in advanced economies about 2023–2026, when there will be a sufficient proportion of 80% cars to ensure that even badly driven manual cars will find it hard to create crashes. Once 50% or more of cars are autonomous and networked, then car crashes will only occur due to software bugs or hacking or poor maintenance or roadside objects or manual cars driven erratically.

This concept can be applied to other insurance types, though there are less networking effects with personal insurance.

Telematics and Turnover Rates

The next issue to be examined is the rate that telematic devices and other technologies can be introduced into the market. In this case, the rate that 80% crash avoidance technology will be introduced into the automobile fleet. The faster the introduction of pre-installed telematics and the higher the automobile turnover rate, the faster is the impact on insurer cash flow.

Some commentators argue that telematics with not be widely used in automobiles because, based on current black-box telematics, they are too expensive for all but the highest risk clients to install. This ignores the fact that increasingly cars are being manufactured with quite detailed telematics pre-installed. The increasing use of these devices is leading to their cost to start to drop sharply. When Google first built their autonomous car the LIDAR system cost more than $70,000. Today, that same hardware can be purchased for $250 and is expected to fall to $90 soon. Even low-end cars will soon have these devices installed. In 2017, 83 million cars with smart functions will be sold. Top-end cars are also increasingly being data networked, though at this stage only within the manufacturer's network. Note that, that all cars produced since 2006 include an OBD chip, so for basic dynamic insurance there is no need for expensive sensors.

Given that it will be low cost for insurers to access these networks and gather data from pre-installed telematics, why wouldn't they? This linking to telematics is happening now in the commercial fleet, which is where these techniques will be trialed.

The turnover rate (replacement of old cars by new ones) of automobiles between countries varies greatly. In the USA, it is approximately 11 years. In general, if we use existing turnover rates, then cars with 80% avoidance technology and telematics will not constitute over 50% of the vehicle fleet until after 2028. This has led to commentators arguing that change will not be substantial until about 2035. However, within an exponential change, a forecast based on a linear projection of past trends is dangerous, so insurers are likely to be surprised and thus wrong-footed. And, as noted above, the tipping point for a rapid decrease in auto-insurer cash flow occurs at about 50%, or around 2028, with sharply increased competition five years earlier.

It needs to be noted that the inclusion of telematics has increased the cost of cars, especially exposed components like wing mirrors or windscreens.[2] The installation of these has become more complex and expensive. This has led to a temporary rise in crash payouts. However, by about 2020, the rate of crashes will decline faster than component cost will rise.

---

[2]Windscreens increasingly carry many sensors and even small errors can results in substantial misalignment in ADAS systems.

For personal risk insurance, external telematic devices have a low cost, and a group of customers have been voluntarily buying them. Hospitals will soon start issuing these to high-risk patients, so they can be monitored at home. There will be some delay for internal devices as medical testing is required. This use by high-risk patients will enable producers and insurers to gain experience and thus to lower costs and create stable systems. Widespread introduction can thus be expected to start after 2025.

For house and contents insurance, there is a first mover issue as currently homeowners have little incentive to pay more for smart connected appliances, thus installation rates are low, so there are few incentives of the insurer to invest in telematic-based service systems. Once one firm moves in with an attractive offer, then homeowners can be expected to switch rapidly, especially at the top end of the income scale. Insurers who do not respond will be left with lower income clients.

Electric and Automatic-Drive Vehicles

A related issue linked to turnover is the rapidly decreasing drop in the cost of electric vehicles (EV) against the cost of internal combustion engine vehicles (ICE). Tesla has been an EV innovator, and while still a niche player is raising genuine concern among the incumbents. Realizing that the main cost was the battery pack, Tesla has built an extremely large battery factory. Given that batteries are about $12–14k of the cost of a $35k car, a halving of the battery cost makes the car competitive. By the end of 2017, Tesla's Gigafactory will be approaching or below $100/kwh as production ramps up. Continuing cost reduction will make EV cars cheaper than ICE cars after 2020. EV range is also rising rapidly, with Tesla predicting a driving range equal to ICE cars by 2020 and double the ICE range by 2028. Tesla's success has motivated competitors to step up their game. BYD, Foxconn, LG Chem, Nissan, Dyson, Apple, and Samsung have all made announcements with plans to build large scale battery factories. BYD's plans are the most aggressive - a goal to add 6GWh of production per year, hitting 34GWh by 2020 (matching Tesla's 35GWh capability). This manufacturing attention could accelerate the cost curve downward even faster.

Car purchase costs are not the only factor, as most ICE cars cost owners over $10k in annual running costs. Given that EVs have a about 90% lower fuel and maintenance costs of ICE cars, with superior performance, it can be assumed that once they can be purchased at a similar price to ICE cars EV cars will probably be purchased as fast as they can be produced. Current trends indicate that somewhere between 2020 and 2025 is the tipping point - the point at which it would make no financial sense to purchase a new ICE vehicle for the average vehicle buyer. These predictions do not lie in the success or otherwise of Tesla to meet production targets. And, they also do not assume that individual ownership will decrease. The prediction is based on the immaturity of current EV manufacturing and the expected rapid drop in price as technology improves. Fundamentally, EV are substantially easier to manufacture than ICE cars. FoxConn, a contract IT manufacturer, estimates that by 2025, it will be able to make family saloon EVs at a price of $US15k.

This replacement of ICE cars by EV cars is a one-off disruption, which will jump the turnover rate substantially within the next ten years. The main limiting factor will be the speed at which incumbent manufacturers can respond by switching production to auto-drive EVs, at that price range. Assuming all these cars will come equipped with an inbuilt advanced sensor and auto-drive systems then the tipping point to auto-insurance viability in cash flow terms could occur surprisingly soon.

Progress to date with 100% automatic-drive systems has been slow due to physical issues with car telematics. These have been largely solved, so delays from this year will be primarily related to AI experience. AI progress depends on accumulating sufficient training data. Given that Tesla is collecting driving data from all its cars, Elon Musk predicts that software issues should be primarily solved by 2020, for areas without extreme winter conditions. Note that networked cars are not stuck with the auto-driving ability possible at the date of their manufacture, as software downloads can regularly improve that performance. Within an EV future, cars become software devices on wheels.

Given the exponential rates of software improvement, it would be a brave insurance manager who would argue that auto-drive cars will not be introduced rapidly. If the auto-drive software capacity doubles and telematic cost halves every two years (say), then why would crash rates and associated premiums not start to drop by 10–15% per year?

It needs to be remembered that any technology offering a substantial reduction in the costs of car accidents is likely to be proactively embraced by both the public and regulators. Europe is likely to ban the use of non-auto and non-electric cars by 2030. Turnover rates are thus likely to sharply rise.

It also needs to be remembered the change to safer telematic linked EV cars will occur first for rich and upper middle-class clients. This implies that insurers who do not provide a dynamic networked product will be left competing for a shrinking pool of lower income clients driving old manual ICE models.

An increasing trend in large cities will be the use of car or ride sharing Apps. Already car ownership rates have peaked in key demographic urban categories. In particular, these groups will be less likely to buy a 2nd or 3rd car. The net impact of this is still unknown, but since profit margins on fleet insurance deals are low, the impact on premium flow could be noticeable.

Rapid Innovation Switches

The time it takes for an external disruptor to enter is shrinking; it took Uber only 4 years from its foundation in the USA to start to disrupt the Australian market. Examples exist of unexpectedly rapid technology switches. For example, urban transport in cities went from 99% horses in 1900 to 95% cars by 1912. The key is the pace at which technology advances - cars were a new technology that was faster, cheaper, longer living, and always followed directions. These benefits were so overwhelming that a technique of travel that humans had been using for millennia disappeared in a little over a decade. The lesson here is that once a disruptive technology reaches a particular tipping point, it doesn't just take market share incrementally from the incumbent industry but rather completely rapidly replaces it.

Another example is the German electricity sector. In 2010, the major companies regarded their market as stable and secure. The threat of distributed solar power was regarded as a minor issue. By 2015, both EON and RWE were in internal crisis and announced that they were spinning off the fossil- and nuclear-dependent parts of their businesses so they could focus on renewables and producing consumers, 'prosumers.'

As an important enabler of innovation, insurers could evolve with technology and even thrive. Some cars today can tell when you're drowsy, or if you don't have a hand on the wheel, or if you're speeding, and so on. These are enabled by listening devices, biometrics, and telematics in your car - monitoring you and your driving habits.

Given this flood of real-time data that cars can generate, the current model of charging annual premiums seems so last century. Dynamic insurance is the future. These are complex issues and all should be debated by insurance strategists. However, I would argue that it is better for insurers to be prepared too early than to be rushing to catch up. Assuming no change is the risky choice. There is a lot of money currently going into InsurTech. Are auto-insurers willing to bet their firms on the unlikeliness of disruption not occurring over the next 5–10 years?

Barriers to Entry

The insurance industry has traditionally had higher barriers to entry by new firms that other industries do. These include financial, data, experience, reliability, switching costs, and regulatory barriers. The auto-insurance market, because it is a temporary and simple product where switching is easy, has substantially lower barriers than other insurance sectors. This reinforces its role as the leading edge of reform.

Personal insurance is, by nature, a long-term contract. Once a customer has taken out a life or health policy, then any health conditions which subsequently occur, would be covered by their existing policy but excluded if they switch. They are thus locked into their existing supplier for life. Because of this, customers must trust their insurer to continue to exist. Switching is also not straight forward as there may be medical questions or tests required. Regulators thus require insurers to hold long-term capital and guarantee stability. Incumbents also have a data and underwriting experience advantage. Because of these hindrances emerging InsurTech firms are unlikely to poise a major threat in the personal insurance market until they have grown to be large, trustable companies in other sectors. Competition is more likely from large firms in other sectors who add an InsurTech option to their existing product line.

These hindrances are not as important in the P&C insurance market. Customers face few barriers to switching their car or house insurance, and telematic users like Octo or Tesla have the data and experience advantage. Bankruptcy of an insurer is, thus, not a serious problem for customers, nor are regulators as strict. Dynamic insurance also offers more in the P&C sector. For these reasons, auto-insurance will be impacted by external disruptors before other sectors are. I would argue that while InsurTech start-ups have entered via niche markets, there are only limited barriers to their expansion outside those sectors, especially if they have a substantially lower cost model.

The major barrier to entry to the new world of insurance will be (i) an automated end-to-end processing system, (ii) expertise with AI analysis of real-time big data, (iii) a large relevant data set, (iv) an ability to transform as successive waves of innovation roll in, and (v) experience with engaging and delighting customers. Incumbent insurers do not rank well in terms of these attributes. Large Internet platforms do.

Regulation

There has been commentary that the introduction of autonomous cars will be held up by conservatism on the part of legislators in passing the necessary laws. However, the relative safety of autonomous cars versus the dangerousness of the current human drivers will provide enough impulse to push through the required legal and cultural changes. Worldwide more than 2 million people are involved in car crashes, with a total cost exceeding US$212B. Each year in the USA, 30,000 people die. If auto-drive cars reduced this by 90%, it would be brave legislators who would oppose restrictions on the use of manual drive cars.

In fact, cities could well ban self-drive cars from the CBD, and countries could ban them from expressways, probably by 2025. There will be a strong incentive for smaller countries or states to promote themselves as 'autodrive' friendly via enabling legislation, in an effort to attract investment and workers into their jurisdiction. This is why the change may occur first somewhere like Singapore, where regulation can be trialed easier. Within fifteen to twenty years self-driving a car could become a quaint sport like horse riding - something rich people do on weekends on an enclosed track. After all, people still own and run antique or classic cars for fun. They are just not used for normal commuting and do not constitute a large insurance sector.

Reference

Cognizant. (2017). *The work ahead: Seven key trends shaping the future of work in the insurance industry*.

8

The Response of Incumbents

Incumbents

As explained a perfect storm of technological disruption is about to hit the insurance industry. A key question is thus - 'are existing incumbents able to respond fast enough to avoid being swept away?' The main issue for incumbents is that they are set up to run their existing activities as efficiently as possible, as well as respond to any immediate, real, crisis. They thus do not have the existing spare resources, the spare money, or personal, or the intellectual flexibility, to respond to medium term possible crises and to remake their business while also running the existing business. It's like trying to rebuild a car while it's driving at speed.

A company subject to disruption is hard to manage as the core business is suffering decline yet still produces the bulk of revenue and employs the bulk of staff, whereas the expanding business is a cash drain and requires skills/culture which may be foreign to existing staff. This is worse if the disruption sector is exotic to the company culture and disruptor is still minor so the threat is potential rather than actual.

Added to this is the fact that most possible threats don't eventuate, so that executives who focus on looming possibilities and divert scarce cash

M. Naylor, *Insurance Transformed*, Palgrave Studies in Financial Services Technology,
DOI 10.1007/978-3-319-63835-5_8

and personnel to combat something which doesn't eventuate, risk being seen as over-reactive. Incumbents thus have to determine if a threat on the horizon actually exists or is noise, and if it will involve a small change, a major change, or a complete reimagining of the industry. Yet it is impossible to determine if a looming threat is disruptive or hype until it impacts on existing cash flow in a major way. Who could have imagined in 1990 that the phone industry would destroy the film industry?

As explained earlier, an issue is that management response to disruptive change cannot be the same as the response to incremental change. Disruptive change will require transformation of processes and culture. The strategy that got you to the top is probably not the strategy you'll need for the road ahead. This change has to be substantial, as there is a big difference between 'an insurance company which does digital' and 'a digital company which does insurance.' It is hard to switch from one to the other.

The problem is that because of the nonlinear nature of disruptive change, by the time cash flow is affected, it is probably too late for a company to react. Late adoption is thus often not viable. Therefore, businesses can either (i) adopt early and become part of the disruptors, or (ii) downsize and try to survive with the old model, or (iii) shut up shop, maybe by sale to the disruptor. There will often be instances when no viable path of transformation exists for the incumbent.

It needs to be understood that an incumbent following best practice for their current sector is not going to save the incumbent if a disruptor uses a different business model. Incumbents may have to imagine an alternative approach to their current business model and disrupt the market themselves.

Stages of Disruption

Capgemini (2015) argues that there are three stages to technological disruption by an external entrant. These are (i) *onset* - typically within the first year and is marked by the entry of the external disruptor (ii) *spread* - typically takes place with the first two or three years, when the disruptor starts to grow in popularity, which leads to multiple me-too entrants, and (iii) *mainstream adoption* - the disruption technology achieves widespread acceptance, typically within four years from entry.

Capgemini's analysis shows that only 26% of incumbents respond to the disruptive entrant during the onset stage, with 35% responding during the spread stage, and a worrying 38% responding during the mainstream adoption stage. Needless to say, the substantial majority of incumbents who went bankrupt were those who responded late.

Capgemini argues that there are five reasons why incumbents tend to delay responding to disruptive entrants.

1. *Slow Decision-making Cycle:* Traditionally, companies have used an annual planning and strategy cycle. Satell (2012) shows that the technological cycles are becoming, on average, shorter than annual and are becoming increasingly shorter as the IT revolution progresses. Companies are thus finding that their markets are becoming disrupted before they have had a chance to analyze the change. An example is Uber, which spread worldwide within 18 months of establishing itself, well before taxi companies could think about and react to its entry.
2. *Complacency about Existing-Business Model:* Management typically fails to sense the need for drastic change due to inertia. This occurs because management tends to focus on improving the efficiency of the existing successful business model. Their position in their market sector during the onset stage is often unchanged and initially shows no sign of strain. The disruptor is small and it is easy to ignore or pretend it will come to nothing, especially as most new technologies do fail. The disruptor often has an entirely new business model which incumbents cannot visualize. Often the disruptor has not quite worked out how to make a profit, so financially switching seems idiotic. Thus, very few companies ever question their business model until it fails. Even technically savvy companies can fail to foresee disruptive changes. For example, RIM/Blackberry ignored the technological challenge posed by the all screen iPhone as they remained the market leader in their business market sector, failing to see that Apple's new approach was destroying that market sector. Because the

change is exponential, it is easy to initially assume the threat is over hyped, and then be surprised when a tidal wave of change hits.
3. *Fear of Cannibalizing Existing Business:* Most companies' initial concern is that new business models will destroy existing cash flows. As this is true, a choice has to be made between current profits which may disappear and uncertain future profits. An example here is Kodak who delayed investing in digital despite their initial technological lead, vs Fuji, who invested heavily in digital processing machinery.
4. *Lower Margins in the Transition:* Digital businesses often have lower margins than traditional businesses, so that moving into digital is normally perceived as a risky bet on future revenues. An example is newspapers which have been reluctant to move into digital since the advertising revenue is a lot less. The heavy investment required in new areas often means they run at a loss for a lengthy period.
5. *Key Resources unaligned to Opportunities:* The siloed nature of most companies, where unit size equates to manager salary and prestige, tends to mean that no manager wants to contribute cash or material to a new unit. Managers thus tend to try to retrofit new units into the existing structures, failing to realize the essential cultural and business model changes required to make the new technology successful.

The ideal response to disruption is to treat the new-area business with a venture-capital style management, so that growth rather than cash flow is focused on, and flexibility is stressed. The existing-business area should have private-equity style management, with a focus on cash flow and efficiency. An incumbent can then disrupt itself, using the new area to destroy the existing area.

Unfortunately, what tends to happen in practice is that the new area is treated with suspicion and endures a high level of scrutiny, particularly if cash flow estimates are not meet, while the existing business is treated leniently. Existing-business managers have been right in the past and events will show them to be right until they are wrong, whereas new-area managers have no history of success to build on. The skill set which made existing-business managers successful is unlikely to be the skill set which works within the new area, so existing-business managers may not recognize or value the new-area manager skills. This tends to delay a successful response to external entry until the threat to cash flow realizes, and then the transition has to occur within an environment of rapidly declining existing-business cash flow.

It needs to be remembered that in the initial stages of the revolution, the external disruptor will only impact on the poorer quality firms, so that the better firms can tell themselves that they will survive intact. As long as you're not the weakest firm, you may not be under imminent threat. An analogy here would be a herd of wildebeest being chased by lions. An individual wildebeest can tell itself that as long as it runs fast enough to stay in front of the slowest runners, it won't be eaten. What it fails to recognize is that as the back wildebeest are eaten, the lions are getting larger and faster and its own turn will come sooner than it thinks. The best survival is to go early, learn to run faster, and try to transform into a lion.

This relationship between the old and the new business areas is made even more difficult because the main target the new area wants to disrupt will be the old area. Basically, customers have to be migrated to the new area as fast as possible, even though profit margins in the new area may be initially far lower than profit margins in the old. The impact of this on the state of the accounts can cause huge internal management disruption and needs strong leadership to ride out.

Capgemini (2015) argues that there are four ways of successfully responding to disruptive entrants:

a. *Acquiring digital talent:* hire appropriately skilled staff. This was used by 48% of successful responders.
b. *Mimicking:* deploying significant resources to create similar products and business models. Used by 32% of successful responders.
c. *Acquisitions:* purchasing new entrants and then using them. Used by 36% of successful responders. Note that the incumbent has to use the acquired firm to change existing core business culture or the acquired firm will ossify and employees will leave. New competitors will arise.

d. *Judicial/regulatory*: new entrants often have new business models which are not covered by regulation, so incumbents raise legal or regulatory concerns. Note that this can only delay disruption and can slow down incumbent adoption until change occurs with a tidal rush. Used by 32% of successful responders to give them time to react.

Note that these methods can be used together and are the only effective long term if they aid the incumbent to transform its business model. Ultimately, successful responders need to embed a culture of open digital innovation and customer centricity within a new business model. Management needs to be constantly looking for possible new disruptive elements at an early stage and prepare for them. The pace of technological disruptions will increase in all sectors and will increase at an increasing rate.

Business as usual is not an option. Existing business units will have to be evaluated and ones which are not useful for the future need to be sold-off while they still have value. McKinsey (2016a) argues that the senior management and board need to step back and ask fundamental questions—'do the businesses we own make sense in the new world which is unfolding, and are they going to create value, and are we the best owners of those businesses to maximize value, and what else could we be investing in, what's the bar on the capacities which we have, and how much has it gone up, and are we up to scratch or are we going to end up being out-competed by someone else who's just reconceived what's possible?' Given that during a disruptive transformation, the future will be unusually hazy; this strategic thinking has to be done via loose scenarios, rather than precise spreadsheets. The board needs to focus on lost opportunities in the new area, rather than threat to revenue in the old area. The culture needs to change from a '*Fear of Making Mistakes*' mind-set to a '*Fear of Missing Out*' mind-set.

The role of the CIO is vital and probably too important to be left to existing CIOs. This is because traditionally CIOs have been routine and reactive, focused on efficiency and trouble shooting. What is needed for IT transformation is a person who can combine IT knowledge with a strategic overview and focus on innovative and proactive initiatives. In particular, the job of establishing IT as the core element of an insurer will need close integration of IT development with all sectors of the firm and with customer groups, with a special focus on usability and visualization appeal.

Cultural issues at board level are a problem. This is because the existing board was chosen for their skills at evaluating and running the existing business with its well-understood model and stable cash flow. The new-area business will probably require a different set of skills from board members, more attune to those of a venture capitalist board. It takes a courageous board to approve management investing heavily in terms of personal and money in ambiguous projects in areas where the outcome is uncertain, cash flow is unstable, and the pathway to success subjects to unexpected shifts. For this reason, survivors are more likely to be incumbents who were in trouble and therefore had a board prepared to gamble, than the best-run and most-profitable incumbent.

Increasing investment in the new area and declining cash flow from the old area mean that profits will probably drastically shrink and the fall in dividends may trash the stock price. Stock investors who liked the old cash cow model will become disgruntled. The board may be tempted to underemphasis the financial pain necessary during the transition phase, which only leads to a larger crisis later when the scale of problems is realized. Survival may thus require a different class of investors.

An additional problem is that boards often have a 'group-think' and thus may fail to see problems which would be obvious to a person from an external sector. Thus, a shake-up in board membership may be an essential part of survival. The introduction of experts in disruptive transformation and in the core skills of the new area is required, as well as a deliberate increase in the diversity of board member worldviews. Disruptive thought leaders should be prized, yet they are usually not selected because their presence makes other board members uneasy. Strong and decisive leadership at the top is essential. New board members should be chosen because they make current members uneasy.

Oligopolies and Disruptive Entry

A lot of the description in this book, about what will be required in the immediate future from insurers in terms of new patterns of management behavior, will strike many currently in the insurance industry as fantastic speculation - they will respond that the described changes seen as essential will never occur because they are so far away from current modes of behavior. Some participants will, however, not find it unrealistic as they will either already be starting to engage in these behaviors or will have already contemplated these issues. Readers in disrupting sectors may regard my speculation as trivial and old-dated. This contrast in reactions is not unexpected as such dichotomy is the norm during revolutionary upheavals.

The unique convergence of the technical innovations outlined in an earlier chapter will create an unprecedented period of change in service administration across all industries, a period when there will not only be a major change but change will occur at an increasing rate; exponential change. As outlined in figure 1.1, the human mind cannot generally cope with this kind of change, initially being disappointed that change is occurring at a slower than expected change, before being shocked by the unexpected rapid change. The natural reaction is to initially dismiss exponential change as ridiculous, then to fight it, before reluctantly and belatedly rushing to catch up, and lastly accepting the change as normal, and finally wondering what the fuss was about.

The pace of change in the insurance sector will probably be faster than most participants expect. Internet giants and platforms suppliers are already starting to move into the insurance sector, and their data analytical skills should make them strong competitors. Insurers are starting to be forced to learn big data and social network skills. The base concept is that these two sectors, Internet technology and insurance, are starting to converge in terms of the fundamental skills required. Insurance has two basic skill sets: (i) data analytics and (ii) customer relationships. These are also the core skill sets of many IT sector firms, and in general, Internet technology firms are generally more efficient at these two skills. Insurers are definitely playing catch up.

Customer reluctance to use out-of-sector firms is also dropping. Capgemini/Efma (2016) shows that one-quarter of Generation Y customers and nearly one-half of Latin American and Asian-Pacific customers say they are very likely to purchase insurance from a technology company.

It also cannot be understated that the scale and speed of the combined changes amount to a revolution in the way service administration is carried out. It also needs to be repeated that there is no visible end to the process of change, in that it will not be a series of discrete changes with a defined end date, a one-off change. It instead seems to be a permanent increase in the rate of change, a new norm which businesses will have to adjust to. Insurers cannot thus just visualize the change as one of moving from their old arrangement to a new stable arrangement - they will have to reconfigure themselves to accept permanent change.

All service sectors will be impacted by these changes but insurance will be impacted more than most service sectors because (i) other sectors, like banking, have made more adjustments already, whereas insurance has stayed fairly traditional; (ii) insurance depends more deeply on skills in data analysis than most sectors (iii) insurance is inherently relationship and trust based; and (iv) insurance in most markets tends to be traditionally less competitive. The finance sector, for example, has moved away humans trading; it has extensively disintermediated and has coped with extensive changes in company ownership and structure. Insurance has done none of these.

How quickly the insurance sector in each market reacts to the growing pressures to evolve will depend on local market structure. Many markets are oligopolies with a small number of firms dominating. These markets are not subject to intense competitive pressures, with market participants able to reach de facto understandings to only engage in certain types of competition. Innovation thus has tended to be limited.

In many markets, this has limited the introduction into the insurance sector of a range of technological changes which have impacted on other service sectors. It is thus easy for these insurers to conclude that they will remain safe from the onslaught of technological innovations discussed. The reverse is true, however, as escape is impossible from a

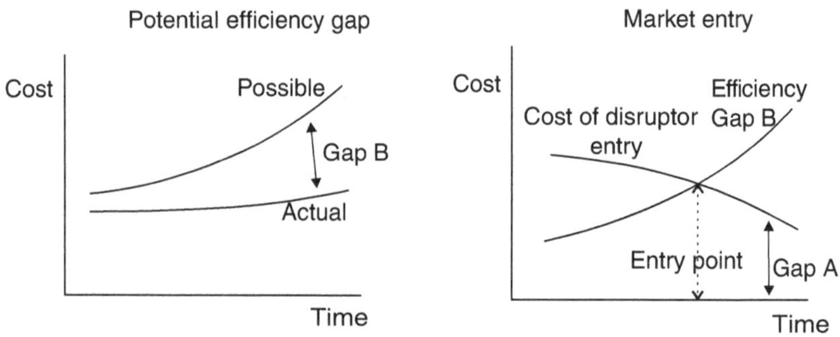

Fig. 8.1 Market Entry Dynamics

wave of innovations which are of a type which effect a broad range of administrative processes, as well as a range of customer behavior patterns, especially when these innovations both cut internal costs by a substantial magnitude and intensify customer acquisition and retention processes.

What the differing types of market structure will affect is the type of disruption experienced. Within competitive markets, firms are used to responding to changes in the business environment and thus will be prepared to ditch existing frameworks faster. This higher efficiency reduces the scope for an external disruptor to enter. Within less competitive markets the cozier an oligopoly is, then the slower the rate of internal sector change will be, thus the more the sector will fall behind the general service sector norm, and therefore the more attractive the sector becomes to an external disruptor and the less that existing firms will be able to compete with that external entrant. Thus, in competitive markets, change will tend to come by competition forcing existing firms to adapt to the required changes, whereas in less competitive markets, change will tend to come by the entry of external firms who are strong in the new skill sets and the subsequent disappearance of existing firms. It is up to insurers to decide which fate is theirs.

The basic concept behind disruptive vs evolutionary change is illustrated in Fig. 8.1. There is a cost to entry imposed on a non-sector outsider, PV amount A. The dynamic changes discussed above mean that this cost of entry will probably decrease over time. There is a gap between efficiency/profit generated by best practice and efficiency/profit generated by existing firms, PV amount B. This increases over time if existing firms do not innovate. As soon as amount A is less than amount B, it is profitable for an external firm to enter and disrupt the market. This is the 'Uber moment.' As time passes, the gap gets larger so the chance of change by disruptive entry rises.

It is useful to note that the rate of disruptive entry is increasing in all industries and the rate of established company bankruptcy increasing, as shown by the five-year mortality rate for US public companies now running as high as 33% overall. Even for the largest established firms, the rate is around 20%. In 1958, S & P500 companies, on a rolling seven-year basis, remained in the index for 61 years, but by 1980, it was down to 25 years and, by 2011, was down to 18 years. From 2000 to 2015 52% of Fortune 500 either went bankrupt, were acquired, or ceased to exist. Realistically, it can be expected that over half of all currently listed insurance companies will not be listed by 2027, due to bankruptcy or takeover.

It is vital to realize that disruptive entry does not have to involve one major external disruptor. It can equally involve many small firms attacking the more profitable parts of a value chain and forcing incumbents to disintermediate. This is particularly true in smaller markets. The disruptor also does not have to be the major world leader, as once a business model is established, third-party innovators can establish in smaller markets before the international giant has a chance to expand there.

The insurance sector is also highly prone to disruptive entry as their return on equity has been persistently below the average with the US property and casualty insurance sector falling below the average more than 85% of periods during 1955–2010. They will thus struggle to obtain the extra equity they require to make the large investments needed to support the large increase in innovation needed.

The Economics of Digital Disruption

McKinsey (2016b) argues that the task of trying to prepare for future innovations is very complex as companies not only have to examine current trends, current industry competitors, and possible external disruptors, companies also have to predict trends which have yet to occur. This involves understanding 'what-we-do-not-yet-know'. This is vital as the ultimate aim of insurance survivors should not just be to survive against waves of disruptors, it should instead be to get on top of yet-to-occur trends so the incumbent insurers can become the disruptors. This requires an understanding of the deeper forces, that is, not *which* companies or technologies will disrupt, but *why* the disruption will occur.

For an external disruption to be successful, there needs to be a 'disruption point'; some aspect of the value chain which the disruptor can carry out substantially better than incumbents can. Some disruption points are

1. *Unused inventory:* Amazon, Uber, and Airbnb have thrived because they are better able to organize inventory, which existing suppliers left unused.
2. *Information aggregation:* Disruptors can organize production or client information better than incumbents
3. *Reputation:* Incumbents have low reputation and trust levels.
4. *Cost-plus pricing:* Incumbents are using cost-plus pricing. An example is the way Space-X is transforming its industry by reducing cost to less than 10% of the hide-bound incumbents
5. *Low marginal cost:* Disruptors can automate processes so each activity has an extremely low marginal cost, thus enabling them to both undercut the incumbent and to offer customization.

Incumbents need to decide in which area of their value chain they are vulnerable and start to disrupt their own model.

McKinsey (2016b) argues that there are two primary sources of digital disruption, each with three sub-elements:

1. *Modest changes:* These tend to cause smaller changes in market structure.

    a. *Unmet demand* caused by changes in customer expectations. Changes in technology reveal that customer expectations are not what incumbent companies thought they were. For example, music was delivered as albums as this was the most cost-effective supply mechanism. Digital downloads revealed that customers actually prefer to buy single tracks. Do customers want to own cars or do they merely want to use private transport services? Do customers want insurance on a permanent annual basis, or only when they engage in particular activities? Companies are vulnerable to disruption if some customers subsidize others, or if customers have to buy a whole product to get the part they want, or if customers can't get what they want when they want it, or if the customer experience doesn't match the global best standard.
    b. *Exposed new supply* because digitization allows new sources to enter product or labor markets. For example, Airbnb unlocks the supply of previously unrentable lodging. Companies are vulnerable to disruption if customers only use a product partly, production is inelastic to price, supply exists which is currently unusable, supply can be utilized in an unpredictable new way, or fixed costs are high. An example here would be Web-based peer-to-peer insurance.
    c. *Market makers* enter to match unused supply to latent demand. For example, Wikipedia allows people to learn about a topic without buying a large encyclopedia set. Companies are vulnerable if there are; high information asymmetry costs, or high search costs, intermediaries who impose fees, or long lead times to complete transactions.
2. *Extreme changes:* These tend to cause substantial market disruption and normally involve external disruptors using a different business model.

    d. *A new value proposition* is created due to customers' expectations evolving past what present suppliers can deliver. This often involves new suppliers providing what customers weren't aware they needed. For example, the ability to search the Web from a pocket phone. Customers and thus producers were not aware that they wanted phones to do anything apart from talking to other people. Companies are vulnerable if increased information would greatly enhance your product, your physical product is not connected, there is a significant lag between when customers purchase your product and when they receive it or the customer has to go and get the product.

e. *A reimagined business system* is offered by new suppliers. Incumbents often focus on perfecting their supply chains, so are stunned when an external supplier introduces a completely new way to make money. For example, Hard-drive manufacturers focused on efficiency before Amazon came and transformed data storage from a product to a service. These new approaches often transform the scalability of cost structures, driving marginal cost toward zero, thus flattening the supply curve. Companies are vulnerable if there are redundant value chain activities, or well-entrenched physical distribution networks, or higher than average distribution costs. Do customers want compensation after an adverse event or do they want help to ensure that event does not occur?
f. *New suppliers transform the industry* by scaling the quantity and breadth of production up by previously unimagined multiples and thereby blurring industry boundaries. For example, Amazon introduced the Kindle mainly to sell digital books rather than make money from physical sales. This allowed them to move onto the sale of services. This disadvantaged Sony, who had to make money from sales of Kobe. These disruptions normally involve the creation of a digital platform, which binds chosen suppliers into an ecosystem dominated by the platform supplier. Within the car industry, the company which is best placed to offer car insurance is the player with the best data, which is likely to be the company which supplies and operates the telematics platform.

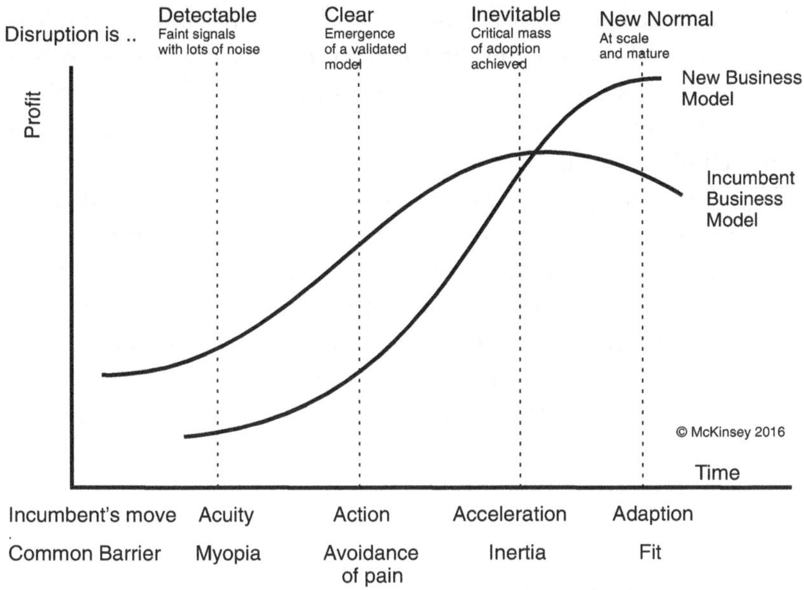

Fig. 8.2 Stages of Digital Disruption. *Source* McKinsey (2016a)

Stages of Disruption

McKinsey (2016a) argues that there are four stages to digital disruption. These can be graphed by recognizing that all businesses involve technology which grows matures and then ages over time. This can be visualized as an S-shaped curve. The only question is - Are you on the old or new technology curve? McKinsey argues that we can visualize disruption by overlapping the old and new technology curves, shown in Fig. 8.2.

- *Stage One: Signals amidst the Noise* - In the first stage, the new technology is just evolving. A clear-sighted incumbent could spot the possible change and react to it early. However, because the environment is so noisily, which hundreds of possible threats, it's nearly impossible for an incumbent at the time to decipher which technology will thrive from the hundreds which will fail. Incumbents, however, need to be aware of the likelihood of some technologies being successful and being prepared to react swiftly. Scenarios based on possible disruptive challengers will often highlight vulnerabilities. Those incumbents who do spot possible threats and prepare to react are well placed to survive.

- *Stage Two: Change takes Hold* - In the second stage, the trend is clear. The incumbent needs to commit to nurturing multiple new incentives. They need to invest in the most likely new directions and be prepared to cannibalize existing businesses. This is difficult as the threat is still distant and may not seem important to stockholders. For example, when Netflix moved from DVDs to Streaming, its stock price fell by 80% because of a sharp drop in current cash flow. Most incumbents thus dabble, making only small investments, and focus on protecting the existing business.
- *Stage Three: The Inevitable Transformation* - In the third stage, the future has arrived and new technology is rapidly gaining market share. Incumbents have to massively shift resources to the new area. This can be difficult if they do not already have experience in managing the new area. It is made even worse because old-business cash flow will be dropping, so firms focus on cutting back rather than on making the large investments required. Top management and boards, who are normally sourced from the old business, often view the crisis as temporary; one they can live through if they focus on old-business efficiency.
- *Stage Four: Adapting to the New Norm* - In the fourth stage, the new technology is dominant, so incumbents have become disruptors or have to focus on the best way to exit. Often all that is left of value is the brand name and legacy.

Digital Strategy's Double Game

BCG (2015) argues that because of the exponential possibilities and economics of new technologies, companies need to create defined 'digital strategies' to enable them to continually adapt to and seize new opportunities. This means playing a 'double game': Making the most out of today's contests, while positioning themselves to win in tomorrow's contest. They have to rebuild their new business while running their old one.

BCG argues that companies have to ask three strategy questions:

i. *What can I forecast?* Companies need to analyze what is possible in the future; explicitly stating the most likely scenarios and conclusions, but also running scenarios about any possible outcomes, even if very unlikely. This reduces surprises about future and prepares companies to act on any outcomes with decisive speed.
   For example, automotive companies have been contemplating a future with autonomous vehicles for decades. But because their business focus was on efficiency, global expansion, and electric cars, they were surprised by the rapid emergence of an autonomous-vehicle prototype by outsiders, Google and Tesla, and the broad embrace of the concept that they generated. The industry is thus urgently playing catch-up.
ii. *Where can I be disrupted?* Companies need to examine all areas of the supply chain as well as customer requirement. It is because an external disruptor has a very different perspective on customer needs that they are successful. Who knew that phone customers wanted to play games? For example, buyers of cars do not want cars, they want mobility, which is not the same thing. Car insurance customers do not want 24/7 insurance, they want insurance only when they drive. Would customers prefer to buy PAYG insurance from their mobile data provider? Thus, companies need to explore the attacker's perspective. They need to examine adjacent industries for new moves which could endanger their current business. They need to be aware of the activities of disruptors in all sectors. They need to actively imagine multiple possible futures.
iii. *What can I shape and where do I need to adapt?* Existing supplier advantages, brands, distribution networks, supplier relationships, strong capabilities, and superior cost positions, etc., do not disappear in a digital world. Companies need to examine how they can draw on existing or latent strengths to acquire new capabilities or adapt to ambient forces. BCG cautions, however, that CEOs often

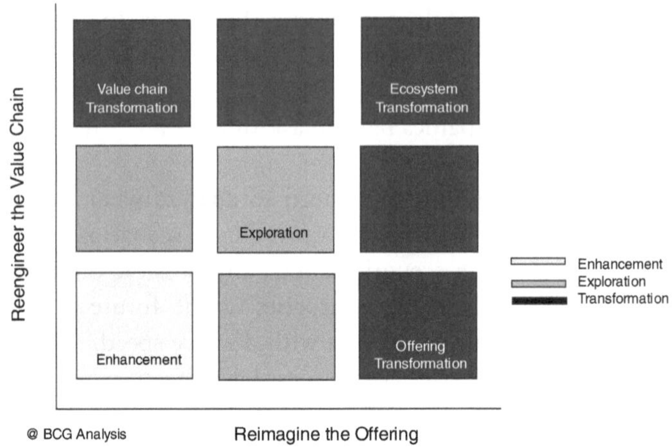

Fig. 8.3 The Digital matrix. © Boston Consulting Group, used with permission. *Source* BCG (2015)

> overestimate their ability to predict and shape their environment, underestimate the power of disruptive trends, and consequently lead their companies astray.

BCG (2015) argues that charting the current and future playing fields is necessary but insufficient. It's also essential to frame, explore, and prioritize strategic choices. An intuitive tool is BCG's digital opportunity matrix, shown in Fig. 8.3, which comprises two axes: (i) *Reengineer the value chain* - state-of-the-art IT has become flexible, intuitive, powerful, and accessible. Data analytics that improves sales effectiveness across physical, mobile, and online channels can promote significant value creation. (ii) *Reimagine the offering* - whereas reengineering is largely a linear process in search of efficiency and effectiveness, reimagining is more open ended, requiring creativity and vision. Digital also creates ample opportunities for novel products and services. These innovations typically exploit new data and powerful analytics.

The BCG diagram has three stages that are represented along the diagonal in the digital opportunity matrix.

1. *Enhancement*: Strategically, enhancement is about extrapolating from your current position. Start with where you can create immediate value. While this is the least radical stage of digital opportunities, it can improve the organization's digital skills and provide tremendous and immediate value creation that can fund the broader digital journey. Examples include predictive maintenance, streamlined digital links to suppliers and customers, and recommendation engines.
2. *Exploration:* Exploration requires investigating offerings adjacent to the current business or pursuing larger adjustments of the value chain. Exploratory digital strategies become executive topics. Companies need to invest significant resources in digital businesses and closely track their performance. In many cases, companies can develop a portfolio of venture investments to establish beachheads in promising areas.
3. *Transformation:* Transformation is an all-encompassing strategic move that has the greatest potential to generate competitive advantage, often over several years, but also the greatest risk. From a strategic standpoint, executives need to reimagine a target business model 5–10 years out and then 'retropolate' from that vision back to the present. Transformative change by its nature becomes *the* top CEO priority. Transformation requires major investments and often the development of new partner ecosystems.

BCG (2015) argues that three conclusions arise from this: (i) *Ultimately, strategy is about choice*. Companies cannot do everything, and they cannot even do all the things they should do simultaneously. Strategic choices are required to prioritize and stage initiatives. (ii) *Conventional wisdom can be generally right but specifically wrong.* In a fast-moving environment, even winners stay vulnerable. Data in particular is a problem because it is new and growing exponentially. The most valuable data doesn't rest in dusty databases but has yet to be created. (iii) *Practice playing the double game.* Sustained success requires actively managing a portfolio of initiatives across time, running the old and new side-by-side.

Companies find implementing these strategies hard. Managers are increasingly nervous about the lack of progress in their digital initiatives

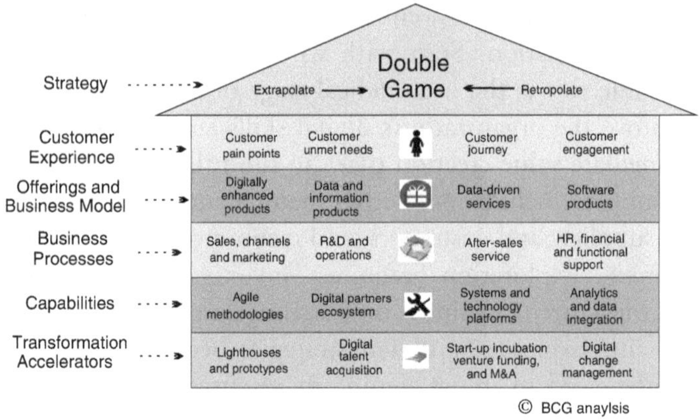

Fig. 8.4 The Action Space for Digital Transformation. © Boston Consulting Group, used with permission. *Source* BCG (2015)

and consequently merely add 'digital pixie dust' to traditional processes or engage in a frenzy of digital experiments and ventures, designed to look good rather than being effective. Rather than drive competitive advantage, these efforts leave companies more vulnerable.

Insurance customers do not want an insurance product, they want an insurance service. Insurers need to reimagine their entire business model.

BCG (2015) argues that companies need to operate in an action space consisting of six interdependent layers as shown in Fig. 8.4. A complete digital transformation requires playing in all six layers.

These layers are:

- *Defining the strategy* focuses on building competitive advantage in the double game. It provides insight into short-term 'no regrets' moves as well as more-transformative plays. These decisions establish the path for the other five layers.
- *Reshaping the customer experience* explores how to eliminate pain points and how to surprise customers with new levels and forms of service today, while achieving quantum improvements in customer experience tomorrow.

- *Reimagining offerings and business models* prepares companies to create novel products and services, often by exploiting new data and powerful analytics.
- *Reengineering business processes* entails adopting flexible and intuitive digital technologies to simplify processes and increase efficiency.
- *Building capabilities,* often by working with outside partners and creating new platforms, enables companies to develop new ways of working, new business models, and other building blocks of digital transformation.
- *Accelerating the transformation* involves devising new approaches to speed up learning, ramp-ups, and transformational plays.

BCG (2015) argues that delivering a superior customer experience is a natural initial goal of many digital programs. New offerings designed to retain or increase the share of wallet of current customers and to win new customers are at the heart of many digital programs. Allowing customer to interact with quality Web systems can enhance their experience and transform neutral customers to enthusiastic advocates. While quality is vital, however, speed is more important. A common mistake is letting perfection stand in the way of progress. It is more important to launch minimally viable offerings, even if faulty, and then to upgrade them quickly in response to customer feedback than to let time and opportunity slip away. Customers have proven to be highly collaborative - accepting initial imperfection and suggesting practical product improvements - when their feedback is acted upon.

Speed and flexibility are more important than perfection. In today's world, it is more important to be wrong fast than right too slowly. It can also be useful to set impossible targets and deadlines, even if these are not met, as this focuses executive minds on how to get there, rather than on the precise details of the journey. Strategies do not have to be precisely mapped out, designations can be fuzzy, methods can be flexible, and targets can be missed - what is important is momentum.

Business processes need to be reengineered. Rather than thinking creatively about how digital technology can support novel approaches to work or production, many companies simply digitize the legacy processes. Companies also need to quickly find or train candidates to fill new job profiles. Without active management of workforce issues, fundamental reengineering will almost certainly stall or even fail. Experienced digital transformation managers are particularly hard to find. Very few executives, for example, have industry experience and deep knowledge in prototyping and agile methodologies.

Playing the double game in this area is challenging because it requires simultaneous action to maintain legacy technologies, embed new digital tools, and introduce a flexible and scalable new digital architecture that will pave the way for an even more radically redefined future. IT departments and external partners can be critical resources in this undertaking, or they can be a hindrance if their specific skill profiles, business practices, and interests do not sync with what is needed - so IT processes will probably need transformation.

Companies are adopting various practices to accelerate their digital transformation, including rapid prototyping, incubators, M&A, and the acquisition of digital talent, as well as traditional change management levers. Many of the most effective accelerators call for new ways of working and new forms of behavior, such as cross-functional, self-directed, teams and collaboration built around agile software development methodologies.

Innovation Traps

Kanter (2006) argues that faced with disruptive changes, firms fall repeatedly into the same innovation traps. She identifies four waves of competitive changes in the last 25 years: (i) the dawn of IT in the late 1970s when PCs started to take over from mainframes, Japanese style total quality management became the fad, and new industries were established. Firms responded by creating product innovation 'garages' modeled on firms like Apple. (ii) The takeover scare of the late 1980s, when financial innovation gave corporate predators more power and state-owned enterprises were privatized. (iii) The Digital Mania of the 1990s, based on the threat of firms associated with the newly created Internet. (iv) The mid-2000 consolidation following the dot.com crash.

Kanter (2006) argues that each wave has started with enthusiasm but has been derailed by similar problems. The main tension is between protecting revenue streams from existing businesses and supporting new concepts which could potentially dominate future revenue streams. This tension creates internal resistance to the new innovations which tends to destroy most renewal programs. Kanter notes that this means major innovations tend to occur due to external disruptors.

Kanter observes a repeated pattern of mistakes in four areas:

Mistakes in Strategy

1. Executives declare that they want innovation but are refuse to support new programs unless other incumbent firms are doing something similar.
2. Executives tend to focus on opportunities for large gains, even if risky, rather than opportunities for smaller, more certain gains.
3. Executives screen out opportunities which do not promise a revenue gain within two years, even if it has the potential to disrupt the industry.
4. Executives tend to focus on new products instead of realizing that innovations can be as important in areas like production or administration or transport or CRM.
5. Executives impose too tight controls.

In the 1980s, Procter and Gamble failed to develop a new type of toilet bowl cleaner as analysis showed that returns were uncertain and didn't fit traditional market research. They thus lost substantial market share to a rival. In the 1990s, Quaker Oats focused too much on minor tweaks to existing products and thus missed nearly all the more health-focused innovations.

Mistakes in Process

1. Executives strangle new innovations by applying traditional planning and budgeting controls to new products.

2. Executives apply existing metrics and performance reviews to innovations. They want innovation managers to stick to plans, even if innovation has gone in a different direction.
3. Employees tend to be rewarded for doing what they are committed to do, rather than acting as changed circumstances would suggest.

In the 1990s, Ocean Spray grabbed the radical paper-bottle market because its larger competitors were not prepared to fund uncertain innovations outside their budget cycle.

Mistakes in Structure

1. Executives are unsure of how closely to link the innovator unit to the mainstream, making it either too loose, thereby generating misunderstanding and resentment in the mainstream, or too tight, thereby stifling the innovation team with bureaucracy.
2. Executives can create two classes of conflicting corporate citizens: those who have fun innovating vs those who make the money. This conflict is worsened if the innovation unit has a markedly different culture and type of employee.

In the mid-1990s, AT&T worldwide refused in invest sufficiently in an Internet service provider unit because existing managers were reluctant to provide funds or personal, as they were convinced it would never generate significant revenue. Once it was a going concern, it was brought back into the mainstream budgeting process and starved of funds.

Mistakes in Skills

1. Executives tend to undervalue and underinvest in skills relevant to innovation. They tend to put the best technical person in charge of innovation units and not the best leader.
2. Technical executives tend to undervalue the importance of communicating results to non-innovation units, tend to empathize tasks over relationships, and do not build team interpersonal skills. Innovators tend to like to work in isolation and undervalue the need to get

corporate-wide buy-in, and the need to present the radical in familiar terms.

3. Executives tend to rotate staff too quickly. Research shows that innovation staff are more productive after two years, yet tend to be rotated every 18 months.

In the early 2000s, Timberland developed an innovative new line of modular travel shoes within a separate innovation unit. However, existing units had not been included and the sales force refused to promote the product.

Kanter argues that there are thus four remedies to create successful innovation:

1. *Strategy Remedy* - Firms need to widen the search for new ideas and broaden the scope. They should create a pyramid of innovation, topped by a couple of long-shot ground changing ideas, but cascading down to multiple smaller ideas. Company-wide calls should be made for new ideas in all areas, not just products. While dedicated groups pursue big projects, temporary groups can pursue smaller ones. This allows a lot more employees to be involved and embeds a culture of innovation and dynamic change.
2. *Process Remedy* - Flexibility is required in planning and budget cycles. Special funds should be set aside for use if ideas arise mid-cycle. Budgets and plans need to be changeable if innovations take new directions. A cross-department team of flexible thought leaders needs to allow exemptions from normal processes.
3. *Structure Remedy* - Links between innovators and mainstream units need to be tightened, especially human links. Productive conversations have to be created between innovators and mainstream units, with senior leaders actively encouraging mutual respect. Innovators need to understand that they are there to serve the mainstream business, and the mainstream units need to understand that innovators are securing their future. Tesla insists its research engineers' work in the middle of the production floor.
4. *Skills Remedy* - Firms need to emphasize that the most important company asset is the level of skills within its workforce. Continual

retraining will be required as activities are lost to software. Employees need to feel part of an ongoing team.

New Entrants/Innovators

Current indications are that the majority of existing insurers will be unable to make the required transition successfully against competition from outside firms, due to their inability to break from traditional modes of behavior.

An example of this inability to break traditional bounds is Google's failure to find an insurer prepared, or even able, to underwrite road tests for its self-drive cars, despite this being an ideal opportunity to gather innovative data. The essence of accurate risk pricing is data, and the increase in real-time driving data collection being generated by sensors currently embedded in modern cars means that within a few years, car manufacturers will have a better source of driving data than insurers and will thus be able to price risk more accurately. Manufacturers will also be able to establish real-time proactive customer contacts. Why would insurers not want that data experience even if it is money losing?

Once real-time feedback is perfected, insurers will be in the position of needing to work with car manufacturers to survive, yet car manufacturers will by then have the capacity to establish themselves as the platform at the center of business ecosystem, with its profitable value-adds. This relegates insurers to the margins, as suppliers of low-value products with little direct customer contacts. Insurer cash flow will drop and car manufacturers will be able to play insurers off against each other. Insurers need to understand their potential positions within business ecosystems and what they can offer partners. They need to create skills which are useful to potential partners.

It is vital to recognize that insurance is a key end-market for data from telematic producers and as such, insurers need to insistent that telematic sensors are incorporated into consumer, health, and home products as fast as possible. Given that integrated use of telematics is the core aspect of intensifying data collection and use, and therefore vital for dynamic premiums and substantially lower cost adminstration, insurers who do not proactively innovate and cooperate will be at a severe competitive disadvantage. If current insurers do not proactively engage, then there will be a strong impulse for these telematic suppliers to approach newer, more innovative, insurance competitors.

Disintermediation is also a major threat. A growing trend has been for IT developers to develop stand-alone modules for various components of the insurance supply chain. For example, Guidewire offers a core processing suite for P&C insurers. New entrants with existing customers will therefore be able to buy in the technical capacity which they may be lacking, adding modules from a network of suppliers, effectively creating an 'insurer-in-a-box' to add to their suite of products. SAP is an example of a firm which already offers a comprehensive IT insurance package. They can add to this by contracting with firms who offer actuarial, or CRM, or claims, or other sector-specific expertise. Insurers who aim to survive the coming perfect storm therefore need to ensure that they leverage off their expertise and deeper understanding and therefore are able to offer a superior value proposition than an 'in-a-box' solution provider can. Given that the cost of processing via IT software is expected to fall by about 20% per year, this will be a sizable challenge.

The shorter product duration cycle in P&C means that these changes are both likely to impact there first, and that it will be easier for existing insurers to migrate clients to a new IT system. While life and health insurers may be less exposed, they face more issues with migrating long-term policies, probably already located on multiple legacy IT systems, to a new system.

Canas (2015) argues that the likely failure of insurers to respond will mean that change will probably come from an outside disruptive technology innovator, similar to the way Uber is disrupting the taxi industry, a process now called 'uberization.' These new entrants will probably be existing technology firms with high social capital. The entry point will probably be first via comparison quote engines, then purchase of e-aggregators, then purchase of product creators. A growing alternative new entrant is Web-based group schemes, 'peer-insurance,' which is similar to old-fashioned mutual insurers. These trends will mean that existing multiple-task insurers will have to fight strong disaggregation trends, as new entrants cherry-pick profitable tasks.

Equinix (2014) argues that given that the core competencies of insurers are abilities to aggregate, predict, and manage financial risk using data analytics, then outside organizations which possess these skills are potential rivals. The core business of companies like Google and Amazon is data analytics, their customer relationship skills are superior, and they are technological leaders in core areas like big data, AI, and telematics. It is easier for these companies to add insurance to their product mix than it is for current insurers to remedy their limitations in AI data analytics and customer relationships.

Possible Future Pathways

Morgan Stanley/BCG (2014) foresees seven possible scenarios for insurers subject to technological disruption:

1. *Status Quo* - insurers continue to offer the whole value chain. This is seen as unlikely.
2. *Insurer-based ecosystems* - insurers create the platform which is the core of an ecosystem and thus continue to dominate the value chain, as well as expand into related areas. This is the best outcome for insurers but seen as unlikely due to lack of platform expertise.
3. *Traditional Partnering* - insurers work with an adjacent entrant, possibly a bank, to offer insurance via the partner. The problem with this is that traditional partners for insurers may also lack platform skills.
4. *Complementary Platform* - insurers seek a suitable ecosystem platform to offer complementary services. The insurer loses control but is a part of a dynamic ecosystem which has a higher chance of success that a go-alone policy offers. This is the most likely outcome for survivors.
5. *Value chain disruption* - insurers work with partners along the value chain but face erosion of its value chain as more suitable adjacent entrants expand into the insurer value chain.
6. *Disruptive ecosystem entry* - entrants from adjacent ecosystem sectors expand into parts of the insurance value chain. This is already happening in some sectors.

7. *Disruptive entry* - entrants from outside sectors offer a new model of insurance cover and squeeze the insurer out of significant parts of its market, destroying scale, or attracting prime clients. This is the most likely result unless insurers are proactive in removing the opportunity.

One of the key points which Morgan Stanley/BCG (2014) makes is that any pathway which separates insurers from contact with their customers and the resultant feedback exposes insurers to a significant risk of gradual erosion of its role in an ecosystem to being that of a margin-squeezed processing component supplier, so that client contact is not maintained.

IAIS (2017) discusses three contrasting response scenarios. The superior route for incumbents is that of intensifying both the spread and depth of client contact and data and then leveraging of this to create deep client engagement, directly useful products, and value-added services. This kind of deep authentic branding is, however, still largely absent in the insurance sector so they lack experience.

The current response of many incumbents is to buy or partner with a start-up or disruptor. This can be successful, though the track record of incumbents in other industries gaining from these is patchy. The reasons for this, as laid-out above, are that (i) the incumbent needs to transform its IT system to reduce its marginal costs enough to make use of the start-ups technology (ii) the incumbent's culture needs to be transformed, or the innovativeness which created the start-up withers. The same arguments apply to start-ups the incumbent creates itself. Responding to disruptive innovation is difficult.

Disruptive Innovators

Canas (2015) highlights examples of seven innovative firms disrupting existing insurance markets. These firms can't be regarded as perfect in all areas, but they are useful examples.

1. *Zenefits* - founded in 2013, this cloud-based company is transforming the HR business, by giving away its software and making profits

instead from commissions on health insurance sold via its HR software. Because it is software based, it has low costs and can undercut all its insurance competitors, as well as the advantage of being embedded within the client's core software.

2. *BizInsure* - founded by an online business insurer and a leading US broker, BizInsure enables clients to explore policies, to obtain quote, buy instantly, and get them all declarations and policy details in their email inbox within 10 minutes. They also offer phone or email access to a licensed agent able to answer any queries, at any time.
3. *MetroMile* - connects clients to insurers who offer vehicle cover by the mile driven, not on a time basis. It is a software-based downloadable app which can be installed on most current vehicle models. The company has very low costs per client and has been advertising heavily at those who drive less than 10,000 miles per year. It also offers companies the ability to track their fleets and create online vehicle usage and cost reports, as well as discounts on maintenance, and information on the best parking deals. It has teamed up with Uber to be the default insurance supplier to all Uber drivers.
4. *Evosure* - provides a Web-based platform for commercial brokers to outline the types of client risk they want to be covered and to receive specific quotes from underwriters.
5. *Friendsurance* - arranges peer-to-peer personal risk insurance cover by creating groups of people with similar risks, normally via existing social connections, and then offering this to underwriters. Pools with less than expected losses are given a refund, while pools with higher losses face no increase. The business concept is that using groups of friends sharply reduces fraud and improves risk selection, as the group jointly wants a refund.
6. *Social Intel* - underwrites risk by using software to analyze people's social media posts rather than traditional metrics like driving history or credit record. This cuts data collection costs sharply without reducing underwriting quality by much. By being software driven, they can provide underwriters with real-time updates. This leads to interesting concepts like the insurer knowing that a client is at a 'rave party' and can therefore cancel the car insurance for 24 hours, while arranging an Uber driver.

7. *Policy Genius* - founded by two ex-McKinsey consultants who considered current insurers very backward and disagreed with the concept that insurance 'had to be sold.' Instead, they thought that provision of the right information would inspire clients to purchase online, as they did for other products. An example of this is providing information on what 'people like you' need cover for and linking this to a client friendly checklist which takes 5 minutes and leads to a summary and a link to quotes and online purchase. It builds trust by pointing out what kinds of insurance you don't need, as well as how need for cover changes over the life cycle. It has strong appeal to the younger digital natives.

Other firms of interest are:

8. *Aspiration* - offers financial advice linked to investment funds. It is predominantly software based and is aimed at middle-class investors with between $500 to $100,000 to invest. It charges no fees and instead asks that investors to 'pay what you think is fair.' This surprising concept has led to a rapid growth in investment funds.
9. *Lemonade* - a P2P insurer. They take a flat 20% of premiums as a fee, use 40% for reinsurance (internal and external), and 40% as a small claims pool. Any profit above that is given to nominated charities. These arrangements disincentive fraud. Adminstration is based on an intensive software-based system, with 80% of most client activities requiring no human involvement. Claims are nearly all automated, with one claim paid in 3 seconds. Feedback from customers indicates that the ease of application, lack of paperwork, rapid query feedback (usually chatbot based), and speed of claims payment have generated very high social media rankings and 'makes incumbents seem like they are from a past century.'
   Lemonade involves three aspects which are different from the incumbent model: (i) P2P is simply a return to the old mutual insurer model, so nothing new. The issue with the mutual insurer model was a lack of capital, which Lemonade solves by their financing set-up. (ii) Reinsurers play an increased role, which may not be as cost effective as an internal capital model. (iii) An intensive software admin system is the real innovation. Most incumbents will struggle to adjust legacy systems to Lemonade's low admin costs and fast processing.

10. *Insure-the-box/Drive-like-a-girl* - these sister companies offer cheap car insurance by requiring all clients to install a telematic box device which monitors driving. Clients who do not fulfill cautious driving parameters are dropped or required to pay hefty surpluses. The better the driver behaves, the lower the premium drops. The device sends real-time reports, instantly alerts a staff member to any crashes, and sends a crash report which includes data on aspects like location, speed, force of impact, direction of impact, and engine condition. A staff member can then alert emergency crews with the car location and likely extent of injuries. The increased speed of response has already saved lives. The company is especially popular with young drivers who can prove that they shouldn't have to pay the extremely high rates generally imposed on them. Since driving frequency and location are recorded, infrequent drivers or those in rural areas can be offered substantial discounts. If the car is stolen, the location can be tracked in real time. Note that the company only attracts low-risk drivers, leaving high-risk drivers to traditional companies.

11. *Bought-by-many* - this is an aggregator firm who finds and groups people who have unusual insurance needs, for example, diabetics who want travel insurance. It finds these groups mainly by using algorithms which are designed to respond to Web searches by people looking for insurance. These people are offered customized policies at no extra cost, and insurers are offered a block of clients with a specific risk profile.
12. *Tokio-Marine* - has partnered with mobile phone operator NTT DoCoMo to offer limited time insurance for specific events arranged and paid for via a mobile phone-based app. This can normally be obtained on the spot, just before a purchase is made or an activity takes place. An example is a non-car owner who borrows a friend's car and needs cover for ½ a day. The target is uninsured younger participants in active events and costs are heavily reduced by piggy-backing on existing NTT software with invoicing via NTT's payment system. NTT gets extra business at minimal

cost, and Tokio-Marine has access to NTT's 60M customers. This approach has seen sales rise by at least 22% per annum across the range.

13. *Oscar* - this is a rapidly growing New York health insurer, based on an online only platform. Insurance can be obtained rapidly, which a quote offered in 5 clicks. Oscar offers free phone calls to doctors and a Google-map-based doctor-finder, as well as health price-comparison tool.
14. *Youi* - is a South African-based insurer which uses an intensively underwritten model to provide customized quotes and thus skim off good clients. It has a high social media presence including allowing customers to post unedited reviews on its Web site in real time. Currently, user satisfaction on its Web wall stands at 85%, and Youi is rapidly expanding internationally.[1] [1]Note that Youi has suffered from regulatory action in Australia and NZ over dubious sales practices.
15. *Allianz* - this German insurance giant is trying to transform into a digital business model. It is spending €500M on IT per annum and has 5 key initiatives (a) digitization of all business processes; (b) enabling online research, quotation, purchasing, and servicing; (c) standardization of data and policies so data for a customer can be viewed in an integrated manner; (d) standardization of Web platforms worldwide; and (e) establishment of an experimental center for new ideas. Key decisions were to re-create products as modules which can be assembled in different packages and to change culture by employing a substantial number of staff from social networking companies. Allianz is a good example of a company which is overcoming the inherence of running a legacy model while transforming.
16. *Wells-Fargo* - has used the Stagecoach Island social media game both to teach 16–24-year olds financial literacy and to cheaply acquire tens of thousands as new clients. The accumulated emails enable them to run a successful educational social media service.

17. *Progressive Insurance* - pioneered dynamic car policies based on telematics, via Snapshot which offers drivers discounts depending on when and how well they drive. They have signed up 3 million customers since 2008, collecting a massive archive of driving data from onboard black boxes. This data has enabled them to identify potential customers by risk type a lot more finely than competitors can.
18. *Brolly* - a UK InsurTech start-up which offers a digital agent focused on helping customers, understand, manage, and buy insurance. The App helps clients gather all necessary financial and lifestyle information and then compares these to existing insurance policies, examining cover levels and conditions in order to spot coverage gaps or negotiate better policy terms. Customers are offered detailed feedback and explanations and can then OK a search for better policies. While personal details are not provided to insurers, customers as a group can be underwritten more accurately due to qualitatively higher quality profiles.
19. *Octo Telematics* - is the leading global supplier of telematic devices for the auto-insurers. They have 4.8 million connected users and 380k crashes analyzed. From this, they have developed a range of data algorithms and provided in-depth accident-causal data to clients.
20. *DBS bank* - this Singapore bank is not an insurer, but it is an example of how a large incumbent can embrace the challenge of a digital future. Keys to this are ensured the central software system was recreated end-to-end, focused on the customer experience, and on the required cultural change. They found that setting up a separate R&D unit failed, so they embedded innovation into every employee's job. Every employee was taught how to be technology creative and required to run experiments. A separate online only bank in China has been established, which aims to cut admin cost by 90%. Bancassurance market share has doubled.
21. *L&T General Insurance* - this Indian insurer was faced with the problem of reaching customers spread across a subcontinent with poor roads and few bank accounts, when skilled staff were hard to find. Its solution was an end-to-end IT system which handles all customer contact and payments via a mobile phone App. This has

ensured low costs and enabled low-value micro-policies to be issued. It is scalable and handles sizable regional fluctuations in demand for services. All customers get proposals and automatic translation enables policies to be offered in the preferred language. New products can be launched very fast. Growth in India has been fast, and the model has the potential for use across all emerging markets.

Keys to Insurer Success

When current company mortality rates are low, existing companies can fall into a 'success trap,' that is, focusing on exploiting existing opportunities and being as efficient as possible, rather than understanding that existing opportunities will soon disappear. Management focus should instead be on exploring and creating new opportunities. The creative destruction of existing management structures and replacement by flexibility and innovativeness have to be the key to success.

PWC (2014) argues that there are ten attributes which will mark out the future survivors in the insurance sector from those who will fail.

1. *Contextualized* - matching the customer experience with their individual preferences, by using digital interaction to know customer preferences and modifying the buying experience to suit.
2. *Optimized* - continually testing and enhancing the interaction with the customer, by individually asking for feedback, and modifying interaction to increase the effectiveness of capturing leads, closing sales, and managing contracts. This has to be open and two-way, so the customer needs to feel in charge of the engagement style.
3. *Engaged* - creating a compelling reason to buy by increasing customer understanding and engagement. This should be benchmarked against best IT sector practice.
4. *Targeted* - turning the increased insights into customized products by recognizing what features customers value and then expanding services. Expertise in predicting customer behavior is critical, as is dynamic pricing.

5. *Guided* - helping customers decide what the correct choices are, by using a dynamic structured decision-making process.
6. *Synchronized* - creating a seamless, customer-lead, multi-channel experience, including online, social media, and human. The customer has to choose the mix of channels. Personal advisers should be available via multi-channels, phone, Skype, live chats, texts, Facebook messaging, social media, as well as face-to-face.
7. *All-embracing* - reshaping the entirety of company processes toward being customer focused. Every aspect of a company's operations needs to be re-examined so that the new approach is embedded in every area, and all managers need to be comfortable with the big-data decision-making style.
8. *Nimble* - leading rather than following the changes, taking control of the market place rather than reacting. Perfection is not as important as speed, and ability to change. A learning culture is vital and staff need to be allowed to fail.
9. *Efficient* - delivering more for less, by pricing risk more closely to customers, and using efficient internal processes. This does not mean the cheapest product, if customers understand choices.
10. *Sensitive* - clarity about what the company is doing with data and why. Data should only be collected if there is a reason clear and beneficial to the customer, and privacy is critical.

To this could be added 11. *Diversity* - an inherent ingredient of flexibility and innovativeness is employees who can approach an issue from multiple directions. It is thus vital to avoid creating a monocultural workforce with a dominant shared worldview. Instead, companies have to deliberately diversify their workforce in the right way. This then creates an internal richness of approaches and closer understanding of a diverse client base. It is vital to understand that this is not a simple matter of employing and promoting across ethnicities and both genders, as there is no guarantee that employees from different ethnic groups actually have differing worldviews. It is more about deliberate recruiting people who think differently. Important external stakeholders and paradigm thinkers need to be involved. It is also vital that existing management culture is supportive of this diversity and encouraging of more complexity in internal decision making.

A simple example of the new approach would be the integration between the Web site and the call center, so when a customer phones the employee knows which aspects of the product the caller has been searching, or if quotes have been received, so that they don't have to force the customer to repeat the procedure or re-input information. Then prospective customers can get information and initial quotes on the Web site, with the always available option of a virtual or human adviser on standby.

Value-Added vs Commodity

The key thread throughout this book is that a large part of the process of administration for insurance products is replaceable by software which has a very low marginal cost and few barriers to entry. Thus, the inevitable result is that insurance administration will become commoditized and therefore low profit. The profit, as always, will be where insurers can add value to those products by creating a deep brand which is in-tune with client intuitions. McKinsey (2012) argues that correct use of social media within a deep brand can increase margin by up to 60%. McKinsey, however, then argues that while insurance as a product has a high potential for capturing value, current insurers are among the worst sectors at achieving that.

It is vital to note that in a world of social capital based on business ecosystems, insurers cannot take heart in the idea that they can just reach agreements to supply product to other ecosystem members to distribute to clients. This is because once they lose client contact they (i) become invisible and therefore highly likely to end up trapped in a low-value commoditized market, (ii) do not get the data they need to grow into the data analytics area, (iii) will therefore find it hard to expand into the growing value-added areas of the ecosystem, and (iv) will drastically shrink in terms of employee size as core functions disappear into software.

In terms of pricing, three differing price models come to mind: (i) The core insurance products and the added services are all provided at a profit-margin about average total cost; (ii) the core insurance services are provided at a profit-margin about average total cost, with the added services provided at a very low marginal cost, or free, as a product purchase inducement, or more revolutionary; (iii) the added services become the core product priced at a profit-margin above average total cost, with insurance product provided at a substantial discount, as a service purchase inducement. Given that the services are likely to be more intimately integrated into customers' lives, and therefore valued more, option (iii) has more to recommend it than traditional insurers may consider.

A Vision of Dynamic Insurance

As John leaves his house, the sensor at the garage door notes that he is leaving and instructs the house to make sure that everything is secure until his wife, Helen, gets back at around 5 pm. The house bids him a cheery farewell in the sultry voice which John prefers.

His car welcomes him in a deep masculine voice as he gets in and adjusts settings to his preferences. He tells the car that for a change he'd like to manually drive. He glances at the dashboard indicator which shows that his car insurance has switched from his house insurer, which handles his insurance while his car is parked at home, to his driving insurer.

As he accelerates onto the expressway, he notices that the dashboard indicator shows that his current insurance risk rating has jumped. Several voice commands later he is scanning his recent driving record and concludes that he has recently been heavy footed on the accelerator, and his insurer has concluded that he is higher risk. He pushes the black button to put the car into auto-drive and sighs with relief as the risk indicator plummets to 10% of the manual drive rating. He watches as his car slides over into the fast, auto-drive-only lane, slots itself into a coordinated convoy of cars, and accelerates to 150 m/hr. He idly wonders whether he should only manually drive on weekends, since the car is safer and faster than he is.

He switches his attention to the car's built-in screen and sees that his life insurer has sent him congratulations for his recent avid gym attendance and has cut his weekly premiums by 15%. He scans his personalized news and reads an article sent by his health insurer outlining research showing the benefits of a new kind of berry and clicks on the button to receive his free sample pack. He thinks about the coming family vacation, considers the recommended insurance add-ons, and asks the system a few questions, before going to the insurer store to make his choices.

He notes that his food cupboard and fridge have been talking to his health insurer's computer and have agreed that if his family lifts their consumption of greens by another 10% then the health premium will be dropped by 8%. He notices a linked offer from his life insurer.

He opens a pop-up from Google Insurance offering driving insurance for the next week at a 30% discount if he agrees to not drive manually. He accepts the offer with a click and happily watches the dashboard rating indicator drop even further.

He surfs his favorite Web sites until the car informs John that he has reached work. Just before he hops out, he tells the car to go park itself at the Uber car park and to accept any fares. He watches the dashboard indicator switch to Uber insurance. He knows that auto-Uber use doesn't always go smoothly but he likes the extra income and remembers an accident the prior month, caused by a third-party manual driver, and how the Uber insurance computer informed the police of exactly how the crash had occurred, arranged his car to be repaired, and provided him with a backup car for two days, all set up according to his specifications. All this before he had finished work.

John briefly stops to talk to his friend Eric. They discuss how Eric's employer, who is a major player in the mobile messaging industry, has been recently gaining substantial market share in the health insurance sector, due to their superior social media software. Eric expresses his relief that he left his old insurance company when he did and describes with disbelieve how its dinosaur approach to technology led to its recent bankruptcy.

As they entered the office foyer and chat, they passed Eric's favorite café. The barista handed him his morning double-decaf soy latte, which his car had arranged via the café app. Both men agree that times had certainly changed for the better.

Conclusion

The CEO of Lloyds, Inga Beale, announced in a speech on July 2015, that the disruption moment in insurance was 2015, when irreversible forces were being set into motion. She said that non-traditional holders of customer information like supermarkets, or social networks, had an in-depth understanding of and contact with clients, which insurers did not. She also said that insurance was rapidly globalizing so that the disruption will probably come from foreign providers.

The future of traditional insurance is looking as bright as the future of Kodak was in 1995. Note that Kodak was the inventor of the digital camera, but executives choose to delay its development because they feared its impact on their existing business model of cheap cameras and expensive film. Insurance CEOs are similarly worrying too much about destroying their current cash flows to see the larger threat from not investing in the management changes required to meet disruptive technology. In general, there are currently two types of insurance executives: those who believe that their sector is facing disruptive transformation and those who are not paying attention.

One of the key reasons for the inability of existing insurance companies to react successfully is that the people in charge have achieved their success by acquiring and displaying the attributes best suited to the past environment. Within a new environment, they may be no better able to acquire and display the new skills required than subordinates are and probably less than outside entrants. This is a major problem given that the key to insurer survival is a complete cultural transformation. This need for managers to transform themselves is difficult for existing companies and the major reason why they are normally out-innovated.

This is particularly true when shape of the future is still undefined and therefore insurers are unsure which new skills they have to acquire and can be sure that whatever choices they make now will probably be faulty. In this new fluidity, the ability to experiment and restructure rapidly is more important than perfection. Insurers need to create a Google-X style experimental unit which requests 'long-shot' ideas from staff and trials them. They need to adopt Google-X's mantra of 'fail fast, fail often, fail forward.' The acceptance of a culture of creative failure is, however, a huge cultural change for insurers to achieve.

There is a positive feedback loop to database size, as more information on clients enables an insurer to price more finely, and therefore sell more, and therefore collect more data. This gives a huge first-mover advantage, and therefore stragglers will disappear. Insurers need to actively collaborate to create across company and across industry databases, they need to be constantly developing new analytics ideas and they need to manage data as trustees.

McKinsey (2016b) sees four key areas competitive advantages in the new digital era:

1. *Distinctive technology* - obtaining proprietary low-cost or base technology
2. *Distinctive data* - obtaining propriety data and using this to provide innovative customer service.
3. *Platform providers* - creating broad-based software enabled platforms upon which third parties can build applications.
4. *End-to-end solutions* - customizing products to provide customers with unique complete solutions.

Successful survivors will have to understand that (i) competition is global, (ii) social engagement is vital, and (iii) creativity is essential. Insurers have to be constantly inventing and trialing new products, new services, new customer connections, and expressing ideas clearly and imaginatively. They have to reward staff for being creative and experimental. Customers have to be actively engaged and connected in ways which make clear insurers' value proposition.

What insurers need to do to react to the looming technological perfect storm is reasonably clear. It is also clear that few insurers are even aware of the issues, let alone are transforming with sufficient speed. PWC (2014) argues that the key issues holding insurers back are: (i) a preference for incremental over radical innovation, (ii) legacy systems - heavy investment in upgrading existing systems which leaves little room for new systems, (iii) constantly moving performance targets, (iv) inexperience of actuaries and underwriters with big data, and (v) success being gauged on product development and sales rather than smart solutions and enduring engagement. Most insurers also feel lost and inadequate in possible growth areas like cyber-insurance. They are also unlikely to be able to excite enough innovative young IT graduates to join them and thus will not be able to create the required skills base.

In the past established insurers have been protected from new entrants by the high fixed costs of developing systems and distribution capacities. In the new digital era, however, these barriers have disappeared, as many IT-based companies have better existing systems than insurers do, making it easier for new entrants to develop the required systems than it is for existing insurers to transform their systems. Given the abysmal level of social capital of most existing insurers, new entrants may have a distinct competitive advantage.

The insurance companies who survive the coming perfect storm will be those who recognize that they are no longer primarily insurance companies, but that in the future they will be primarily information companies specializing in analytical risk-based client services. Insurers who aggressively build the richness of their data and its analysis will find new sources of profit mushrooming. Insurers need to reimagine their industry.

References

Boston Consulting Group. (2015). *The Double Game of Digital Strateg'*, P. Gerbert, C. Gauger, & S. Steinhäuser, BCG Perspectives, Oct 16.

Canas. T. (2015). *What will be the Uber of Insurance?* Insurance Thought Leadership, PWC, July 22.

Capgemini Consulting. (2015). *Strategies for the Age of Digital Disruption*, Digital Transformation Review, No 7: Feb.

Capgemini/Efma. (2016). *World Insurance report*.

Equinix. (2014). *Challenge to change: three-part series*, Acord/Global Futures & Foresight.

IAIS (2017). *FinTech Developments in the Insurance Industry*, International Association of Insurance Supervisors, Basel, Switzerland.

Kanter, R. (2006). Innovation: The Classic Traps, *Harvard Business Review*, 84 (1).

McKinsey. (2012). *The Social Economy: Unlocking value and productivity through social technologies: consumer financial services*, McKinsey Global Institute.

McKinsey. (2016a). 'An Incumbent's Guide to Digital Disruption', *McKinsey Quarterly*, May.

McKinsey. (2016b). 'The Economic Essentials of Digital Strategy', *McKinsey Quarterly*, March.

Morgan-Stanley/ BCG. (2014). *Insurance and Technology: Evolution and revolution in a digital world*, Boston Consulting Group, USA.

PWC. (2014). *Insurance 2020: The digital prize—taking customer connection to a new level*.

Satell, G. (2012). *Business Models and the Singularity*, May.

9

Regulatory and Legal Issues

Pricing Regulation

In general, governments for reasons of equity have placed restrictions on the ability of insurers to convert information about risk differences between people into differences in rates and premiums. There are three levels of insurer price freedom: (i) *Community rating* - The insurer is not allowed to vary the price between customers based on risk. Often used for health insurance. (ii) *Restricted rating* - The insurer is allowed to vary within set bands, possibly with a small number of groups. Often used for workers' compensation. (iii) *Unrestricted* - Insurers are free to set rates as they wish, either by groups or individuals.

For dynamic insurance to work, insurers do not have to have complete price freedom, they merely need the ability to vary rates or offer conditional discounts by an amount large enough to induce the desired behavioral change. Research clearly shows that a substantial proportion of customers respond in behavioral ways to small price differences.

This will probably take the form of rate reductions for positive changes, rather than rate increases for adverse changes. Governments can be expected to be cautious about allowing rate freedom for risk

M. Naylor, *Insurance Transformed*, Palgrave Studies in Financial Services Technology,
DOI 10.1007/978-3-319-63835-5_9

factors which are unchangeable, e.g., genetics, and bolder in allowing rate freedom for lifestyle choices. However, choices will have to be made. Does the government allow insurers to price young drivers who display very poor habits out of the market, or reward those who undertake regular exercise so substantially that the unfit feel discriminated against? Because telematic feedback is tied to individual activities, it is likely to generate a powerful nudge effect toward better individual choices. Tying this feedback to small monetary inducements should have a beneficial impact.

If the rates discrimination induces positive behavioral changes which can be shown via research to contribute to reducing social ills and therefore reduce government costs, e.g., by reducing car crashes or reducing health costs, then regulators can be expected to be more supportive of rates freedom than they have been previously. When Progressive increased auto-insurance premium rates for its worst 5% of drivers, (who cause a high proportion of crashes) there is no reaction from regulators.

Customers have, in general, been supportive of linking discounts to telematic feedback, so political reaction should be minimal for well thought through proposals. After all, the current factors used for underwriting are broad classes, and customers often feel aggrieved - Why should a careful young driver pay more for auto-insurance than a careless middle-aged driver? Telematic data would provide a detailed breakdown of the individual's risk factors and therefore provide moral justification. Dynamic insurance, which gives feedback via changes in rates, will create a strong sense of moral justice and an obvious reward for good behavior. Complexity will arise, however, when big data analysis discovers correlations between multiple factors and beneficial outcomes, and where the logic is unclear. What is the link between early evening shopping and car crashes?

There are, however, many legal and ethics issues with the increasingly sophisticated use of data. One issue is that customers need to be able to understand what factors their premiums are based on and why weightings on those factors are fair. There may need to be causation and not just correlation. This can be very difficult to achieve if sales staff or even underwriters find it hard to understand the models, and nearly impossible if dynamic multi-causal models are used. A related issue is that insurers have to be able to show that banned discriminatory factors like ethnic origin are not proxied by a closely correlated factor. Another issue is that insurers have to be able to show that data is being protected, and this is difficult if data is sourced from or used by external firms or connected ecosystems. There are particular issues if data is sourced from social media, as is increasingly common. One known complication here is that users often lie or are deliberately malicious on social media postings.

Data Law

The creation, storage, and use of personal data raise many legal, ethical, and regulation issues. What right does each of the parties have in respect of the raw, aggregated, and processed data; what uses should be permitted; and in what circumstances? What rights exist to control the use of data across ecosystem companies, when the customer is unaware of their existence or data usage intentions?

A wide range of legal rights and obligations is developing in relation to data, based on traditional intellectual property rights, contract law, and regulatory law. This means that use of data without the right licenses or permissions can lead to large damages claims. Meanwhile, regulatory data protection liability is being expanded.

Therefore, insurers need to make sure they have all the rights they need to all the data they use and in all the ways they use it. In legal terms, this means licensing it, processing it and using it correctly, and, especially with personal data, obtaining the explicit informed consent of the individual concerned in order to comply with data protection law. This requires a structured approach to data use and governance.

It is useful to classify commercial data into four groups:

1. *Metadata*: data about the data. For example, not the details of a phone call, but when, where, and for how long.
2. *B2B Data*: data about individual businesses, which are suppliers or customers.

3. *Anonymized B2C Data*: data about individual customers but with individual identifiers removed.
4. *Personal Data*: data about individual customers, which has individual identifiers.

Nearly all big data analysis only requires one of the first three groups, as outside of telematic or purchase data, it is rare for data to need to identify individuals. Most big data analytical systems don't use individualized data, they use data about 'someone like you', and so it is about slotting individuals into a tighter category than currently. Data analysis is about assessing correlations about how 'someone-like-you' suffers adverse events. Only data involving identifiers will face legal issues.

Insurers will need data law managers. They will have to understand the data analysis structure in terms of: (i) *data inputs* - Where does all the data, the structured data sets (industry, marketing, and personal) and unstructured data (social media, mobile, and Internet) come from? (ii) *data processing* - How does the business intelligence software that analyses the input data work? and (iii) *data outputs* - Where (internally and externally) do the data outputs go, who uses them and how?

This requires close cooperation between the insurance company's legal team and its technology group. These groups will have to assess the IT system structure maps in terms of the flow of information. The structure map must enable tagging of all the characteristics of each type of data and map it to all the relevant licenses, permissions, and consents that attach to it. The legal team needs to understand the technical vocabulary of IT architecture and the technology team needs to become familiar with the concepts of copyright licensing, confidentiality, contracts, and explicit informed consent under data protection law.

Four steps are required to ensure legal compliance: (i) *A 'deep dive risk assessment'* examines current data use; reviewing and assessing it, then reporting back to senior management on issues and solutions, (ii) *A big data strategy* should then be created by a senior management team. This should include members from all business areas and should clarify and formalize the Data Strategy as a written statement of high-level objectives, goals, and relevant considerations, (iii) *A big data policy* is then created, which is a high-level plan showing who's doing what, when and how, and (iv) *A policy and procedures plan* is then created, setting out how data governance should be handled.

The insurance of drones raises a number of additional as yet unresolved issues, especially as regulation is currently unsettled. Apart from physical damage to drones, drone operators can potentially be sued for trespass, nuisance, and privacy invasion. Insurers will have to determine how to insure the innocent use of drones but exclude the ill-intended use. Given that drones with cameras can survey neighboring land even when not passing above them, areas like trespass will not be easy to define. In general, while there is no right to privacy if a person is in a public place or in a private place which is easily viewable from a public place, a drone can view a high-level apartment or see over a high fence - this can easily be defined as an 'unreasonable' breach of privacy. Potentially, a drone operator could be sued for invasion of privacy every time they operate a drone in an urban setting. Failure of a drone could mean damage to people or property below it.

Policy terms will have to be precise, and insurers will have to clearly decide what areas they do not want to insure, yet insurers who do not offer a wide enough definition will not find customers. Does any liability from drones arise for house contents insurers?

Data Privacy Issues

Three approaches have been used to collect individualized data: (i) *A free market* - whereby firms collect and sell whatever data they can collect, (ii) *an opt-out system* - whereby data can be collected unless customers actively refuse, and (iii) *an opt-in system* - whereby data is only collected if customers positively agree. A mix of these three is used in most countries, though the USA tends toward (ii) and Europe toward (iii).

Dynamic insurance is only possible if data is willingly shared. This will only be possible if customers give their informed consent, which they will only do if they trust the insurer, if there is established social capital. An alternative is for data to be held by a neutral body and used by insurers on a regulated basis.

The main issue is that legislation to enforce opt-in is difficult to enforce in practice as data users often do not need to deal directly with the public. Insurers are able to buy data sets from venders or receive it from ecosystem members. Data vendors use schemes like free surveys to gather data. Many Apps include cookies, the uses of which it takes an IT expert to understand. Many Apps use a tick-in contract to ensure legal opt-in, but 99% of users never read the terms and conditions. Thus data law can be obeyed in letter but not in spirit.

The collection of data is, however, not as much of a concern as the public often thinks as data privacy concerns and regulation mainly revolves around personal data, and most data analysis does not involve this. Thus, in general, individual privacy will not be compromised.

Data privacy systems will need to set rules around: (i) *storage* - what data is stored and for how long, (ii) *access* - which type of employees have access to what data elements, (iii) *sharing* - what types of data can be shared within the insurer and with what external parties, (iv) *merging* - what data should be linked or amalgamated, and (v) *reacting* - how each data element should be acted upon. These rules have to cover both positive and negative information or behavioral predictions. For example, insurers have to respond cautiously to buying patterns, which indicate pregnancy or adverse health conditions, as the client may not have informed friends or their spouse. The behavior of others with the client's social network is often vital to buy decisions, yet care is needed when contacting a client because of the actions of their friends.

With regard to personalized data, there are two areas of concern. One is that data analysts have shown that it is possible to combine non-identified data from a range of sources, including political affiliations in the USA, and get close to identifying preference types by street or house. This can then be linked to browser history to actively, in real time, understand, and monitor personal preferences. For example, only 15 minutes of real-time driving data is enough to identify individuals from a selection of possible drivers. There will need to be regulation around this.

The other area of concern, which is important for dynamic insurance, is telematics data. If this is linked to underwriting or services then individual identifiers will be required. In addition, analysis of data may give insurers substantially more information about a customer's risk factors than the customer pocesses. Insurers can then be seen as ethically bound to inform the customer of the risk factors they face or ways they can reduce risk. This could be complex for genetic or other health factors where the factor only shows a tendency rather than a high probability, or where there is a complex and poorly understood but robust, correlation between multiple factors.

Telematic, browsing, or other individualized data is thus a major privacy issue and of deep concern to many people. If it identifies your location in real time it is a private security issue. Health data may also involve intimate and sensitive information. Used inappropriately these types of data can be used to harass or blackmail people and thus this area can cause general unease.

One suggestion is for individualized data to be held by a regulated 3rd party and provided to ecosystems under strict conditions. This has strong merit. For individuals concern about insurer use of data will probably not revolve around the data held but around the uses to which it is put. The problem is that understanding this involves examining the validity of AI algorithms and 99% of the public have no capacity to scrutinize those. For example, one suggestion is for governments to require insurers to provide to individuals all the information held about them, so they can correct errors. However, customer access to their own individualized telematic data may be problematic because: (i) they can't access it without data warehouse programs, (ii) its size will exceed individual's capacity to cope, (iii) it can't be understood without using data algorithms, (iv) big data analysis often involves indirect correlation between two variables, which have no causal link but proxy for an unknown third variable, thus causing confusion, and (v) it will not tell a customer how the insurer uses the data, especially the weights the insurer's systems places on differing aspects of the data, which is commercially sensitive. What will be of more use to a customer is to know their ID data and a summary of the assessment of their risk, which the insurer has discovered from their own analysis.

It needs to be noted, however, that the urge for privacy is not inherent but cultural. Before the 16th century a lot of activities, which we currently regard as private, like toileting or sleeping, were public or done in groups. Today's younger generations, who are growing up in a globally connected world with significant moments posted online, tend to regard freedom as not bound up in self-contained autonomy, but in enjoying access to others and in inclusion in a global public life. Research does support this, showing that there are generational differences in data privacy assumptions. The younger generations are thus less likely to forego the benefits to be gained by agreeing to share data. The assumptions which European Commission (2013) make about the inherent need for data privacy may not be shared by these younger generations. The website Patientslikeme.com shows that at least some of the public are prepared to make detailed health information publicly available in an effort to find a cure for their conditions.

Hacking of data is a serious concern. The possibility that hackers could take control of health or car telematics is real and can be used to terrify, blackmail, or for terrorism. This could lead to increased auto-theft by hackers as well as hacker-caused auto-accidents. Insurer data security is thus a serious concern, both from an operational and a legal angle. Insurers will have to work closely with smart device manufacturers to ensure data privacy is maintained. Does a homeowner's failure to secure their smart devices from hacking breach the conditions of their house or contents insurance? Who is liable if a telematic device gets a health metric wrong?

Any unauthorized access to or public release of data or illegal use of data will expose the insurer to legal liability and destruction of their reputation. Given the need for increased trust outlined in earlier chapters and the increased ease of customer switching, a serous data breach could lead to bankruptcy.

Issues also arise around the use of autonomous digital agents by customers. The interaction between these and insurer IT systems, with a mutual exchange of data which is not actively supervised by humans, requires robust procedural safeguards. Savvy customers are increasingly using these agents to control access to personal data and, in some cases, attempting to charge firms for their use of data in analysis.

System and Flash Crashes

As IT systems become more complex they create the possibility for unexpected but sudden cascades of failure. Complexity leads to unpredictability. It is impossible for codes to be created which are bug-free, as no single person fully understands the millions of lines of code. Certain combinations of events can lead to system freezes or adverse reactions, as has occurred in stock markets. Algorithms are not open to public inspection and verification.

If these crashes are linked to telematics or to auto-drive cars then the consequences could be serious. This will impact in two ways: (i) The insurer admin system crashes, preventing the insurer from continuing normal business, and (ii) telematics crash, individually, or as a networked group. The insurer or its clients would then be liable for a mass adverse event. A few car crashes caused by software errors might not be fatal to the autonomous driving industry. But if autonomous cars are also connected, via car-to-car systems, or car-to-infrastructure, then a systemic problem could bring down a whole network of cars. These are all insurer legal nightmares.

The Ethics of Insurance Bets

Insurance has traditionally been based on the concept of a 'fair-bet.' Neither you nor the insurer knows what your future holds, so premiums are based on broad generalized groups. Insurance markets exist because no one really knows whether or not some bad event will happen. We may know the historical odds, but we can't accurately predict the event for particular instances. Pools of policy holders were thus traditionally created with premiums sufficient to cover the payouts for accidents that will eventually occur within the pool as a matter of statistics.

Moving to individualized premiums, based on real-time behavior breaks this concept, the equity of this 'fair-bet' - you are charged your actual risk level. This raises a question about ethics: is it problematic to offer insurance bets when the outcome is increasingly certain? If one party has much more information than the other party, 'asymmetric information,' is an insurance transaction morally questionable? If insurers can know everything about customers related to risk, and the insurer knows that the individual's chance of an a specified event is extremely small, then it doesn't seem fair to charge a customer anything. If the customer knew they had no risk, they wouldn't want to pay anything.

Increasing asymmetry of information may erode the moral justification for insurance markets to operate as they currently do.

Traditionally insurance law and regulation have assumed that individuals know more about their personal risk than the insurer does, so that law requires individuals to disclose relevant data. In an age of big data, however, the insurer may know a lot more about the risk that some individual faces than that individual does. The insurer can then set up a biased bet. Regulation will be needed to ensure the insurer provides a summary of the risk factors which the customer faces.

Privacy Legislation/Regulation

The European Commission (2013) argued that the Internet of things will require strict privacy protocols and extensive security. Creating restrictive data regulation, however, can be a major competitive hindrance for a countrys' insurance industry. For example, EU directive 95/46/EC (Data Protection Directive) requires that personal data is only collected for 'specified, explicit, and legitimate purposes' and requires that it must be 'adequate, relevant, and not excessive' in relation to the purposes for which it is collected. Typically, regulations require that data only be kept for as long as it may be lawfully used, only be used for the purposes which the individual consented, and the insurer must be satisfied as to the information's accuracy.

These rules contradict the requirements of big data analytics, which involves collecting the maximum amount of data from the largest range of data sources and then using that data across a range of purposes, often seemingly unrelated to the initial reason for the data collection. For example; shopping data used in an algorithm to predict car crashes. The EU has thus modified 95/46 by adopting the General Data Protection Regulation, which relaxes these restrictions. A part of this, however, involves stricter conditions on 'profiling' purposes, whereby individuals have a right not to be subject to a decision based solely on automated algorithms. Profiling based solely on sensitive data, such as health data, is prohibited. Profiling based on pseudonymous data is allowed. GDPR also requires a more active consent process, including express consent for data to be processed. Organizations must be able to demonstrate the individual really understands and is in agreement with how their data will be used.

The issue is that big data analysis inherently involves the merging of data from a large number of individuals and the insurer than exploring the data in new and innovative ways, which will not have occurred to insurers at the time of gathering data. Data may also be gathered by other firms in the ecosystem, or automatically via telematics, a lot of which may be rough and uncertifiable as 100% accurate. The data pool will also be too large to allow extraction of individualized data. It may thus be impossible to ensure strict security and a balance will be needed between privacy and the advantages of the coming technological revolution. Choices will have to be made between insurance innovation and privacy. It needs to be understood that for big data, there is no need for 100% data accuracy as each item of data plays only a minuscule part in creating a risk profile, unlike the current situation.

A general restriction on data use is thus likely to halt domestic insurer innovation and lead to their replacement by disruptors from less strict jurisdictions. The EU's GDPR may thus prove difficult for insurers and may hamper InsurTech within Europe. Data controls need to be only applied to data which directly identifies individuals. There is increasingly regulatory competition between countries, with jurisdictions like Singapore proactively introducing regulation reforms to attract InsurTech innovators.

More importantly in an age of big data and AI analysis, regulation should not be about the use of pieces of data, but be focused on regulators examining the algorithm code or AI settings, so the privacy or ethical dimensions of the insurers' IT system can be examined. After all, in an age of big data, human analysts do not look at the raw data, what they do is set the framework of AI decision making. Regulation relating to algorithms is more important than regulation relating to data. Regulation is required around the aggregation of data and its use to back-identify individuals or vulnerable groups. Regulation is also needed around data breaches and the on-sale of data, or its transfer after takeovers or bankruptcies.

Another issue is that current regulation assumes large vertically integrated insurers who perform all roles. If disruption leads to extensive disintermediation and therefore a fragmented market, there will need to be regulation aimed at specific roles within the market. For example, regulation covering; client acquisition, customer relationships, underwriting, claims assessment, and payments.

Unavoidably Higher Risk Customers

As discussed in an earlier chapter individualized pricing and the associated incentives will reduce the average risk and spread risk. This will increase the group for whom insurance may be unaffordable. For those for whom their higher risk is due to factors over which they have no control, insurers or governments may have to consider how to protect them. There three main ways to do this: (i) impose restrictions on the ability of insurers to set premiums based on individualized risk factors, (ii) develop market-based risk sharing schemes, and (iii) create a government agency to act as an insurer of last resort.

General Regulation Recommendations

Regulation should be digital-friendly, technologically neutral, and future proof. It needs to be principles based and flexible. Regulation needs to stop being based on insurance type, but become activity based, applying to all insurance activities and providers, regardless of size or origin. Regulation has to be internationally agreed so that national regulators have to exchange data and experiences. Data and privacy protocols have to be international.

Regulators need to support innovations and allow failure, which is against the traditional regulatory culture. To do this regulators need to: (i) create an innovation 'regulation sandbox,' where insurers can trial new ideas for a while outside existing regulations, (ii) create a team who understands technology and the innovation process, (iii) lower licensing barriers, (iv) help small innovators comply at minimal cost, (v) allow heavily automated insurers to use third-party sign-offs on organization competence requirements, (vi) allow ecosystems to be licensed as group or allow the insurer to certify data or procedures provided by non-insurer parties, and (vii) weaken merger and cooperation regulations to allow ecosystems to strengthen relationships or use pricing/procedure agreements.

Auto-Insurance Vs Product-Liability Insurance

In the short-term, major liability issue arises from a mix of auto-drive and self-drive - how to partition fault if the car was in auto-drive but the driver was inattentive? Level 3 and 4 cars will be a major issue - drivers will not be paying attention to driving and cannot be expected to take over in an emergency if the software defaults to them. Longer term, for level 5 cars the turning point for insurers will occur when owners start to send cars off by themselves, to pick up the children, or a pizza, or to find a car park. If there is a crash when no one is in the vehicle, then it is obvious that the product producer is to blame, via product liability. How can laws which assume a 'driver' is responsible for errors work if there is no one in the car driving?

Insurance for level 4 or 5 auto-cars will thus eventually move from being covered by drivers under auto-insurance to being covered by car-manufacturers, or software producers, under product-liability law. Insurer cash-flow will drop as profit margins in product-liability cover are significantly lower than retail insurance margins. There is an issue for older auto-cars as telematic degradation can be expected over time. Given that telematic sensors need to be keep clean and correctly aligned, insurers may need to set conditions around maintenance. Therefore, there is a scope for liability to increasingly shift to telematic maintenance companies. There will always be a need for residual auto-insurance to cover damage by external objects, flood, bushfire, terrorism, etc.

Brookings Institute (2014) argues that the USA has a robust product-liability regime used to adapting to technological challenges and should cope well. ABI/Thatcham (2016) points out that other countries may need to upgrade their product-liability legislation. In particular: (i) product liability needs to be compulsory, (ii) liability for personal injury under product liability needs to standardized as per current auto-insurance cover, (iii) careful consideration is required as to the duration of product liability cover, (iv) product liability has to include damage to the product itself as well as other products, (v) product liability will not cover external causes unrelated to the product, (vi) product liability will not cover if poor maintenance is an issue or sensors have not been cleaned. ABI/Thatcham thus argues that auto-drive insurance needs to be covered by separate legislation and regulation to existing product-liability legislation. There are strong arguments in favor of this idea.

A major complication will come from level 3 or 4 cars where drivers may switch between fully auto-driving and manual modes. If an auto-drive car finds itself in a crisis not of its own making, and defaults to the driver who finds themselves unable to cope with an sudden emergency, is the product or the driver liable? This may come down to—'would a reasonable driver have been able to cope?' 'Was it reasonable for the AI to default back?' As mentioned earlier, it is clear that humans are weak at manually driving cars, but are terrible at paying attention to what is happening when the car does 80% of the driving. How much can the product be expected to ensure the human is paying attention, so they can take over if need be? If a human being repeatedly refuses to watch the traffic after repeated warnings, is the car entitled to stop and refuse to auto-drive any further?

Therefore, legislation and regulation need to initially make a distinction between level 3 and 4 cars with advanced driver assistance systems (ADAS) and level 5 fully automated driver technology (ADT), as only in the latter case can any fault on the part of the driver be excluded. The distinction between these two will fade, however, as manufacturers will steadily upgrade ADAS cars so that they approach ADT capacity in all but extreme cases.

Product liability will also be a complex area because multiple parties are involved. Should a particular crash be covered by the car manufacturer, or the telematic supplier, or the AI driving-system supplier, or the tire manufacturer, or the road marker supplier, or car maintenance workshop, or the owner for poor cleaning? Manufacturers will not cover post sale modifications, or for faulty telematic maintenance.

The defendants in auto-accident lawsuits will change. Rather than going after drivers and their insurance companies, plaintiff personal injury attorneys will target vehicle manufacturers, software companies, producers of vehicle sensors, maintenance services, or even for councils for not maintaining smart roadside telematics. Accident claims will grow much more complex, with more subrogation claims, as the parties try to shift liability to others in the vehicle service stream.

Note, however, disputes about the facts of a crash will be easier to solve, because of the large amount of real-time data collected by the car on its actions, the actions of the other cars, and the environment. Thus, while some litigation may become more complex, overall a high percentage of crashes will be handled by data exchange between the two insurance company computers.

Adjuster investigations for these crashes and accidents are increasingly going to shift from disputes about fact controversies, like who really had the green light or right of way, to disputes about software glitches or collision avoidance systems and what kind of malfunctions in those systems caused the collision. The auto-insurance adjuster profession as it exists today, could thus become obsolete. Rather, there will be product-liability adjusters who will need a much different skill set than traditional auto-insurance adjusters possess.

Issues Around Autonomous Drive Programming

There are major as-yet-unsolved legal and ethical problems for insurers, producers, or programmers of self-drive cars. Many unthought of ethical issues arise for software coders. For example, how does the software faced with an unavoidable impact, decide between minimizing harm to its passengers vs minimizing harm overall, e.g., what does the software embedded in the two cars jointly decide about an impeding head-on crash if one car has one occupant and the other has six? Does the software avoid the crash by sending the one occupant car off the edge? What if the car has to choose between hitting two different pedestrians? This is called the 'trolley problem' which predates self-drive cars. We need to teach AI systems some ethics.

Most manufacturers, like Mercedes, have announced that they will set up their software rules so the car occupant is always given priority regardless of the level of harm to others. Manufacturers have no choice, as who would buy an auto-drive car which may decide to sacrifice you? This will require regulation setting the parameters for autonomous car ethics, even though the issues could get very complex. Future lawsuits for software producers could be media minefields. Given that automobile trade is international there is an urgent need for an international regulation agreement. In 2016, the Federal Automated Vehicles Policy started the process by disseminating a set of proactive safety guidelines to provide safety through autonomous innovation, recognizing that 'automated vehicles hold enormous potential benefits for safety, mobility, and sustainability' but raise many legal issues.

Issues arise if an unoccupied car is involved in a crash. How do the police deal with the car? How do the police deal with a driver-less car if its software is misbehaving? What if a fleet of cars is hacked and used as a weapon? The answer is that police will obviously need a software override to control programs. Note that for fully automatic cars, there will be no need for an occupant to have a driver's license or be able to drive or to be sober. This means that police need the ability to correct any issue with a malfunctioning car and get the occupant to their designation.

Another issue is that auto-drive cars are currently set up to be very passive in traffic, obeying rules, trying to avoid crashes, and always giving way. Experience with Google cars indicates that manual drivers recognize this and learn that if they drive aggressively they can always bully the Google car to give way.[1] This could be frustrating to owners, so they may start to demand the ability to adjust the car's passivity setting. Insurers have to be aware of this and adjust premiums accordingly. Owners who are bullied will have the data to send to police to show the manual driver's rule breaking. Regulation may be required around modifications in this area.

Another major legal issue is the possibility of cars being hacked and taken over. In theory, someone with knowledge of coding could control a rich person's car, lock the doors, drive to a remote location, and demand a ransom. The perpetrator could be anywhere in the world, outside domestic jurisdiction. Burglars could also hack car software to tell if a family is at home.

It needs to be remembered that crashes will still occur with auto-drive cars as the technology will never be perfect. Even with perfect programming, self-driving cars rely also on sophisticated hardware. Improperly maintained equipment, such as mud covering a sensor or a sensor misaligned by a big bump in the road, could mean incomplete or

[1]A crash involving a Google car occurred because a bus driver tried to force the car to give way.

wrong data, and that could cause an accident. Redundant systems and sensors reduce those odds, but the odds are still not zero.

There are indications that the public may be less forgiving of these crashes even if the overall crash rate is a lot lower than the manual drive rate, as increasingly they expect more of software that they do of humans. This may lead to media controversies and liability issues. Tesla has already faced several auto-drive law suits.

To enable a self-drive system to work successfully a substantial amount of data is required. To get to that Level 5 autonomy goal, manufacturers will collect data as cars drive in level 2 or 3 modes, comparing driver reactions to that of machines, known 'Shadow Mode.' Currently only Tesla and Progressive have enough data to enable self-drive at level 4 or 5 by 2020. Insurers who want to survive will have to negotiate access to these data sets.

References

ABI/Thatcham. (2016). *Pathway to Driverless cars: Proposals to support advanced driver assistance systems and automated vehicle technologies*, Association of British Insurers.

Brookings Institute. (2014). *Product Liability for Driverless Cars: Issues and Guiding Principles for Legislation*, Centre for Technology Innovation.

European Commission. (2013). *Digital Agenda for the Future: A Europe 2020 Initiative*, Brussels, Belgium.

10

Consequences for Insurance Workers

Introduction

There has been much discussion and fear of the impact of disruptive technology on the level of employment. A lot of this discussion has, however, been uninformed. It is useful to note that every technological change in history, from the invention of the wheel, to the spinning machine, to the petrol engine, to the computer, has raised employment questions, yet there are still enough jobs to go around. During the initial industrial revolution this was called 'the machinery question.'

In general, the conclusion from research into past episodes of disruption finds little net long-term impact on the overall level of employment. This is because the disruptive changes mean a reduction in the price of many goods or services and this increases demand for those goods, and for substitute goods. Overall demand for workers remains unchanged, with employees in nicer jobs with higher incomes. There is, however, a distinction between successful survivor companies who respond to disruption by actively retaining, retraining, and reallocating staff, and the laggards who respond by reducing cost and retrenching staff, and thus slowly shrinking into obviation.

M. Naylor, *Insurance Transformed*, Palgrave Studies in Financial Services Technology,
DOI 10.1007/978-3-319-63835-5_10

It needs to be noted that just because a human doing an activity can be replaced by technology, that doesn't mean that will be. Five factors are involved: technical feasibility, costs to automate, relative scarcity, skills, and cost of the workers who would be replaced. Many activities which could be replaced won't be for a while.

The question is more one of transition, as many jobs may have to be drastically rearranged and some workers may have to change industries or face substantial reductions in earnings. Not every employee may have the capacity to make a smooth transition. While the outcome is speculative for insurance workers, there are several principles which are of relevance.

Kelly (2016) argues that there is a recurring pattern to worker reaction to the threat of computer replacement;

1. A robot/computer cannot possibly do the tasks I do.
2. *[Later]*—OK, it can do a lot of those tasks, but it can't do everything I do.
3. *[Later]*—OK, it can do everything I do, except it needs me when it breaks down, which is often.
4. *[Later]*—OK, it operates flawlessly on routine tasks, but I need to train it for new tasks.
5. *[Later]*—OK, it can have my boring old job, because it is obvious that was not a job humans were meant to do.
6. *[Later]*—Wow, now that the robot is doing my old job, my new job is much more interesting and pays more!
7. *[Later]*—I am so glad a robot/computer cannot possibly do what I do now.

Mechanical vs. Analytical

The faster growth in software development than mechanical development has complex consequences. In the 1980s, most of the occupational disruptions due to IT innovations occurred in jobs which involved a definable set of routine procedures, like assembling a car. These could be easily replaced by a mechanically simple robot obeying simple software. Thus, the blue-collar workers were affected more than the white-collar workers. The increasing use in the immediate future of smart robots may in contrast be beneficial to Western blue-collar workers as reduced marginal cost and increasing demand for flexibility will induce producers to switch production back from emerging countries.

Management ranks were until recently, largely left untouched. While typists were impacted from the 1960s, and book keepers from the 1970s, it was only from about 2000 that software started to affect the ranks of lower middle managers. Even here, the rule has been that software has been focused on the routine and by provision of better information has expanded the role of analytics. In general, the overall process has been good for office workers, making jobs more interesting and better paid.

The rise of AI software has recently, however, started to impact on higher level administrators. In the future, as software tackles ever more complex tasks, higher and higher levels of management occupation classes will be affected. For example, IBM has used what it learnt developing its Jeopardy software to expand into offering legal research and health diagnosis services. They have started to make this expertise available to everyone by renting software on-the-cloud by the minute.

Conversely, jobs like office cleaning or gardening, which involve reasonable complex manual dexterity, which robots currently find difficult, should be replaced at a far slower pace, at least until the cost of renting autonomous robots reduces below the minimum wage.

Fluff Not Stuff

Given that most physical goods have low-income elasticities of demand, the world is consuming ever more intangible material rather than physical, fluff not stuff. Thus, most of the increase in future income will be reflected in an increase in service employment, especially areas like health care or entertainment, rather than industrial employment. Jobs for cafe waitress are probably secure while demand for animators and YouTube clip producers will boom. Who knew that you could get rich by home-making short clips about makeup in your own bedroom?

The USA has been particularly successful at expanding into innovative new services. Progressive Policy Institute (2013) found that the creation of smart phone Apps had by 2013 resulted in the employment of over 750,000 extra people in the USA, even though it was only five years since Apple launched its App store. For countries which support it, this increase in employment due to software demands will vastly exceed any losses due to the use of robots.

Note, however, that the drastic reduction in the cost of international communications means that workers in the West will have to offer something extra in terms of creativity or cultural connectivity then workers in Bangalore or Chengdu can offer.

Complexity

The level of difficulty in replacing a human activity by software or robotics is determined by a mix of the mechanical aspects of the job, the analytical complexity, and the human interactions. It is easy to understand that truck driving or being a plane pilot has a limited future, as it is already largely mechanized and involves regular routines. Already major mines as well as ports are using autonomous vehicle fleets. Conversely, courier delivering may expand (though the deliverer may not do much driving), as it involves complex last step deliveries, irregular routines, and customer interactions. Call center workers have a limited future, as 90% of calls are routine and voice recognition software can handle them, without those accent issues, or the need for breaks. Sales or persuasive calls are unlikely to be automated.

The important aspect is not the complexity of the job, but the predictability of the activities. Jobs with set rules are fairly simple to automate from the software angle. The main difficulty involves mechanical innovations, which are making slower in progress. An area like retail is more complex. Cashiers are rapidly being replaced in supermarkets, as are warehouse and shelving staff. 'Shopping' itself is, however, changing from a necessity to an entertainment, with high street shops becoming demonstration centers linked to resultant online purchases or automated cashiers. Engaging with customers to motivate them to buy or chatting to them in the café queue is unlikely to be automated. A lawyer may seem to have a complex job, but a lot of legal analysis is finding the relevant information and then applying well-specified rules, which AI software tends to do better than humans. From a software angle, the law firm cleaner's job involves more complex, unstructured, activities than the lawyer's job does. In addition, since the lawyer is paid more, there is also more incentive to replace them.

Many clerical jobs involve the organization, storing, and retrieving of information. These are tasks that computers handle particularly well, and so the demand for clerical labor has fallen. It is useful to note that while all decision making, and therefore most jobs, involves information processing of some kind, computers are not better than humans at every kind of information processing.

Levy and Murnane (2004) draw some useful distinctions between three types of activities. (i) Simple activities which require '*rules-based logic*' can be easily delegated to machines. A problem is broken down into a sequence of statements, the truth or falsehood of which can be unambiguously assessed. Many activities using data can be broken down into a sequence of decisions, culminating in a final decision. These kinds of tasks have already been largely replaced by software. (ii) Some activities may seem more complex as they involve '*pattern recognition,*' by which is meant the ability to assess a situation and determine if it fits a previously encountered pattern. Until recently, these activities were thought to be too complex for computers. However, AI can handle most of these, as long as the required patterns are clear. Software only struggles when ambiguity is present. In the work of automobile mechanics, computer diagnostics can identify many problems previously encountered by car owners. Novel problems would require human intervention. (iii) Harder is '*expert thinking*' which involves assessing a body of knowledge and building the experience necessary for specialized pattern recognition. This is unlikely to be impacted in the medium term.

The key question to be asked is - are changes to the capacity of analytical software able to be handled by incremental change within existing management structures or does it involve disruptive change which requires new management paradigms?

Because of the expanding ability of software to handle many professional level occupations, especially those which involve pattern recognition, Martinez (2016) argues that in the future software will no longer fill selected *hard* gaps in a human workflow; instead, humans will fill the gaps in an IT workflow which computers find hard. Marc Andreessen, co-creator of Netscape, argues that 'in the future, there will be two types of jobs: people who tell computers what to do, and people who are told by computers what to do.'

How much occupational disruptions will there be elsewhere? The drastic change could be most disruptive in areas which can be handled by analytical AI software. This can tackle a lot of jobs which now require a university level education, but involve fewer issues with mechanization. Even in these very complex cases, because computers will access to an exponentially growing database of similar cases worldwide and can search and analyze these faster than humans can, software will become better at recognizing complex patterns based on inadequate information than human experts are. Software is making an increasing number of decisions around loans, mortgages, and replacing tax accountants. Examining x-rays or MRI scans is likely to be increasingly automated, as the latest software is better than humans. Medical software is now equal to doctors at diagnosing illnesses and by 2020 will exceed even specialists.

Before the Darpa auto-driving ah-ha moment it was assumed that only jobs involving repetitive actions were at risk, after the moment it was obvious that jobs involving complex analysis are at risk. Why can't software do 90% of the job of a lawyer or accountant or doctor? The software industry itself will be disrupted, as programs are proving more effective and reliable than humans in writing generic code, in debugging, and in creating large programs. A key reason is that humans are unable to cope with tracing logic strands over millions of lines of code.

Degree of Creativity or Human Interaction

The activities most immune to a takeover by software are those which require 'complex communication' - the ability to convey and understand nuances and subtle differences in meaning between statements that may sound very similar. In face-to-face or telephone communication, this skill may involve reading meaning into voice tone or body language.

Jobs differ in the extent to which they involve complex social skills. Humans in general prefer human company. Software is still facing large challenges in the area of social interactions, with particular difficulties in recognition of human emotions and the ability to respond appropriately to these. Software has, for example, so far been unable to detect sarcasm or irony, though programmers are working on this. Thus, human interactions with software will seem formal and 'stiff' for at least another decade. Occupations where persuasion or selling or empathy is involved have a high level of required social skills which are very hard for a computer to replicate, at least for face-to-face communication. Thus, occupations involving high levels of human interaction or persuasion or social intelligence are unlikely to be at immediate risk.

Occupations involving creativity are also unlikely to be impacted. Software can only predict based on the data it has and can only be creative to the extent that it can find hidden trends in huge data sets. Software cannot predict new products, nor can it assess whether humans will find a new product 'cool.'

Thus, the kitchen hand will be replaced but the waiter won't, and a barrister is less likely to be replaced by a program than a solicitor is. This is why an insurance broker or financial adviser is less likely to be replaced than an underwriter. Personal Assistants are less likely to be replaced, nor are wise-cracking bar-tenders. While a small but growing percentage of routine business and sports journalism in the USA is now computer written, interviewing and investigative or political journalism will still require people.

In the longer term, however, this will change as digital avatars are improving in their ability to recognize emotions and respond appropriately. IPSoft's *Amelia*, for example, can be taught using employee training manuals and scenario training to continually improve its client interactions and is able to handle e-mails, Skype, and phone calls, recognizing natural languages expressions, searching files for answers, and knows when to transfer queries which it can't handle to a human. She then learns from the advice given by that human. She is able to recognize most emotions from faces or text, even analyzing the rhythm of your key strokes, and is able to respond in the most emotionally appropriate manner. She is also fluent in 20 languages and works 24/7, never getting bored by repetitive tasks.

Types of Jobs

Kelly (2016) argues that jobs can be broken down into four categories;

1. *Jobs that Humans can do but Machines can do better* - Humans can weave cloth, but automated looms are better. While handmade cloth is still produced and is prized for its imperfections there is little reason to value imperfections in driving software or X-ray analysis. Machines improve these products.
2. *Jobs Humans can't do but Machines can* - Humans can't produce computer chips or search the entire web to find a precise page. Most of the jobs software now does are jobs humans could never have done.
3. *Jobs we didn't know we wanted done* - One hundred years ago nobody asked if they could watch moving pictures while in their carriage, or if they could find imaginary creatures on a small screen while walking. Each innovation creates entirely new classes of occupations to fulfill needs we didn't know we had.
4. *Jobs only Humans can do, at first* - The one thing software can't (currently) do is decide what humans want to do. Industrialization has enabled us to feed and clothe ourselves with less than 20% of the workforce. This has enabled an ever greater proportion of people to decide to do other things, like musicians, yoga teachers, fan-fiction authors, makeup bloggers, game developers, night-club reviewers, or travel bloggers. When each of these tasks is taken by a robot, other areas will open up.

Increasing Income Inequality

During the initial stages of the looming revolution, workers whose skills are in short-supply, like data analysts, may find their income sharply increasing, while workers unable to adjust may suffer hardship. Given that a substantial proportion of these affected workers will be middle-income professionals this has major implications for social stability and politics.

The high level of skill required to take advantage of the new opportunities imply that more developed countries will initially gain more than less developed and that countries which aggressively welcome the new changes required by technological innovations will gain a lot more in the long run than countries which restrict the changes. McKinsey (2015), however, notes that developing countries will have the opportunity to leap intermediate stages of technology and not face the problems of resistance from sectors hurt by the decline of the old. This is similar to the way many developing countries without landline phones have moved straight to mobile phones, and have developed more innovative phone-based payment and other systems than exist in developed markets.

The Overall Job Market

Of course, jobs in general won't disappear as many commentators' fear. Economists call the idea that technological changes mean the disappearance of work in the general the 'lump-of-labor fallacy' (which is the idea that there is only so much work so if machines do more, workers do less). It is a fallacy because work as such never disappears.

What actually happens is that IT intensive workers will earn more, and thus spend more, and this extra spending will provide demand for displaced workers. There will thus be the equally rapid creation of completely new occupations. Overall there will be increased GDP growth, and therefore, increased demand for goods and services. In the end, there will be far more wealth, far higher average wages, and demand for nearly all workers who want a job. What is more difficult is that some workers will need to change sectors or change location or be forced to enter occupations they have no natural talent for.

A lesson from history is that automation of activities within a sector does not automatically translate to a lack of demand for workers in that sector. This is because the sharp drop in the price of the activity should create a substantial increase in demand for that activity, and thus a demand for experienced workers to supervise the software.

It is vital to understand that 'jobs' don't disappear, what happens is that particular work 'activities' disappear. An example of this would be typing, an activity which used to be very common, but which computers have minimized. Typing, of course, replaced scribes. Yet demand for clerical workers has remained strong.

Some activities will shrink, some activities will be unaffected, whilst some activities will grow in demand. The consequence for individual jobs is dependent on the specific bundle of activities which make up their work. Things may thus not be so nice for some individual workers. It also needs to be remembered, however, that if costs drop drastically for a product due to software, then its price will drop, and demand should rise. If price or income elasticity is high enough, then demand for workers in a heavily impacted area may well increase.

What is unprecedented about the looming waves of disruptive innovation is the size and speed of the disruption, as it will occur at a far faster pace than the two earlier industrial revolutions did. Frey and Osborne (2013), in an in-depth study, assessed that about 50% of all jobs are at high risk of being eliminated by 2030, with 30% of entire occupational classes going the way of typing pools or supermarket cashiers. McKinsey (2016) estimated that by 2025 about 60% of all current work activities could be replaced by automation with an average saving in excess of 30%. It is hard to survive in a job when the cost base of your software competitor is halving every year. The impact will be felt across society, with white-collar jobs at particular risk. CBRE/Genesis (2014) states that some experts predict that up to 50% of current job areas will either disappear or be radically transformed by 2025. McKinsey (2015) argues that up to 45% of all work activities can be automated *right now*. CitiGPS (2015) argue that 54% of finance and insurance jobs are at high risk, while another 17% are at medium risk.

In contradiction to these reports, Arntz et al. (2016) focused just on the impact of movable robots and broke work down into activities which repetition versus those which involved group work or face-to-face interaction, and estimated that only about 9% of jobs faced an immediate risk of more 90% of their activities disappearing. They note however that jobs may disappear because employers rearrange the remaining activities into fewer jobs, or decide to forgo the face-to-face interaction which is routine in some areas, but which customers may choose to forego. An example of this is the use of grocery self-checkouts.

Overall, workers will have to adjust, moving from their current area, at which they may be quite skilled and well paid, to a job with may involve a drastically different skill set, a drastically different work environment, and possibly substantially reduced pay. Older workers unwilling to adjust may face early retirement. This is similar to the disappearance of the 1960-style typing pools or phone operators, but at a greatly increased scale.

The scale of the looming jobs transformation thus may prove very socially disruptive as required new skill sets may be well outside the displaced workers' comfort zones. Incoming young employees can expect to have their role radically transformed every decade or so.

The change may occur faster than workers can be re-skilled or re-educated. Autor and Dorn (2013) argue that the work force is being polarized with demand for the elite and for manual service workers, and less demand for the middle. MGI (2013) argues that over the next decade or so sophisticated algorithms will replace 140 million knowledge workers worldwide. I would argue that what history does show is that even if skilled workers do lose their jobs, as long as their skills are generalizable, they are more likely to find re-employment than lower skilled workers.

The revolution is also international, which implies that jobs lost by a worker in one country may be easier picked by a worker in another country than a worker in the same country. Worker flexibility and innovativeness will become a vital attribute to the success of countries. Countries with inflexible work environments may lose entire industries.

Lessons from the Professions - the importance of programmable rules

The high-level jobs most at risk will be in job areas where routines, complex as they are, can be reduced to a set of programmable rules. The jobs least at risk will be in areas which involve mental innovation, or intense human interaction, or which have a wide array of activities. Stock-market floor traders have largely disappeared, to be replaced by traders skilled in creating trading programs. Banking has also undergone a large transformation in work activities, though far larger changes are to come. Software is unlikely to replace barristers, as persuasion is their key skill, though the paper-shuffling juniors who accompany them may disappear. Solicitors are at high risk.

A large proportion of accountancy work is already disappearing to software, with successful accountants rapidly moving from routine account preparation to overall business management advice. Expert estimates are that demand for the activities accountants traditionally do may drop by 50% or more over the next decade. Survivors will morph in business consultants and financial advisers. Surgeons are beginning to be replaced by far more precise robots. The work of general doctors is likely to be replaced by computerized expert diagnosis systems, with estimates of up to an 80% reduction in demand. Survivors will focus on offering sympathy and psychological aspects of their service. They may, however, find that a skilled nurse can operate the diagnosis system at a far lower cost and will thus screen clients, leaving only the more difficult cases or client reassurance to the doctor. Software is more likely to replace a highly skilled radiologist, who does a narrow range of routine activities, rather than their PA, who does a wide array of activities.

It is important to understand that impacts can be complex. For example, Markoff in 2011 found that law firms faced with legal analysis software initally drastically reduced their demand for law clerks, as the software could far more effectively search case databases using language analysis to identify general concepts, during a better job at a fraction of the cost, and with no risk of getting bored and missing things. The increasing language ability of software even allows them to read documents for tone and spot unusual conversations. However, the drastic drop in the price of 'discovery' led to a substantial increase in client demand for it, and since the software still needs to be supervised, demand for law clerks is currently actually rising by 1.1% per annum. I would argue that a similar trend is likely to occur for accountants, if they creatively use the increased richness of data.

University academics are at risk in areas of routine teaching and marking, with software being able to adjust the teaching pace and amount of problems asked based on student feedback and performance. Conversely, academics capable of innovative research are unlikely to be replaced.

The Economist (2016) pointed out that in the USA there has been a trend since 1990 for non-routine jobs to grow in demand while routine jobs have stagnated. In the future, routine jobs should start to shrink. The issue is that it is nearly impossible to predict what types of jobs will be created though we can be certain that many new types of jobs will be created. After all, who would have predicted 20 years ago that you could make a living being a professional video game player or YouTube star?

Careful assessment of internal insurer administrative functions in terms of which exhibit the type of programmable rules required for the role to be capable of being handled by software in the short-term and artificial intelligence (AI) systems in the long-term, indicate that approximately 60% of all insurance administrative functions are potentially replaceable by software within the next five years and up to 80% within the next decade. The key point is that if a function is programmable and costs of software are dropping by at least 10–15% per year then that function will eventually be handled by software.

It is important to note that by 'programmable' I don't just mean able to be written into a codeable preset sequence of steps. Modern advances in Artificial Intelligence mean that software can learn by doing, so that even activities which seem complex and require intuition can now be classified as programmable if an AI system can be correctly guided through a learning process. Amazon has shown that AI systems which control networks of machines are generally more efficient than average humans and the efficiency gap is increasingly increasing. An important new area is the development of natural language capacity so that answering phones, writing reports, or creating video presentations are now areas which are programmable. This implies that professions may be more at risk of disruption in the future than the average low-wage job.

McKinsey (2015) argues that 'steeper declines will occur in more saturated markets, products with declining business volumes, and, of course, the more predictable and repeatable positions, including those in IT. The broader corporate functions including these roles will lose jobs overall. Other roles, however, will experience a net *gain* in numbers, especially those concentrating on tasks with a higher value added. Some activities will be engines of job creation—these include marketing and sales support for digital channels and newly created analytics teams tasked with detecting fraud, creating 'next best' offers, and smart claims avoidance'. John Cusano, in Accenture (2013), argues that 'technology will change many insurance jobs and even eliminate some. But a much bigger trend is the support that technology will provide, enabling professionals to spend less time on routine administrative tasks and more time adding value; engaging with customers, solving problems, making better decisions.'

To meet these challenges, insurers will need to source, develop, and retain workers with skills in areas such as advanced analytics and agile software development; experience in emerging and web-based technologies; and the ability to translate such capabilities into customer-minded and business-relevant conclusions and results. McKinsey (2015) argues that there will be a 25% drop in insurance jobs overall by 2025, with minimal change in product development and sales support, a minimal drop in IT, a 25% drop in operations staff and a 45% drop in administration staff.

I would argue that an overall drop in insurance sector employment is unlikely, as new opportunities at successful insurers will grow fast. It needs to be remembered that during the initial industrial revolution employment in the hardest hit sector, weaving, quadruped between 1830 and 1900, despite mechanization. This is because the cost of cloth dropped by 98% so demand within the clothing sector boomed. Where insurers may struggle is in attracting sufficient data-skilled employees, as competition for STEM graduates is exceeding supply and surveys show that less than 3% of graduates regard insurance as an attractive sector. Insurers are not seen as offering engaging activities or being 'cool employers'.

One of the differentiating factors between insurance incumbents who will survive and those who wouldn't is that the non-survivors will focus on cutting costs by reducing staff, while the survivors will focus on adding value by reallocating staff.

References

Accenture. (2013). Closing the gap: How tech-savvy advisors can regain investor trust.

Arntz, M., Gregory, T., & Zierahn, U. (2016). The risk of automation for jobs in OECD countries: A comparative analysis. *OECD Social, Employment, and Migration* (Working Papers, #189), OECD.

Autor, D & Dorn, D. (2013). 'The growth of low skilled service jobs and the polarization of the US labor market', *American Economic Review, 103*(5): 1553–1597.

CBRE/Genesis. (2014). *Fast forward 2030: The future of work and the workplace.*

Citi GPS. (2015). *Technology at Work: The future of Innovation and Employment.* Citi GPS Global Perspectives and Solutions.

Economist. (2016). *The Return of the Machinery Question.* Special report, June 25, UK.

Frey, C. B., & Osborne, M. A. (2013). *The future of employment: How susceptible are jobs to computerisation?* (Working Paper). UK: Oxford University.

Kelly, K. (2016). *The inevitable: Understanding the 12 technological forces that will shape our future.* USA: Viking.

Levy, F., & Murnane, R. J. (2004). *The new division of labor: How computers are creating the new job market.* USA: Princeton University Press.

Markoff, J. (2011, March 4). Armies of expensive lawyers replaced by cheaper software. *New York Times.*

Martinez, A. G. (2016). *Chaos monkeys: Inside the Silicon Valley money machine.* London, UK: Ebury Press.

McKinsey. (2015). *Four fundamentals of workplace automation.* McKinsey Quarterly, November.

McKinsey. (2016). *Automating the insurance industry.* McKinsey Quarterly, January.

MGI. (2013). *Disruptive technologies: Advances that will transform life, business and the global economy.* Tech. Rep. McKinsey Global Institute.

Progressive Policy Institute. (2013). *752,000 App Economy jobs on the 5th anniversary of the App Store.* www.progressivepolicy.org.

11
Impacted Occupations

Actuaries and Underwriters

Two of the occupations likely to be immediately impacted are actuaries and underwriters. Actuaries will find 95% of their training on small data increasingly irrelevant and will have to rapidly retrain in big data skills. In this area, they will face sharp competition from graduates in the new Masters in Data Analytics programs currently being launched.

Underwriters have been listed in most reports as one of the 'ten likely-to-be-impacted occupation classes.' This is because the job has traditionally been composed of analyzing data for trends which may impact on risk levels, selecting key indicators, and matching these to the selected characteristics of applicants for cover. These are routine and rule-based so involve areas which software can easily replace. The need to underwrite all clients and customize at a minimal cost means that humans cannot be involved. Automated underwriting software is already being extensively introduced, as noted in SwissRe (2013).

It is important to note, however, that things are not this simple, as decreasing demand for the current work done by underwriters does not automatically translate to a lack of demand for underwriters.

M. Naylor, *Insurance Transformed*, Palgrave Studies in Financial Services Technology,
DOI 10.1007/978-3-319-63835-5_11

This is because the rapidly decreasing cost of using software to underwrite clients means that the amount of underwriting undertaken will explode, as nearly all clients will be underwritten, and in a more intensive fashion. The new style underwriting will become dynamic and real time so that rates will change based on client activity rather than just the rate just being set at contract creation, so that as the actions of clients change, they can be moved between risk classes and differing premiums charged for differing activities. These considerations imply that there will remain amble jobs in the area of underwriting.

The employment issue is that these new underwriting jobs will demand strong computing/mathematics/AI skills as underwriters will generally not directly underwrite but will be involved in overseeing and improving the underwriting programs, as well as setting the rules for when software marks a potential client as unusual and thus requiring human consideration. New style underwriters will thus have to understand big data and algorithms, as well as skills in creating user-friendly interfaces, and display the creativity to use the ever-expanding richness of data in ways which are novel and client-relevant. Whether individuals currently employed as underwriters can make the transition is a moot point. I would argue that because underwriters have experience with customers and with products, it is essential that they are available to guide new big data graduates in creating useful insights from algorithms. Aviva UK, by contrast, has substantially reduced the underwriters it employs and increased data analysts.

Administrative Staff

One of the first areas to be impacted will be administrative systems, with the administration functions of insurers likely to be severely impacted. By 2025, a substantial proportion of insurance administration staff are likely to find the activities they carry out in their jobs drastically changed or gone, as the rapidly dropping costs of computerization impacts on administration processes.

The best estimates are that 95% of current administrative activities within insurance companies follow programmable rules and therefore will ultimately be handled by software. It is not a matter of going digital or going paperless, it is creating integrated end-to-end software systems capable of handling all client requests at minimal cost for all but the most complex of client situations. Analysis shows that about 70% of all current job activities in insurance administration will undergo profound disruption, with these staff expected to adapt to fundamentally different roles and expectations.

Note that this is best examined in terms of 'activities' rather than 'jobs,' with employees seen as performing a range of activities, which will each be disrupted at differing times to differing degrees. Thus, software will not replace jobs but will replace some activities. Insurers will have to continually rearrange employee roles to expand newer activities and reduce shrinking activities.

However, again, this does not mean that these workers will face unemployment, as these systems will still need to be supervised, and demand in other areas of work will open up, for example engaging in social media. After all, the disappearance of typing pools has not led to a decrease in office employment, and there has been an increase in banking sector employment as computerization has spread. The ability of employees to interact with and oversee software processes will be vital, as will the ability to interact with big data and social media.

This disruption will include a number of fairly senior management jobs, and not just junior positions, as many senior roles involve analytical activities which can be replaced by AI agents. Morgan Stanley/BCG (2014) estimates that automated administrative processes alone will cut insurer costs and thus premiums by around 25% by 2019, while at the same time as speeding up response times to clients. The impact is likely to be closer to 60% by 2025. Note that this doesn't mean eliminating human response as most digital natives expect the availability of humans or advisers as one of the many channels available.

Many of the surviving administration jobs will involve a high level of interaction with social media or CRM systems, as insurers need to evolve a deep understanding of digital natives and social capital, and then either create a dedicated social media presence and strategy or quickly become irrelevant. Given the demand for rapid 24/7 responses and intense monitoring of social media, insurers will not be able to reduce response staff by the same proportion as customer calls reduce. The nature of those jobs will, however, fundamentally change as most insurer staff will have to work closely with software, so that extensive retraining to a higher level of technical skill will be required.

Most industry observers argue that jobs which depend on analyzing statistical trends will die, as they will be replaced by expert system AI programs. CBRE/Genesis (2014) thus lists underwriters, fraud assessors, claims clerks, and appraisers, as among the top 20 most-at-risk of all occupations in the next few years. Even software coding jobs may shrink as high-level software takes over.

I would argue that these expectations are wrong as a more astute observation would that the nature of insurance data jobs will drastically transform, with a rapid expansion of analytical jobs overseeing AI programs as well as dealing with the resultant outputs. The range of new insights available will actually increase demand for analytical activities. There will have to be a corresponding expansion in strategy jobs, in terms of trying to understand the insights from the rapidly expanding big data systems and the application of these, especially roles involved in converting the new insights into profitable services. This will imply faster revision of IT-based administration systems, and a large expansion of software related jobs.

One of the largest changes will thus be the heavy increase in the need for regular staff retraining. The idea of staff being trained in higher education and then being suitable for a job for life is already archaic. Staff can be expected to experience a drastic upheaval of their role at least once a decade. The newness of most of the challenges means that there will be a scarcity of already trained staff. This implies that employers will need to allocate substantially increased resources to staff training and an expansion in training roles. The survivors will be those companies which have deep and wide continuous retraining programs. Even new graduates will need to be retrained within the first decade as their knowledge will date fast. The ability to learn will be more important than deep knowledge.

If the insurance employer responds to the increasing opportunities to engage with clients, then the increased demand for staff in the expanding areas will mean that overall employment may increase rather than shrink. Insurers who proactively move from product selling to services supply should employ more staff. It would be a major mistake for insurers to view the digital transformation as an exercise to reduce staff numbers, rather than a process of transforming staff skill sets. Incumbents need to remember, however, that the new entrants will have a need for experienced staff and will try to attract the most competent employees with a more exciting work environment.

The key issue for staff is thus their capacity to adjust to a new job and new skill sets. Those staff who are flexible enough to pick up new skill sets in new areas as they are invented will thrive. Given the pace of change, employees can expect a substantial change in their employment activities at least once a decade. Those staff who are incapable of adapting will lose their jobs. Employers who do not ensure their staff feel confident enough to retrain will face bankruptcy.

Robo-advice and Brokers/Advisers

Overview

SEI (2015) claims that software innovations aimed at the financial and insurance planning/advice industry are now being created faster than the industry can adapt to. The limiting factor in technological change for advisers/brokers is thus now the ability of advisers/brokers to adopt their culture to use the innovations. Firms which adopt faster will have an increasing competitive advantage.

Arthofer (2016) argues that insurance agents/brokers are uniquely vulnerable to tech-based external entrants because (i) they are aging and thus less in touch with modern customer demands, (ii) the next wave of insurance customers will be millennials, who expect an omni-channel response, (iii) entrants have an integrated, front-end-to-back-office IT system, (iv) customers are being expected to take more responsibility for their purchases, which they do by going online, (v) goods similar to insurance are already sold online in many markets, (vi) online disruptors provide a better education experience, and (vii) online disruptors use their CRM systems to provide superior customer service. Arthofer argues that most of the older advisers/brokers will be unable to adjust to this radically different world.

What does this mean for financial and insurance brokers and advisers? Lessons can be taken from other professions are illustrative. Financial market traders now do very little actual trading, and floor traders have disappeared. Market specialists instead supervise high-speed trading programs. Since this requires IT skills, a substantial number of previously highly paid traders have been forced to find other occupations.

Similarly, modern accounting has very little to do with creating and analyzing accounts, as the routine inputting of data and analysis of the output is now done by software. Accountants in general have responded successfully to the IT challenge by moving into offering general business advice, learning to use the increased data analysis capacity to enhance their capacity to examine business trends, and give sophisticated advice. Accountants have not had to become skilled in IT as the software is user friendly.

Lawyers have yet to be affected as strongly but Markoff (2011) argues that since most legal advice involves knowing existing law and analyzing these to find patterns, the common lawyer is in trouble as 80% of legal advice could be provided by software. Lawyers will have to respond like the accountants and shift into using the greater data analysis capacity to offer substantially more sophisticated advice built on the insights delivered by the software.

Buyers of financial/insurance products who wish to undertake simple purchases or receive generic advice will get this online from well-structured Web sites, especially ones which offer computerized feedback to client questions via verbal or facial response systems. Therefore, brokers or advisers who want to survive will have to differentiate themselves from what software systems can offer. In particular, they will have to understand which aspects of their advice follows programmable rules, and can therefore be replaced by software, and which aspects are too complex or psychological to be replaceable. Involvement in activities which create client trust is the most important concept.

The current state of the broking/advice industry in terms of the IT transformation is however lagging as badly as insurers are. For example, most brokers use their Web page merely for quotes and purchases. The majority do not understand the level of sophistication in adviser-based software response which is required. SEI (2015) found that financial and wealth advisers are currently underestimating the potential impact of AI systems, with very few comprehending the ability of future AI systems to offer competent generic advice to 90% of investors. This is because they are evaluating the current rough state of robo-advice software rather than the rapid exponential pace of future developments. In terms of Figs. 1.1 and 1.2, in the introduction, adviser software is not yet at the inflection point, so while we are disappointed by the relatively slow pace of current developments, we will be shocked by the rapid pace of future changes. The industry needs to prepare for the high quality of what is to come, rather than guessing forward based on what currently exists. It may be a consolation for insurance advisers to know that while their sector needs change, the extent of the required change is less than that required for insurance companies.

Increasingly sophisticated software using voice recognition will be able to offer generic advice and answer routine questions over the phone or a Web site without clients being aware they are talking to software. These programs will even be able to cold call prospects, and offer responsive virtual-reality 'talking heads,' so that Skype calls can be done by software. Obviously, the market share of direct sales Web sites will grow. Most routine clients will thus have little need to talk to advisers, or pay their fees. An area where skilled software will be vital is in handling social media, as brokers and advisers will not have the time to intensively monitor all their customer channels. Therefore, queries and comments will need to be first screened by software and answered by software, with pre-set exceptions passed on to the adviser.

One downside for the established western firms is that programmers in Bangalore could become a major player in the lower-end advice market. Another downside is that technology firms will be able to produce advanced AI software and enter the market. Thus, a substantial share of the providers of robo-advice will probably be new market entrants, firms with an IT background, who can easily program a set of rules based on an extensive questionnaire. As costs drop, banks will find it easier to install an AI booth than retain branch advisers. Since banks tend to offer more rule-based advice than personalized advisers do, they may find their clients more susceptible to the IT competition.

Key Concepts for Adviser Survival

The first key concept for adviser survival is that in a well-run adviser practice, the adviser will have already delegated the routine tasks, like answering clients phone enquires, or tracking transactions, or calculating sums producing reports, to lower paid assistants. They will have left themselves the more productive, more skilled, more interactive areas, like meeting clients and convincing them of the importance of following the adviser's recommendations using persuasive skills.

Thus, the adviser's staff who are currently involved in areas involving routines which follow programmable rules are more likely to be replaced by software than is the senior adviser. The Adviser can use quality admin software from 3rd party platforms to automate most of their administrative tasks, including routine client contact and regulation requirements. This should enable them to cut per-client cost by 60–80% while increasing service quality because they are freed from routine administration, therefore increasing the frequency of meaningful engagements with clients. The upside for adviser survival is that it will be easier for smaller practices to survive by replacing admin or reception staff with software. Most routine regulatory activities can be handled by software. The key here is an integrated end-to-end IT system which integrates everything which happens in the adviser office so each staff member has what they need on screen, so clients feel their queries are intelligently answered by lower paid staff, or can interact via the Web site. Reducing per-transaction cost, increasing customer engagement, and limiting adviser time to high-value activities are keys.

A second key concept is that while previously customers would turn up not knowing much about products or prices, and therefore needed educating, increasingly new customers have done extensive online research and so know a lot more about products and prices and so are more focused on the advice aspect - the 'how do I get to where I want to be' aspect rather than the 'what can you offer me' aspect. Hard-sell skill sets are becoming less valuable than softer persuasion skills. The focus will be on lifecycle advice, not product sales.

A third key concept is that as insurance becomes telematic and data intensive as well as embedded in an ecosystem, advisers will have a role in servicing those telematic devices, in explaining to clients how they can use feedback from telematics to reduce dynamic commissions, and in cross selling additional products or services from related ecosystem providers. Advisers are used to the idea that they offer services and not just products. The key strength the adviser has to offer the ecosystem is their close and personal contacts with clients, and the associated ability to influence them and engage the client in an emotionally successful life-process. Data analytics will offer detailed feedback on the best advice or sales techniques. This will lead to far higher persistence rates for adviser clients. Note that the adviser's IT system will need to work with clients' data agent Apps.

A fourth key concept is that the successful survivors of the industry during the coming IT revolution will be those who ensure financial planning is about personalized advice and associated interpersonal skills, and not about sales or transactions or standardized advice. This is because generic advice follows programmable rules. Aspects of the job which depend on personality skills will survive better than those aspects which depend on mathematical skills. Successful advisers will proactively embrace software advice systems to enhance their advice and their capacity to deal with clients by offering better service. It is well established that the key part of being a successful financial or insurance adviser is not the giving of the advice, but ensuring that clients are convinced to actually make the sacrifices required to implement the advice - the human psychological skills.

A fifth key concept is that AIA/Beddoes (2015) shows that insurance advisers demonstrating that they can manage claims by ensuring hassle-free reasonable settlements is vital to ensuring client retention. Since many claims take place at a time when clients are less able to self-manage, advisers are able to add a personal touch which will result in multiple referrals - good advisers' claims management is much more than just money, it is also dealing with all the other aspects of the clients' financial affairs. Since many brokers and advisers don't advertise this area of their work, new clients often undervalue this advantage of advised insurance. Good advisers will ensure all elements of the insurance chain run smoothly. Successful claims handling is impressive to clients and should generate strong social media ratings.

A sixth key concept is that advisers' currently only service about the top 10% of households by income. The reduction in per-client service costs produced by adviser software will enable advisers to expand their offering down into the middle-income brackets. These lower wealth clients who are currently not serviced due to the lack of fees generated, but can be if per-client costs are slashed. This will expand adviser's potential market size at least 3 or 4 times. This can be done by using a predominately robo-advice approach which is integrated with restricted human-delivered advice. By working alongside quality robo-advice software, advisers will be able to offer a low-touch version of personalized service which is now only available to the richest clients to these middle-income clients. The high-net-worth clients, whose financial lives have complexities not amendable to programmable rules, will still prefer human financial advisers and can now be offered a high-touch, high-tech approach.

It will also be easier for advisers to segment clients by costs and profits, and offer differentiated services. Fidelity's 2012 annual broker and adviser sentiment survey showed that tech-savvy advisers managed on average $8M more in funds than their colleagues. This difference will exponentially grow as more tech-savvy advisers offer a more inclusive and dynamic experience to an increasingly diverse array of clients, while the less tech-savvy collapse under a blizzard of admin and regulation requirements.

A seventh key concept is that the cost of services like portfolio selection or investment selection or policy application will drop more than other areas. Investment-only advisers will be impacted more than full-service advisers.

An eighth key concept is that clients will get comprehensive information on adviser costs and will be better able to hold them accountable. Clients will see all their accounts in one place and will see all load fees and be able to compare high-cost mutual funds with low-cost index funds under a range of scenarios. These costs can be then used to evaluate the worth of an adviser. Quality advisers not tied to a one-product supplier will do better than chain advisers

A ninth key concept is that a quality customer relationship management (CRM) system is vital. There is a need to integrate multiple communication channels in a manner which is easy to use for both customers and advisers. For example, some customers may prefer contact via text messages, and these need to appear on one system alongside e-mail or phone messages, so the adviser does not have to be constantly checking multiple sources. Thus, the CRM system needs to cover: personal interviews, phone calls, e-mails, Web site self-service, Web site life-chat, Skype, mobile Apps, text messaging, online forums, short videos, and social media, and it needs to collect information and provide summaries automatically via key word searches. The CRM then needs to output the adviser's response in the customer's preferred channel. What the adviser wants is to get their message to as many people as possible, for the lowest cost per client, and yet make the client feel like they are getting quick and customized attention, in the way they want to communicate.

There also needs to be an effective interchange of information between staff so the lower cost assistants or software applications can do their job, without constant adviser oversight. The CRM should give feedback to the adviser on which channels specific types of customers prefer, why, and alert the adviser to evolving trends. The adviser can experiment with different client approaches and see which results in the best client outcome. The CRM needs to be open to review by customers and improvement suggestions. Anticipating customer needs and proactively addressing them are a vital part of a superior customer experience. Software providers will need to supply insights gained from the AI analysis of CRM outcomes across their network.

A tenth key concept is the need to create multi-generational client and adviser strategies, with differentiated channels, so that the children of current clients can be retained. SEI (2015) reports that less than 6% of US wealth advisers have a multi-generational strategy, resulting in 94% of firms having a dubious long-term future. A key part of this strategy is nurturing the next generation of advisers. Note that the style and ethnic/

gender composition of these advisers will have to match the increasing diversity of the younger generations. An upside is that today's recruits are the first generation of advisers to start out as trained financial planners rather than being converted from sales-related occupations. The CFP qualification is an essential first step, with a specialist degree increasing common. Being tech-savvy will be a required basic competency.

An eleventh key concept is that while earlier generations of advisers have had to deal with inefficient and non-integrated adviser admin software, the new generation will benefit from high quality modular 3rd party software, which is largely bug-free and adviser/client friendly. The adviser will be able to have this personalized to their practice very easily. Advisers, however, will have to get used to frequent upgrades and presentation changes in their software, instead of the current tendency for advisers to stick with the same package for up to a decade.

The adviser will have to offer multiple channels to clients, as different aged clients may have differing preferences in terms of channels. Younger clients, for example, may prefer more software-based systems. A key here will be to ensure that even 100% digital clients get some human contact so a relationship is built up, and as wealth builds they get used to human-based advice. Advisers can't assume that they can sit back and wait for younger digital clients to 'mature' into behaving as older clients do - they will have to be cultivated.

The heart of this software will be ensuring that the client's goals are clear and that clients receive personalized feedback about progress toward achieving them. This has to include feedback based on behavioral finance concepts using real time telematic data-flow and spending as an integrated aspect of encouraging good client behavior. This should ensure deep and real-time client engagement.

Omni-channel access will allow advisers and clients to work together to establish goals and mechanisms, which is called 'co-planning.' Currently, however, less than 10% of US wealth managers offer an effective client portal which is omni-channel, integrated, personalized, offers collaborative real-time document tools, and is linked to real market data. Very few offer tools such as allowing clients to actively stress test their current and planned portfolios under various potential market scenarios, or run insurable risk scenarios. All of these areas are creatable by a quality software provider, and will be part of superior robo-advice packages within the next decade, so advisers who do not regularly upgrade their CRM systems will be at risk of being 'ubbered.'

A twelfth key concept is that passive investing will increasingly dominate over active. The cost of conducting transaction will also drop by at least 100-fold. Thus, advisers who rely on transaction-related fees for profit will struggle, while advisers who focus on client-behavior-based fees will survive.

A thirteenth, and potentially most important, concept is that current robo-advice solutions tend to assume the problem is one of information, so focus on providing this more efficiently - 'if we have more knowledge and better tools we will all achieve financial success.' However, as any adviser knows, the major problems clients have are actually behavioral. Stage 3 or 4 robo-advisers will start to incorporate knowledge in these areas, including real-time feedback to investors based on telematics or spending. Because investors may feel embarrassed to share failing in this areas with humans they may accept this feedback better from software. Advisers will have to embed these systems in a way which assures clients that their failings are confidential.

A fourteenth key concept is that it is faulty to think there is a dichotomous choice between human and robo-advice. Successful advisers will use a multiple of customer contact channels, human/Web/video/phone/robo, etc., with the choice partly determined by the adviser on a revenue-cost basis, and partly determined by clients. Advisers, for example, may provide generic information via robo-channels once the client has been motivated by human contact, or may use a vibrant robo-web-presentation to increase client numbers. A robo-adviser may help to do the initial screening for return-risk profiling, with a voice activated talking-head taking the client through a questionnaire, with the capacity to answer additional client queries. Given that portfolio construction is increasingly being automated, this could link easily into suggestive portfolios, and then book an adviser meeting.

The switch between channels does not have to be linear, as clients can be given the choice at each stage to switch to a human adviser via a Skype or chat box. Robo-software can analyze client voice patterns in response to questions, to determine stress and comfort, and alert a human at preset levels. A human adviser would oversee the robo-derived choices and intervene at key stages. The key is for the adviser to strategically set up an advice process which minimizes cost, maximizes client engagement, and optimizes client outcomes. The client interface has to be seamless, high quality, and engaging.

A fifteenth key concept is that advisers have generally done a better job of creating close customer relationships than insurers have. Accenture (2013) found that 60% of surveyed US advisers have at least weekly contact with clients through social media. Advisers have been particularly active in use of social media. This puts them in a sound position to offer their expertise in this area to external entrants as well as existing suppliers. Certainly, quality advisers have a far smaller transformation to make than insurance companies do.

Accenture, however, also argues that there are two communication issues, (i) advisers tend to seriously overestimate client investment knowledge so that what advisers regarded as clear communication was perceived by clients as promotional, and (ii) advisers tend to overestimate clients' willingness to take investment risk. These issues create a channel for advisers to offer useful education via social media which will be welcomed by clients. Contacts with clients need to be two-way and group based, so advisers can answer questions.

A sixteenth key concept is that the idea that 'millennials and digital natives do not value advisers and will only purchase on-line' is faulty. Evidence clearly shows that the digital savvy are happy to talk to human advisers, and are happier to pay for this than baby boomers if they are approached correctly. The issue has been that advisers in general are used to dealing with baby boomers and do not know how to relate to millennials and digital natives. The new generations want the same thing the baby boomers want - a relationship with a competent professional they can trust. They just want to build it on a computer first. The older generations can often be quite tech-savvy.

However, younger clients have different customer experience expectations - in particular their activities with the online world mean that they expect excellent service at a low price with extremely fast delivery, via a channel of their choice. Their first impulse is not to phone to talk to a person, but to do extensive net searches first, including reviews of the adviser on social media. Cold callings, direct marketing, and referrals are uncommon. Online articles and blogs are highly regarded.

Education and client stories should be a large part of that. Advisers who do not work in that space and do not offer open two-way reviews, or generate numerous online reviews, do not exist in the new world. If an adviser's business is not visible on a millennial's mobile phone, it doesn't exist. The methods advisers have successfully used to attract baby boomers will not work.

Zaptitude (2016) surveyed millennials in Australia and found that they felt disengaged from the financial service industry, especially advisers. Millennials felt that advisers 'spoke an alien language' which patronized them and pushed them away. Zaptitude found that the most important qualities desired in an adviser by millennials were 'a sense of humor' (68%), 'simplifies the complex' (66%), and 'casual/relaxed' (48%). 'Technical/detailed' was only at 29% and 'wearing a suit' at 26%. Zaptitude argues that 'financial service professionals need to stop assuming they know what is best for the public and start to ask them instead.'

For Millennials and digital natives, direct quotation firms are the only ones to vaguely appeal to the new generations; yet these platforms only generate a low-quality relationship, use insurance as a commodity, and therefore not do have sticky customers. They can be easily bested by quality advisers.

Advisers need to avoid the commodity-price space and create a deep and rich omni-channel experience based on quality advice and quality communication. Part of this is not using a simple price quotation system, as this ignores quality issues. Adviser Web sites should start with an advice-based questionnaire to ascertain client needs and therefore the most appropriate range of products, before price is mentioned. Advisers need to mention products the client doesn't need or how to cut cost and reduce risk. This is also vital as it establishes a trust relationship. Advisers, who are skilled at relationships, will find it easier to establish these omni-channel experiences than large transaction-based insurers will.

Change in Activities

There is thus no reason to expect an overall substantial reduction in the size of the adviser/broker industry as long as the industry is prepared to respond proactively, and understands how to respond strategically to the rise of robo-advice. Effective use of technology will allow advisers to source clients from a wider geographical region, or even internationally, and thus specialize in a market segment.

In fact, as internal software allows advisers to service clients at a low marginal cost and therefore at a lower price, overall demand for advice should increase substantially. One key is to ensure that younger, lower income, clients who will initially use generic robo-advisers, get used to being advised and therefore switch to human advisers as their wealth rises.

The aspect of financial/insurance planning which will be most difficult for programmers to replace will be the client psychology aspect, the understanding of client weaknesses, the understanding of how to persuade clients to act in their own long-term interests, and how to help them overcome those weaknesses in order to become financially successful. It is well established that most clients need external prodding before they will act in their own best financial interest. The key element of being a professional financial adviser is not providing a plan, but in ensuring that clients have the willingness and motivation to carry it out.

Robo-advice software is unlikely to be able to use psychological knowledge to provide this style of advice in the intermediate future. Therefore, advisers will have to place a premium on interpersonal or creative or abstract-thinking skills. Advisers will have to define very carefully how their advice is different to, and superior to, the standard, generic, advice produced by AI software.

It would be a mistake, however, to assume that AI systems will not in the future be able to handle many of the psychological aspects of advice once talking heads are available. Advisers will have to run to stay ahead of an increasingly fast improving competitor.

Successful advisers will have to structure their processes so they are able to attract clients away from software systems, as younger investors will start by using software advice at the stage when they have limited investible funds. These investors may then have a tendency to stick with those systems, even when they reach the stage when they have enough investible funds to be attractive to advisers, normally at about $100,000 in funds, as they will find it a cultural change to switch from a software adviser to a human one. If advisers attract younger clients by offering a free robo-advice platform with generic advice, then they can increasingly offer users fee-based human advice as their wealth grows.

Current advisers who effectively use technology with an advanced data presentation system have found that clients understand their financial situation better and trust the adviser's advice more. Clients feel more ownership of the advice, and are thus more likely to implement it, because they have the opportunity to examine their own financial progress rather than the adviser lecturing to them. Note however that adviser software needs an advanced data presentation system and the adviser needs to know how to use the various data slices effectively.

A major issue is that the current robo-adviser systems, immature as they are, are superior to the Web sites of most advisers and wealth managers in terms of graphical presentation, personalization, and customer motivation and acquisition. Successful advisers will have to urgently learn Web presentation skills if they are to survive against fast improving robo-advisers.

One obvious area of human advantage is during bear markets, when nervous clients may abandon AI systems which do not offer psychological reassurance, or rearrange assets sufficiently to retain liquidity. The use of social media by advisers needs to be handled with care, as there are potential pitfalls. While carefully selected links and postings can add to client understanding and engagement, the adviser needs to be careful not to link articles which could lead to faulty actions by clients if misunderstood.

Note that while there will be a legitimately wide range of adviser responses to advances in technology, with some firms using it intensively for most clients, while others will use it as a supplement to a human-focused practice, advisers will have to pay close attention to ensuring each part of their business is cost-competitive with the rapidly falling cost of robo-advisers to avoid being disintermediated. The best advisers will be those who successfully blend the advantages of the human approach with the advantages of the technological approach to offer clients an omni-channel personalized service which is superior to today's service at a lower price, as well as enabling them to service more clients, serve them better, and serve them with less time. They can service clients in China as easily as they can clients down the road. Less able advisers will face increasing competition from online sites or AI software. Advisers who cannot distinguish themselves from software will exit the industry, as the costs of their IT competitor could be dropping by 30% a year. It is probable that a wide gap will open between the best tech-savvy advisers and the rest.

The Economist (2014) argues that the IT revolution threatens to drastically widen the income and wealth gap between the small number of highly paid IT workers and the stagnating rest of us, as most workers struggle to cope. This is obviously good for advisers who deal with the wealthy, as long as their Web interface appeals to the highly IT literate. An effective IT internal admin system will enhance the abilities of advisers able to work with the new tech-wealthy.

The threat of generic advice from robo-advisers will initially impact most strongly on bank or large chain advisers. This is because the majority of these advisers follow an advice framework handed to them by the institution which is designed to maximize sales. The process does not empower the advisers to form a professional view of what's in the client's best interest. Advisers are also encouraged to accept the client's self-diagnosis of what they need. The focus is on the outcome, the product distribution, not on whether the advice is fulfilling the client's needs. There is no trust relationship established.

The problem is that most clients do not know what is in their best interest - that is why they need 'advice.' What clients need is a professional advice process which follows a guiding set of principles to accurately diagnosis the client's condition and determine the best set of solutions, even if they do not involve a product, or involve a competitor's product, or a non-product strategy like budgeting or savings, or involve advice about what products they do not need. As the adviser environment changes to become more advice and customer focused, banks or generic chain-firms will thus find it harder to compete with robo-advisers than will adviser firms which already offer a professional, client-focused, service. Individual advisers will have to be strategic about which firms they work for and need to ensure that their firm has the capacity to move with the waves of change.

Another key concept for networks of advisers or banks or insurers who offer advice, is the importance of social capital. Advisers and adviser networks are going to have to accept that digital native clients will review their services and Web platforms online in detail and that adviser practices which do not offer a sophisticated, efficient, and friendly service, will be rated down and will struggle to attract new clients. Advisers need to actively encourage unedited reviews by clients.

Advisers will have to use a mix of channels across a range of social platforms and modes. They will have to advertise and participate in social media. Adviser practices will have to actively monitor their social capital and have proactive programs to increase it. Use of informality and humor will have to be selectively used.

They will have to invest heavily to keep up-to-date with the latest trends in Adviser software while offering a client-focused interface which is sophisticated enough to appeal to the IT savvy and yet easy-to-use so that it appeals to the less IT savvy. Their software systems need to be able to offer a 24/7 service, even when no humans are present. Any advisers who fail to consistently uphold the highest level of client service will find their rating on social networks dropping, with a subsequent loss of clients.

Insurance advisers and product suppliers will need to simplify their products and ensure the related fees and commissions are transparent, as robo-advisers will offer simple products with straightforward fees. Advisers need to be able to be proud of the way they are paid, so they can discuss this on social media. Any hint of their advice being influenced by commission and not in the client's best interests could devastate their social capital. Note that it is the response to complaints which matters, not the mistakes themselves.

Given that the adviser market will become inherently international, there will be a need for regulation to dynamically change as the adviser market adapts to robo-competitors, especially if these are foreign based. It will be unfair to domestic advisers if they have to obey expensive rules while foreign Web-based advisers don't. This may require extensive international regulatory integration.

The financial advice profession has demonstrated over the last few decades the capacity to respond positively to industry, regulatory, and market changes, and should have the capacity to respond to robo-advice and digital native clients.

Diagnostic Robo-advice Systems

The majority of current robo-advisors try to reproduce the traditional financial advice process. Specifically, they install a detailed questionnaire on their Web sites, just as if you had gone to the office of a financial planner. They then try to understand your current financial situation; your goals, age, income, risk aversion, etc. They then recommend choices; how much to save; how much to invest; how much insurance you need, etc. Finally, they implement each choice for you. This is the standard CFP six-step process. This suits the majority of traditional clients who do not have much knowledge or confidence.

This approach may, however, not suit the likely first clientele of robo-advice systems, the do-it-yourselfer. Those investors have instead already made their investment choices. What they need is for the robo-advisor system to examine those choices and find improvements. This approach can be described as diagnostic. For these clients, robo-advisers should not use the traditional questionnaire but will instead ask investors why they have made their current choices. *Why are you 65% invested in stocks when your risk profile indicates you should be reducing risk? Why have you chosen an aggressive growth fund and not a conservative? Why aren't you using tax-deductible funds? Here are two reasons why that might be best practice. Does either apply to you? Here are some suggestions to reduce your insurance risk.*

SEI (2014) argues that there are eight actions which advisers have to do:

1. *Co-plan with clients:* Clients have become more astute, so advisers need to work with clients rather than act as an expert who imposes advice from on-high.
2. *Adopt goal-based reporting:* Advisers should embrace total life goals rather than pure financial and assess client progress toward those broad goals, rather than money saved. Understand behavioral investing issues.
3. *Hone the value proposition*: Assess exactly what advantages being human offers over software, and focus on that part of the business, and automate the rest. Being a niche player may be effective as the potential market is now international.

4. *Age and ethnic diversify*: Ensure the firm has as wide a range of possible clients as possible, by hiring diverse younger advisers or those from potential target markets, as investors most identify with a like person.
5. *Optimize operations*: Examine each part of the firm's processes and use the least cost staff possible and look to eventually running firm admin by a software package. Ensure customer contact systems use multiple channels and offer clients at least as good an experience as rivals.
6. *Assess income structure*: Ensure the structure of fees/commissions will survive banks and fund managers offering free Web-based transactions. Know what is best practice.
7. *Become a techno-adviser:* Ensure the firm is aware of the latest software and is at the forefront of adviser-friendly CRM and admin software. Ensure all staff are able to optimize all systems. Create a market-leading client interface.
8. *Outsource*: Outsource everything except your client relationship and value proposition. Don't try to become a chief technology officer - it's not your core skill set.

Revenue Issues

The basis of fee charging will change as investment companies will use robo-advice software to enable investors to trade for free or at very low basis points. Many banks or Internet firms may offer robo-advisers for free as a 'loss-leader.' Thus, advisers will have to move to a fee for advice model rather than one based on assets-under-management.

Current robo-advisers tend to charge a percentage of assets, typically between 25 and 75 basis points (0.25–0.75%). They find it hard to charge any ongoing fee unless they provide ongoing advice. This is the challenge for a diagnostic robo-advice service - how to charge ongoing rather than one-off, or episodic, fees. There are two approaches that could be taken. First, a diagnostic robo-adviser could be embedded in a wider service. It might be bundled with the services of an SMSF administration provider. Secondly, the diagnostic service could be provided at low cost by a private wealth management firm, private bank or even an industry fund as a way of establishing contact with wealthy investors.

For those advisers who do run robo-advisers, they will have to think carefully about charging. While the financial advice sector is moving toward fees for service, many still charge a fraction of funds under advice. Even advisers who claim to charge a fee for service often start by asking the size of funds to be advised on and then work backward to a nominal fee per hour.

What very few advisers do is start by working out fixed (non-time related) and marginal (time related) costs per client and then charging based on a profit margin above that. This can be seen as distinguishing between the costs required to keep the business open even without clients vs the extra costs that each type of client creates. In general, advisers tend to have substantially higher marginal costs than fixed costs. In contrast, robo-advice systems tend to have higher front fixed costs (for creation) and then very low marginal costs. What this implies is that extra (predominately) robo-clients can be taken on for little extra cost. Clients need to be segmented into low vs high-touch. Low-touch clients can be offered robo-mainly advice with low fees, and additional charges for contact with humans. These clients are useful as high fixed and low marginal costs also mean that there will be substantial decreases in per-client cost as the number of clients increase.

This may imply cost advantages to larger networks, but these should be offset by smaller firms buying robo-adviser software from cloud-based 3rd party vendors. These vendors will also be able to supply system maintenance services and unlimited cloud-based processing and storage. These will probably be the same vendors which supply the adviser's administrative systems, so that the results of robo-advice can be inputted directly to client files. This will enable advisers to handle a large book of less-wealthy clients as long as they set restrictions on human-based contacts. Given that these clients are currently unprofitable but substantially exceed wealthier clients in number, this will multiply the client base and spread fixed costs.

Overview

The IT advances will substantially change the world of financial and insurance advisers, but probably not as much as they will change insurance companies. Advisers/brokers who have approached insurance as a volume-based transaction business will find that they cannot compete on cost with increasingly advanced software. Advisers who focus on advice and psychological areas will thrive as adviser software both reduces administrative costs and increases client engagement. The passion an adviser can project to a client is very hard for software to re-create.

It is very likely that the admin cost of offering advice will drop drastically, maybe to 10% of its current level, so advisers will be able to handle more clients with drastically less paperwork. This reduction in cost should mean a sharp drop in client fees and a correspondingly rapid rise in demand for advice. Advisers who are able to ride the wave of change should find themselves with substantially increased incomes and happier clients.

References

Accenture. (2013). *Closing the gap: How tech-savvy advisors can regain investor trust.*

AIA/Beddoes. (2015). *The advice challenge: Understanding what clients value*, Australia.

Arthofer. (2016). Insurance brokerage is broken. *TechCrunch*, May 2.

CBRE/Genesis. (2014). *Fast forward 2030: The future of work and the workplace.*

Economist. (2014). *The third great wave.* Special Report, October 4th.

Markoff, J. (2011, March). Armies of expensive lawyers, replaced by Cheaper Software. *New York Times*. Science, 4.

Morgan-Stanley/BCG. (2014). *Insurance and technology: Evolution and revolution in a digital world.* USA: Boston Consulting Group.

SEI. (2015). *The Next Wave of Financial Planning.* White Paper. www.seic.com/enUS/advisors/14834.htm.

SwissRe. (2013). *Automated underwriting: Threat or opportunity?*. New York.

Zaptitude. (2016). *Investing in Millennials*, Research Report. www.zaptitude.com.

12

Conclusion

There is a perfect storm of technological advances which are about to combine and disrupt both the insurance industry and the adviser/broker industry. The majority of current companies and advisers are technological laggards and will require immense transformation before they will be in a position to combat these threats. The industry is thus wide-open to disruptive external entrants who have leading-edge skills in technology.

Insurers have to understand that, while parts of the technology explored in this book seem extreme to insurance managers, nearly all the technology covered already exists, either in companies in other sectors, or within small new entrants, or in beta form. There is no question about 'what will occur' - there is only a question as to the timing. The insurance industry in 15- to 20-year time will be very different to today and will be continuing to change at an ever-faster rate. The big transformation will probably come from the entry of tech-savvy external firms, firms which will do things completely different - the 'ubers.' The majority of existing firms will probably go bankrupt due to their inability to transform themselves into a client-centered model, while survivors will be so transformed that they may be unrecognizable.

M. Naylor, *Insurance Transformed*, Palgrave Studies in Financial Services Technology,
DOI 10.1007/978-3-319-63835-5_12

Insurance as an industry needs to be reimagined. Insurance is fundamentally a series of services: application, policy maintenance, capital funding, customer relations, claims, which are currently packaged and sold as a 'product.' Insurance needs to be transformed into a series of risk data-based value-added services.

The ability to staff, manage, lead, and transform increasingly automated organizations will be the key future competitive advantage. The biggest change is that insurance will stop being a price-based commodity and become a lot more flexible, and focused on real-time dynamic services. While policies may be simplified, the possibility of individualized underwriting and real-time dynamic premiums mean that clients will feel a lot more engaged with insurance and insurers. Insurers who can build trust and social capital, and can find valuable business ecosystems, will create substantial competitive advantage and cross-selling opportunities. Their future will be rosy. Insurers who persist in using traditional approaches will find themselves in Kodak's shoes.

Insurers need to respond with a proactive structured approach involving five elements: (i) a clear long-term strategy, (ii) mechanisms to capture areas where future value is created, (iii) investment in core technical and change management capacities, (iv) creation of an adaptive, flexibility culture, and (v) a clear road map from here to there, which is clearly understood across the organization.

The More Distant Future

As speculative and extreme as the above advances in IT may seem, the insurance industry needs to understand that an even more extreme future awaits humanity after about 2040. The exponential change curve becomes very steep then. Insurers need to adjust as fast as possible to the more immediate future I have outlined so that they are in the best position to adjust to the more extreme future which will occur after that. I will only outline a sample of speculative future possibilities. Some of these technologies already exist in a trial stage, other are still in the imagination stage. Possible future technologies include:

1. *Hand chip-implants* - microchips embedded in your hand, so that when you shake hands with a similarly chipped human, the two chips pass on each other's essential information. There are already more than 10,000 humans with embedded chips, though most are low-tech.
2. *Stomach micro-chip* - an inbuilt bio-med reader in your stomach which feeds back information to medical professionals on what you are eating and how it is being digested. Research shows that differences in stomach bacteria can mean that drugs work differently for different patients. Already done on a temporary basis via swallowed chips, and in clinical trials.
3. *Networked contact lens* - a contact lens which will record everything that you see as well as display information over your eyeball. Samsung has recently patented this. These and networked glasses are likely to replace mobile phones.
4. *ID forearm chip* - an embedded forearm chip which allows you to scan items and verify your ID at buildings or security. This would allow you to get access to your gym or car. A Swedish office already offers this to tenants to gain entry.
5. *Voice-changing windpipe* - a networked artificial windpipe which allows you to change the sound of your voice or to speak in any foreign language. It is covered in stem cells to avoid reject issues. Still on the drawing board but regarded as doable.
6. *Brain-chips* - a networked chip embedded in your brain which gives you access to information in real time. You can talk to a client while being fed information about them or any topic without the other person being aware. Some chips have already been embedded on a trial basis.
7. *Organ replacement* - the combination of 3D bio-printing and stem cells will allow most body parts to be replaced without any rejection issues.
8. *Exotic bodies* - it is obvious that some people will use 3D bio-printing of body parts and genetic engineering to augment themselves with extra limbs or weird facial features. Already happening in a low-tech way.
9. *Self-aware software* - nobody is able to estimate how smart an AI system needs to be before it becomes self-aware and starts demanding the right to be heard, to claim 'cyborg-rights,' to separate itself from

its programmers, and possibly to register itself as a business and ask for insurance. However, this will occur at some stage, and given an exponential curve, sooner than we think. Some industry experts predict that neutral networks will reach the same level of complexity as the human brain by 2025, be 10x as complex by 2030, and 200x as complex by 2040.

Useful Sources

Abbot, D. (2014). *Applied predictive analytics: Principles and techniques for professional data analyst*. USA: Wiley.

ABI/Thatcham. (2016). *Pathway to driverless cars: Proposals to support advanced driver assistance systems and automated vehicle technologies*. Association of British Insurers.

Accenture. (2013a). *Running business for growth*. Insurance-blogs.

Accenture. (2013b). *Closing the gap: How tech-savvy advisors can regain investor trust.*

ACE Insured. (2013). *Reputation at risk: ACE European risk briefing*. UK.

Actuaries Institute. (2016). *The impact of big data on the future of insurance.* Australia: Green Paper.

Adner, R. (2002). When are technologies disruptive? A demand-based view of the emergence of competition. *Strategic Management Journal, 23*, 8.

AIA/Beddoes. (2015). *The advice challenge: Understanding what clients value.* Australia.

Arntz, M., Gregory T., & Zierahn U. (2016). *The risk of automation for jobs in OECD countries: A comparative analysis*. OECD Social, Employment and Migration Working Papers, #189, OECD.

Arthofer. (2016). *Insurance brokerage is broken*. TechCrunch, May 2.

Autor, D., & Dorn, D. (2013). The growth of low skilled service jobs and the polarization of the US labor market. *American Economic Review, 103*(5), 1553–1597.

M. Naylor, *Insurance Transformed*, Palgrave Studies in Financial Services Technology,
DOI 10.1007/978-3-319-63835-5

Bain & Company. (2013). *For insurance companies, the day of digital reckoning.*

Bain & Company. (2015). *Global digital insurance benchmarking report 2015: Pathways to success in a digital world.*

Barras, R. (1986). Towards a theory of innovation in services. *Research Policy, 15,* 161–173.

Boobier, T. (2016). *Analytics for insurance: The real business of big data.* UK: Wiley.

Boston Consulting Group. (2013). *Telematics: The test for insurers.* BCG Perspectives.

Boston Consulting Group. (2014). *Bringing big data to life*. BCG Perspectives.

Boston Consulting Group. (2015a). *Robo-Taxis and the new mobility.* BCG Perspectives, April 21.

Boston Consulting Group. (2015b). *Revolution in the driver's seat: The road to autonomous vehicles.* BCG Perspectives, April 21.

Boston Consulting Group. (2015c). *Navigating a world of digital disruption.* BCG Perspectives, July 24.

Boston Consulting Group. (2015d). *Man and machine in industry 4.0.* September 28.

Boston Consulting Group. (2015e). *The double game of digital strategy.* BCG Perspectives, October 16.

Boston Consulting Group. (2016a). *How to avoid the big bad data trap.* BCG Perspectives, October 2.

Boston Consulting Group. (2016b). *How digital switchers are disrupting US auto insurers.* July 26.

Breznik, L. (2012). Can information technology be a source of competitive advantage? *Economic and Business Review, 14*(3), 251–269.

Brookings Institute. (2014). *Product liability for driverless cars: Issues and guiding principles for legislation.* Centre for Technology Innovation.

Brynjolfsson, E., & McAffe, A. (2011). *Race against the machine: How the digital revolution is accelerating innovation, driving productivity, and irreversibly transforming employment and society*. Digital Frontier Press.

Brynjolfsson, E. R., Hitt, L., & Kim, H. (2011). *Strength in numbers: How does data-driven decision-making affect firm performance?* Social Science Review Network, April.

Canas. T. (2015). *What will be the Uber of insurance?* Insurance Thought Leadership, PWC, July 22.

Capgemini Consulting. (2015). *Strategies for the age of digital disruption.* Digital Transformation Review, No 7: February.

Capgemini/Efma. (2016). *World insurance report.*

Carr, N. (2003). *IT doesn't matter*. Harvard Business Review, May, 5–12.
Carr, N. (2004). *Does IT matter? Information technology and the corrosion of competitive advantage*. Cambridge, MA: Harvard Business School.
Castriotta M., Floreddu, P. B., Di Guardo, M. C., & Cabiddu, F. (2014). 'Disentangling the strategic use of social media in the insurance industry: A value co-creation perspective', chap. 4 in *Social Media in Strategic Management: Advanced Series in Management*, 63–86.
CBRE/Genesis. (2014). *Fast Forward 2030: The future of work and the workplace*.
CEB. (2013). *TowerGroup wealth management client experience survey*.
Celent. (2014). *The internet of things and property/casualty insurance: Can an old industry learn new tricks?*
Charan, R. (2015). *The attacker's advantage: Turning uncertainty into breakthrough opportunities*. Public Affairs, February.
Charitou, C. D., & Markides, C. C. (2003). Responses to disruptive strategic innovation. *MIT-Sloan Management Review*, USA.
Charitou, C. D., & Markides, C. C. (2003). Responses to disruptive strategic innovation. *MITSloan Management Review, 44*(2), 55–63.
Chartered Accountants ANZ. (2016). *Disruptive technology: Risks and opportunities*.
Christensen, C. M. (1997 & 2011) (4th Ed). *The innovator's dilemma*. Harper Business/Harvard Business School, USA.
Christensen, C. M., & Overdorf, M. (2000). Meeting the challenge of disruptive change. *Harvard Business Review*, March–April.
Christensen, C. M., Anthony, S. D., & Roth, E. A. (2004). *Seeing what's next: Using the theories of innovation to predict industry change*. USA: Harvard Business School.
Christian, B., & Griffiths, T. (2016). *Algorithms to Live By: The computer science of human decisions*. New York, USA: Henry Holt & Company.
CII. (2012). *Future risk: How technology could make or break our world*. UK: Chartered Insurance Institute.
CII. (2015). *Big data and insurance: A conversation*. UK: Chartered Insurance Institute.
CII/EY. (2016). *Insurer of the future*. Confederation of Indian Industry.
Cisco. (2011). *The internet of things: How the next evolution of the internet is changing everything*.
Citi GPS. (2015). *Technology at work: The future of innovation and employment*. Citi GPS Global perspectives and Solutions.

Clemons, E., & Hitt, L. (2000). *The internet and the future of financial services: Transparency, differential pricing and disintermediation*. The Wharton School.
Cognizant. (2017). *The work ahead: Seven key trends shaping the future of work in the insurance industry*.
Cohan, M. (2012). Product performance based business models: A service based perspective. Hawaii Conference on System Science. http://ieeexplore.ieee.org/abstract/document/6149476/.
Corporate Insight. (2016). *The innovation advantage*. White Paper, New York, http://www.corporateinsight.com.
Cusumano, M. A., Kahl, S. J., & Suarez, F. F. (2014). Services, industry evolution, and the competitive strategies of product firms. *Strategic Management Journal, 36*, 559–575.
Danneels, E. (2004). Disruptive technology reconsidered: A critique and research agenda. *Journal of Product Innovation Management, 21*(4), 246–258.
Dataiku. (2016). *Data science for banking & insurance*. USA.
Deloitte. (2013a). *The out-of-sync advisor: Applying disruptive innovation to serve non-customers of wealth management advice*. Deloitte Centre for Financial Services/University Press.
Deloitte. (2013b). *Innovation in insurance: The path to progress, Forward focus series*. USA: Deloitte University Press.
Domingos, P. (2015). *The master algorithm: How the quest for the ultimate learning machine will remake our world*. USA: Basic Books.
Dosi, G. (1982). Technological paradigms and technological trajectories: A suggested interpretation of the determinants and directions of technical change. *Research Policy, 11*, 147–162.
Economist. (2014). *The third great wave*, special report, October 4th.
Economist. (2016). *The return of the machinery question*, special report, June 25th, UK.
Energesse. (2015). *Future solutions in customer experience for health insurers white paper*.
Equinix. (2014). *Challenge to change: Three-part series*. Acord/Global Futures & Foresight.
Equinix Insurance Post. (2016a). *The future of insurance technology: Customer data and analytics*. UK: White Paper.
Equinix Insurance Post. (2016b). *The future of insurance technology: IT outsourcing and the cloud*. UK: White Paper.
European Commission. (2013). *Digital agenda for the future: A Europe 2020 initiative*. Brussels: Belgium.

EXL. (2016). *Robots, smart homes and ride shares: Innovations opportunities in the age of disruption for P&C insurers*. USA: EXL white paper.

EY. (2013). *Insurance in a digital world: The time is now*. New York: Ernst-Young.

EY. (2014). *The future of underwriting: A transformation driven by talent and technology*. New York: Ernst-Young.

EY. (2015). *Leading insurers address reputation and its risks*. New York: Ernst-Young.

Floreddu, P. B., & Cabiddu, F. (2014). *Multi-channel strategy and sustainable competitive advantage: A dynamic capacity approach*, working paper, University di Cagliari.

Floreddu, P. B., Cabiddu, F., & Evaristo, R. (2014). Inside your social media ring: How to optimize online corporate reputation. *Business Horizons, 57*, 737–745.

Forbes. (2014). *Internet of things by the numbers: Market estimates and forecasts.*

Foreman, J. W. (2013). *Data smart: Using data science to transform information into insight*. USA: Wiley.

Foster. (2012). *The customer experience index.*

Franks, B. (2014). *The analytical revolution: How to improve your business by making analytics operational in the big data era*. USA: Wiley.

Frey, C. B., & Osborne, M. A. (2013). *The future of employment: How susceptible are jobs to computerisation?* Working Paper, Oxford University, U.K.

Gartner.com. http://www.gartner.com/technology/research/methodologies/.

General Electric. (2012). In P. Evans & M. Annunziata (Eds.), *Industrial internet: Pushing the boundaries of minds and machines*. USA.

GenRe. (2014). *Marketing to the millennial mindset*. USA.

Gibbs, W. W. (2014). The clock-watcher. Nature, 508.7495 (Apr 10, 2014): 168–170.

Gilbert, C., & Bower, J. (2002). Disruptive change: When trying harder is part of the problem. *Harvard Business Review, 80*(5), 94–102.

Glasmeier, A. (1991). Technological discontinuities and flexible production networks: The case of Switzerland and the world watch industry. *Research Policy, 20*, 468–485.

Gomes. (2014). Driving in circles. *Technology*, October 21.

Halliburton, C., & Poenaru, A. (2010). *The role of trust in consumer relationships*. ESCP Europe Business School.

Horvath, S. (2013). DNA methylation age of human tissues and cell types. *Genome Biology, 14*(10), 3156.

IAIS. (2017). *FinTech developments in the insurance industry*. Basel, Switzerland: International Association of Insurance Supervisors.

Iansiti, M., & Levien, R. (2004). *The keystone advantage: What the new dynamics of business ecosystems mean for strategy, innovation, and stability*. Boston, USA: Harvard Business School Press.

IBM. (2006). *Insurance 2020: Innovating beyond old models*. USA: IBM Institute for Business Value.

IBM. (2007). *Insurance 2020: Now what? Exploring initiatives for innovation*. USA: IBM Institute for Business Value.

IBM. (2015). *Capturing hearts, minds and market share: How connected insurers are improving customer retention*. USA: IBM Institute for Business Value.

Insurance Networking News. (2016). *Strategies: Policy administration and underwriting*. UK.

International Transport Forum/OECD. (2015). *Urban mobility system upgrade: How shared self-driving cars could change city traffic*.

Johne, A., & Davies, R. (2000). Innovation in medium-sized insurance companies: How marketing adds value. *International Journal of Bank Management, 18*(1), 6–14.

Joseph, M., Stone, G., & Anderson, K. (2003). 'Insurance customers' Assessment of service quality: A critical evaluation. *Journal of Small Business and Enterprise Development, 10*(1), 81–92.

Kamiya, S., Schmit, J. T., & Rosenberg, M. A. (2010). *Determinants of insurers' Reputational risk*, Society of Actuaries, US.

Kanter, R. (1990). *When giants learn to dance*. USA: Free Press.

Kanter, R. (2006). Innovation: The classic traps. *Harvard Business Review, 84*(1),

Kelly, K. (2016). *The inevitable: Understanding the 12 technological forces that will shape our future*. USA: Viking.

Komlos, J. (2016). Has creative destruction become more destructive? *The B.E. Journal of Economic Analysis & Policy*: 20160179.

KPMG. (2014). *An industry transforming: Insurers and intermediaries in a fast changing, digital world*, white paper.

KPMG. (2015a). *Automobile insurance in the era of autonomous vehicles: Survey results*, June.

KPMG. (2015b). *Big Data: The big factor driving competitive advantage*, Frontiers in Finance.

KPMG. (2016). *Empowered for the Future: Insurance reinvented*, KPMG International.

Kunreuther, H. C., Pauly, M. V., & McMorrow, S. (2013). *Insurance and Behavioral Economics: Improving decisions in the most misunderstood industry*. UK: Cambridge University Press.

Lepore, J. (2014). The Disruption Machine, *Annals of Enterprise*.

Levy, F., & Murnane, R. J. (2004). *The New Division of Labor: How computers are creating the new job market*. USA: Princeton University Press.

Lloyds Insurance. (2014). *Autonomous Vehicles - Handling over Control: Opportunities and Risks for Insurance*, UK.

Markides, C. (2006). Disruptive innovation: In need of better theory. *The Journal of Product Innovation Management, 23*, 1.

Markoff, J. (2011). *Armies of Expensive Lawyers, Replaced by Cheaper Software*. New York Times, Science, March 4.

Martinez, A. G. (2016). *Chaos Monkeys: Inside the Silicon Valley Money Machine*. London, UK: Ebury Press.

McGahan, A. M. (2000). How Industries Evolve. *Business Strategy Review, 11*(3), 1–16.

McGill, R. (2008). *Technology Management in Financial Services*. London: Palgrave-McMillan.

McKinsey. (2012). *The Social Economy: Unlocking value and productivity through social technologies: consumer financial services*. McKinsey Global Institute.

McKinsey. (2015a). *The Internet of Things: Mapping the Value Beyond the Hype*, McKinsey Global Institute.

McKinsey. (2015b). *An Executive's Guide to Machine Learning*, McKinsey Quarterly, June.

McKinsey. (2015c). *Four Fundamentals of Workplace Automation*, McKinsey Quarterly, November.

McKinsey. (2016a). *Automating the Insurance Industry*, McKinsey Quarterly, January.

McKinsey. (2016b). *An Incumbent's Guide to Digital Disruption*, McKinsey Quarterly, May.

McKinsey. (2016c). *The Economic Essentials of Digital Strategy*, McKinsey Quarterly, March.

McKinsey. (2016d). *Transforming life insurance with design thinking*, May.

McKinsey. (2016e). *Making Digital Strategies a reality in Insurance*, September.

McKinsey. (2016f). *Shifting Gears: Insurers adjust for connected-car ecosystems*, May.

McKinsey. (2016g). *The Need to Lead in Data and Analytics*, April.

McKinsey. (2016h). *A Digital Crack in Banking's Business Model*, April.

McKinsey. (2016i). *How Companies are using Big Data and Analytics*, April.

McKinsey. (2017a). *A Future that Works: Automation, Employment, and Productivity*, January.

McKinsey. (2017b). *The Case for Digital Reinvention*, February.
MGI. (2013). *Disruptive Technologies: Advances that will transform life, business and the global economy*. McKinsey Global Institute: Tech. Rep.
Mitchell, T. M. (1997). *Machine Learning*. USA: McGraw-Hill.
Morgan-Stanley, B. C. G. (2013). *Wearable Devices: The internet of things becomes personal*. USA: Boston Consulting Group.
Morgan-Stanley, B. C. G. (2014). *Insurance and Technology: evolution and revolution in a digital world*. USA: Boston Consulting Group.
Morgan-Stanley, B. C. G. (2015). *Insurance and Technology: The emerging role of ecosystems in insurance*. USA: Boston Consulting Group.
Morgan-Stanley. (2016a). *Cybersecurity: rethinking security*. USA: Blue Paper.
Morgan-Stanley. (2016b). *Insurance – Property & Casualty – Digital disruption in small business insurance*', North America Insight, June 29.
MyCustomer/Microsoft. (2015). *Customer Experience in the Insurance Sector: Insight Report,'* UK.
Nahai, N. (2013). *Webs of Influence: The Psychology of Online Persuasion*, FT Press.
Neirotti, P., & Paolucci, E. (2007). Assessing the Strategic Value of Information Technology: An analysis on the Insurance Sector. *Information and Management, 44,* 568–582.
Nicoletti, B. (2016). *Digital Insurance: Business Innovation in the Post-Crisis Era*. London: Palgrave-MacMillan.
Nordhaus, W. D. (2007). Two centuries of productivity growth in computing. *The Journal of Economic History, 67*(1), 128.
Pearson, R. (1997). Towards an Historical Model of Services Innovation" The case of the insurance industry, 1700–1914. *Economic History Review, L, 2,* 235–256.
Perdue University/ Benchmark Portal. (2014). *Service Centre Industry Report*.
Peters, T. J., & Waterman, R. H. (1982). *In Search of Excellence*. New York, USA: Harper & Row.
Porter, M., & J. Heppelmann. (2015). How smart connected products are transforming competition, *Harvard Business Review*, November.
Progress Corticon. (2014). *Flexibility and Control in Insurance Operations*, White Paper, www.progess.com.
Progressive Policy Institute. (2013). *752,000 App Economy jobs on the 5th anniversary of the App Store*, www.progressivepolicy.org.
PWC. (2012). *Insurance 2020: Turning change into opportunity*.
PWC. (2013). *PwC's NextGen: A Global generation study*.
PWC. (2014a). *Reinventing Life Insurance*.

PWC. (2014b). *Insurance 2020: the digital prize – taking customer connection to a new level.*

PWC. (2015a). *Insurance 2020 & Beyond: Necessity is the mother of reinvention.*

PWC. (2015b). *Insurance Banana Skins.*

PWC. (2016). *Turning risk into opportunity: The changing face of Financial Services: 19th Annual Global CEO Survey.*

Rao, A. (2015). *The Rise of Robo-Advisers.* Insurance Thought Leadership, PWC, June.

Rifkin, J. (2011). *The Third Industrial Revolution: How lateral power is transforming energy, the economy, and the world.* London, UK: Palgrave-MacMillian.

Rifkin, J. (2014). *The Zero Marginal Cost Society: The internet of things, the collaborative commons, and the eclipse of capitalism.* London, UK: Palgrave-MacMillian.

Sabatier, V., Craig-Kennard, A., & Mangematin, V. (2012). When Technological Discontinuities and Disruptive Business Models Challenge Dominant Industry Logics: Insights from the drug industry. *Technological Forecasting & Social Change, 79,* 949–962.

Saporito, P. L. (2015). *Applied Insurance Analytics: A framework for driving more value from data assets, technology, and tools.* USA: Person.

SAS. (2013). *Predictive Claims Processing: Transforming the insurance claims lifecycle using analytics,* SAS White Paper.

Satell, G. (2012). *Business Models and the Singularity,* May.

Schryen, G. (2013). Revisiting IS business value research: What we already know, what we still need to know, and how we can get there. *European Journal of Information Systems, 22,* 139–169.

SEI. (2015). *The Next Wave of Financial Planning,* white paper, www.seic.com/enUS/advisors/14834.htm.

Shirky, C. (2010). *Cognitive Surplus: Creativity and generosity in a connected age.* New York: Penguin Press.

Siegal, E. (2016). *Predictive Analytics: The power to predict who will click, buy, lie, or die.* USA: Wiley.

Stevens, D. (2015). *Prepare to be Disrupted',* 12 March, www.riskadviser.com.

Stewart, R. B. (1981). Regulation, Innovation, and Administrative Law: A conceptual; framework. *California Law Review, 69*(5), 1256–1377.

Summers, L., & DeLong, J. B. (2001). *The 'new economy': Background, historical perspective, questions, and speculations.* USA: Economic Review of Federal Reserve Bank of Kansas.

Susskind, R., & Susskind, D. (2015). *The Future of the Professions: How technology will transform the work of human experts.* Oxford, U.K.: Oxford University Press.

SwissRe. (2013). *Automated Underwriting: Threat or Opportunity?* New York.

SwissRe. (2014). *Insurance and the Rise of Drones*, New York.

SwissRe. (2016a). *How 3D printing will reshape the insurance landscape*. New York: Centre for Global Dialogue.

SwissRe. (2016b). *Sigma 2016*, New York.

SwissRe. (2016c). *The Future of Motor Insurance: How car connectivity and ADAS are impacting the market*. Berlin: SwissRe/Here.

Talla, V., Kellogg, B., Ransford, B., Naderiparizi, S., Gollakota, S., & Smith, J. (2015). *Powering the Next Billion Devices with Wi-Fi*, ArXiv:1505.06815.

Target Group. (2015). *Distribution Channels in Insurance: Understanding the Customer Viewpoint*.

Teece, D. J., Pisano, G. G., & Shuen, A. (1997). Dynamic Capacities and Strategic Management. *Strategic Management Journal, 18*(3), 509–533.

TowerWatson/MergerMarket. (2013). *'Surviving the Perfect Storm: The outlook for Insurance M&A in EMEA'*, UK.

Verint. (2016). *Customer-Centricity in Financial Services: The rules of engagement*. USA: White Paper.

Wernerfelt, B. (1984). A Resource-based View of the Firm. *Strategic Management Journal, 5*(2), 171–180.

Willetts, D. (2012). *Ties that bind: The important of science and technology to the insurance industry*, Thinkpiece no 89, Chartered Insurance Institute, October.

World Economic Forum. (2015). *The Future of Financial Services: How disruptive innovations are reshaping the way financial services are structured, provisioned and consumed.*

Yates, J. (2005). *Structuring the Information Age: Life Insurance and Technology in the Twentieth Century*. Baltimore, USA: John Hopkins University Press.

Yoder, J., & Rao, A. (2015a). *Insurance at a Tipping Point*, Insurance Thought Leadership, PWC, June 20.

Yoder, J., & Rao, A. (2015b). *Reinventing Life Insurance*, Insurance Thought Leadership, PWC, April 15.

Yovanof, G. S., & Hazapis, G. N. (2008). Disruptive Technologies, Services, or Business Models? *Wireless Pers Commun, 45*, 569–582.

Yu, D., & Hang, C. C. (2010). A Reflective Review of Disruption Innovation Theory. *International Journal of Management Reviews, 12*, 435–452.

Zaptitude. (2016). *Investing in Millennials*, Research Report, www.zaptitude.com.

Index

M. Naylor, *Insurance Transformed*, Palgrave Studies in Financial Services Technology,
DOI 10.1007/978-3-319-63835-5